D1451227

UNDERSTANDING
MASS MEDIA

UNDERS

MASS
MASS
MASS

Fourth Edition

TANDING

MEDIA

Jeffrey
Schrank

National Textbook Company
a division of *NTC Publishing Group*
Lincolnwood, Illinois USA

Cover photo credits

Top left and second row left and right: H. Armstrong Roberts
Top right: Laurence Risser, Minneapolis, Minnesota
Middle, second row: Courtesy of Hughes Corporation, Inc.
Right, third row: Brian Seed © 1985 Click/Chicago

Published by National Textbook Company, a division of NTC Publishing Group.
© 1991, 1986, 1981, 1975 by NTC Publishing Group, 4255 West Touhy Avenue,
Lincolnwood (Chicago), Illinois 60646-1975 U.S.A.
Library of Congress Catalog Card Number: 90–60407
Manufactured in the United States of America.

1 2 3 4 5 6 7 8 9 AG 9 8 7 6 5 4 3 2

Preface

That roar you hear in the back of your consciousness as you read this fourth edition of *Understanding Mass Media* is the sound of the twenty-first century approaching. When the current century began, mass media communication was an infant. Yes, books and newspapers were mature.

By 1900, public libraries and news agencies, such as the Associated Press and United Press, were well-established; the popular *Saturday Evening Post*, one of the first magazines in the United States, was already eighty years old.

However, electronic media existed only as eccentric inventions. Samuel Morse's telegraph had been around for a while, but it could not communicate with the masses and it required overhead wires to work. W. K. L. Dickson had developed a motion picture camera, Guglielmo Marconi had a patent for a wireless telegraph, and Thomas Edison had already filed a patent application for something called a "talking machine." As the twentieth century began, these media were dreams. As the century ends, they are a commonplace in even the most remote villages around the globe.

Imagine how mass media will differ by the end of the twenty-first century. Will every person alive be able to communicate instantly with any other person in the universe at the touch of a few buttons? For that to happen, we need to end the divisive medium of local languages. For truly global mass media, we need a global language.

Instead of street addresses and a variety of phone numbers, will each person in the future have a communication identity number that will enable the world to share ideas? And might the combination of a universal language and a global ID number draw us so close together as to make World War III unthinkable? Perhaps.

Or will electronic media become an addictive drug, pacifying the masses into a Brave New World controlled by media dictators? Will giant conglomerates replace outdated nations and dictate how we live?

The fact is, mass media will serve us if we understand their messages or control us if we ignore their power. That fact is why you are reading this textbook. That fact is why the study of mass media is a crucial part of a basic education.

Special thanks go to William Jawitz, English teacher at Manchester High School, Manchester, Connecticut, and John Holmes, Chair of the Broadcasting Department at Marshall High School, Milwaukee, Wisconsin, for their reviews of *Understanding Mass Media* and for their helpful suggestions.

Contents

CHAPTER 3 *Advertising*

CHAPTER 4 *Film*

CHAPTER 5 Comics and Cartoons

CHAPTER 6 News Media

CHAPTER 7 *Newspapers*

CHAPTER 8 *Magazines*

CHAPTER 9 *Radio*

CHAPTER 10 *Recordings*

CHAPTER 11 *Media Control*

CHAPTER 12 Media and Our Image of the World

CHAPTER 13 New Trends and Futurecasting

CHAPTER 1

What Are Mass Media?

WHAT ARE MASS MEDIA?

What do King Tut, Elvis Presley, and the crew of the Starship *Enterprise*™ have in common?

In past centuries imaginative writers described the "world of tomorrow." They pictured time travel as easy as entering a car and dialing a future date. They saw a world in which the touch of a button would transport humans through time and over distance. They wrote of mechanical people, of mind reading, and of instantaneous worldwide communication. Their readers enjoyed such "science fiction," but few believed it would really happen.

In fact, when the future arrived, few noticed. Consider the "Star Trek" series of television shows and movies. The U.S.S. *Enterprise* carries a transporter that casts a shimmering beam to convey people and objects. Crew members stand in the transport room and a beam of light moves them physically to the world below. Fortunately, the beam works both ways and often serves to rescue crew members from nasty interplanetary messes at the last instant by beaming them safely aboard. Perhaps you enjoy "Star Trek" as fiction, and think how much fun it would be to have your own transporter.

The transporter beam was a device to overcome the boundaries of distance. The ancient Egyptians also wanted to overcome distance (and time), so they created a low-tech version of the transporter. They mummified the bodies of kings and queens and built pyramids to put them in. According to religious belief, the pyramid served as a transporter room, as a sacred place from which the dead could move to another world. The Egyptians even packed food for the trip, but no one ever returned to describe the journey. Today we have devices to conquer both time and space. Our inventions, however, are so unlike mummies and transporter beams that we often fail to realize how truly miraculous they are. We dream of the future, but when it comes, it comes in disguise. The future's most recent disguise is telecommunications.

When the future comes, it comes in disguise.

True, we still have no gadget to beam blood and bones instantly through space, but we can move what is more important to humans — we can move feelings, thoughts, ideas, voices, looks, and even facial expressions. We can touch a few buttons to transmit the subtleties of tone and demonstrate our ability to sing or play music. We cannot move our bodies in an instant, but we can move our spirit and image. Through telephones, television broadcasting, printing presses, recordings, and film, we can overcome the limits of time and physical space. We can beam voices and images to millions of people in an instant. Our voices and ideas can be in a thousand cities at one; our pictures can appear in a million households; our spirit can live well beyond the grave.

The history of mass media is the story of the human desire (and practical need) to break the prisons of time and distance. We strive to live beyond our allotted years on the planet; we want to move beyond the few miles we can walk in a day—media technology makes this possible. Right now, as you read this page, more people are watching performances of Shakespeare's plays than ever saw them while he was alive. Right now, over two hundred years after he set the notes to paper, countless thousands are listening to the music of Wolfgang Amadeus Mozart. Elvis Presley lived only forty-two years but, thanks to mass media, he still entertains millions each year. King Tut would be impressed. Twentieth-century celebrities have achieved the immortality of which the Egyptians could only dream. Late-night television is populated by the voices and faces of long- dead stars of the silver screen. The mass media of printing and recording enable creativity to outlive the creator. Space and time are no longer inescapable prisons; we have conquered both through mass media.

Seven percent of Americans say Elvis may still be alive.
—1989 CBS News poll

TO CONQUER
DISTANCE

What are mass media? First, understand that a medium is merely a channel or system of communication. Speech is the most widely used medium. Other media (*media* is plural for medium—there are no communication "mediums") include painting, sign language, the written word, music, images, or even smoke signals. A *mass medium* is a means of communicating to a mass, or large number, of people. Modern mass media include television, radio, newspapers and magazines, books, films, and recordings.

The spoken or written word itself is not a mass medium. If you shout as loud as you can or write a letter, you might manage to communicate with hundreds of people. However, communicating with a large number of people, or mass media communication, was not possible until the invention of the printing press in 1456 by Johannes Gutenberg. With the development of technology—radio, telephone, television, the microchip—mass media communication has begun to reach its full potential. What were the communication media before the development of mass media?

Most common were the town criers, forerunners of today's television news anchors. In medieval times, these loud-voiced representatives of the king wandered town streets literally shouting the news. But town criers were effective only in urban areas, where people lived close together.

Another medium that conquered distance was the runner. Paul Revere was a "news runner," overcoming the barrier of distance as he rode his horse to announce in 1775, "The British are coming." The most famous runner was the messenger Pheidippides, who brought news of the victory at Marathon to Athens in 490 B.C. His twenty-six-mile run is commemorated every time we run a marathon. Runners and criers helped spread the news, but not massively.

In some societies, a drum beat the message of imminent danger; in others, smoke signals spread the word. Both these media communicate over space, but the message had to be a simple one, such as "danger" or "good hunting here." One thousand years ago, however, there was one important reason why you didn't really need *mass* media—there were very few masses. People were not concentrated; the largest cities would still be small towns by our standards. You could spread any message you could conceive by the original medium—"tellaperson." Mass media require the social invention of large cities to take root.

TO CONQUER

All mass communication pushes back the boundary of distance, but hardly conquers it. A runner, town crier, or even a smoke signal had a very limited range. Furthermore, none of these media conquered time. Once the echo of the crier bounced off the last wall, the message was gone forever; even the smoke signal lasted only a few minutes in calm air.

Our ancestor's first attempts to communicate across time were quite simple—they used song and rhyme as memory aids. Thanks to these simple techniques, a story might be remembered for years, instead of being forgotten in days. A minstrel singing a rhyme was a more effective communicator than a town crier announcing the news. Important rules and regulations were often set to rhyme as a learning aid. Today's catchy advertising jingles (the kind you find yourself humming in the middle of the day) have their roots in our early need to communicate in a memorable way—to expand the prison of time.

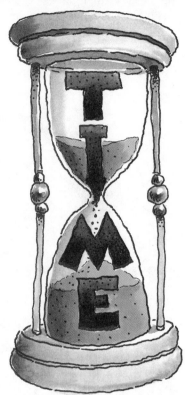

Ancient cultures who mastered mummification and monument-building fought to overcome time. Their buildings and artifacts communicated with future generations, but it was the invention of writing that enabled humans to send ideas into the future, as well as to learn from the dead.

Even the best of archaeologists, however, can't definitely say what our ancestors looked like. We have no photograph of Alexander the Great, or Socrates. Paintings are not totally reliable. How could exact images of the present be preserved for the future?

...little boxes enabled ordinary people to preserve themselves better than King Tut...

Exactly how wasn't discovered until 1835, when William Henry Fox Talbot, the father of modern photography, set small boxes containing a lens and sheets of paper covered with silver halide chemicals about the lawns of his English estate. Talbot, a scientist and country gentleman, waited one-half hour, then brought the boxes inside and opened their doors. Inside each was a miniature picture of the object before which it had been placed. Talbot succeeded on a grander scale than the Egyptians—he invented photography—a way to conquer time, to send images into the future. Now, even the ordinary person's image could be preserved on chemically treated paper for future generations. Alive on earth today is the first generation of humans to know what their great grandparents looked like. William Talbot's little boxes enabled ordinary people to preserve themselves far better than King Tutankhamen or a feudal lord, who could afford the luxury of having their portraits painted.

So what is a mass medium? It's a means of communicating over time or space with a mass of people. And what do King Tut, the crew of the Starship *Enterprise*™, and Elvis Presley have in common? All have defeated distance and time. Their images and, in some cases, their voices are kept alive today on celluloid, in tiny particles of oxide on recording tape, on chemically treated paper, by digital pulse codes on compact discs, or by printed words and pictures.

WHAT ARE BROAD- CAST MEDIA?

Personal communication media include unpublished writing (from a note on the refrigerator door to a letter delivered halfway across the world), a telephone or facsimile message, a snapshot for the family photo album, a tape recording mailed to a friend, or even a home video. All communicate through time and space, but none involves the masses.

Mass media include television, radio, newspapers, magazines, books, recordings, and film. These are media intended for the public, for the masses. You can write a letter (a personal medium) to a magazine that can become a mass medium if published in the letters column. In other words, one medium can become the content of another. For example, a record or compact disc can become the content of a mass medium, such as a radio program. A photograph or film can be content for a television show.

Broadcast media are, specifically, radio and television. Broadcasting means using electric signals to reach a large audience. The word *broadcast* is borrowed from agriculture where it originally meant a way of hand-sowing grain or seeds by casting them broadly instead of planting one at a time. The telephone is a communication medium but it is neither a mass medium nor broadcasting. A telephone conversation is a personal medium, not "cast broadly" for the masses. Since most phone messages are carried through wires, not by radio waves, it is not broadcasting. But if that telephone conversation is part of a call-in radio show, that is broadcasting. Radio is the mass medium used to broadcast the telephone conversation.

A ship-to-shore radio telephone conversation is not broadcasting, nor is a call from a portable phone. Both use radio or microwaves to carry messages, but neither is intended for mass reception. The mass media of broadcasting today include television and radio. Cable television, strictly speaking, is not broadcasting because wires are used to carry the programs to specific households.

New technology has made the distinction of broadcast media difficult to maintain. The word *telecommunications* is often used to include any communication by means of radio waves, electronic signals, wires or cables, fiber optics, microwaves, or satellites.

BROADCASTING
A GLOBAL VIEW

When you think of broadcasting, you picture radio and television as you know them. Radio means mostly music and DJs, with an occasional all-news station or talk show thrown in for variety. Television means daytime drama, sitcoms (situation comedies), adventure shows, game shows, and newscasts—all punctuated by frequent commercials. Large cities usually have at least one channel devoted to cultural and educational programs. But what does broadcasting mean to the rest of the world? What would you find if you became a world traveler armed with a radio and television set?

Nowhere in your travels would you find the variety of choice you take for granted in the United States. You would not find AM and FM radio jammed with dozens or even hundreds of stations—often you would find only one station. In many parts of the world, you would find television stations that broadcast only late in the afternoon and leave the air before midnight. You would even find some radio stations that operate only in morning, afternoon, or nighttime segments.

In many European nations and Canada, you would find more cultural and educational programming than in the United States. These governments feel that advertising should not determine programming content. The British Broadcasting Corporation (BBC), for example, carries no advertising and is supported by a tax paid every time a TV set or radio is purchased. Great Britain, however, does have commercial radio and television with programs similar to those in the United States. In fact, some American series have been successful in England and, conversely, some English programs have proven popular in the United States. The same holds true for Canada.

Some countries establish offices or commissions to act as a kind of "nutritionist" for the national diet of TV and radio. They aim for a balanced diet of programs, without what they view as the American emphasis on "junk food programming."

Television, so often derided in the West as junk food for the eyes, has been the secret weapon of Eastern Europe's revolution.
—R. C. LONGWORTH,
Chicago Tribune,
January 7, 1990

Small countries that strive to provide balanced programming know that viewers want entertainment, but producing TV shows is expensive. So they buy U. S. television shows dubbed into the appropriate language. Government leaders may find American values inconsistent with their own national values; nevertheless, some American TV shows, such as "Dallas," the "Bill Cosby Show", and "Miami Vice," are popular in many countries.

We think of broadcasting primarily as a source of entertainment, but much of the world knows that broadcasting means power. In many Communist and third world nations, all broadcasting is controlled by the government. In fact, governments own and operate most of the world's radio and television stations. In your travels, you would find many radio transmitters guarded by high fences and machine guns. In some third world countries, the government controls both the military and the broadcast transmitters. In newspaper accounts of attempts to overthrow governments, you may read a sentence such as, "Rebels launch a coup to overthrow General (insert name of current dictator) by seizing the radio transmitter." They seize control not because they object to the local DJ but because they know the radio is a way to communicate with the people; it is the nation's electronic drum.

Governments who own broadcasting outlets use the stations to encourage patriotism and to control news. They know that control of broadcasting means control of minds. You may find programming in such countries rather dull—programs promote good citizenship rather than provide entertainment. Since the government owns all broadcasting, there is no competition and thus no incentive to provide "what the people want." Instead, the programs are what government officials deem "good for our people."

In the Soviet Union, there are about 350 television sets for every 1,000 people; in the United States, the figure is about 650 sets per thousand. Part of the difference is economic and reflects problems in production and distribution, but another reason is that programming is not attractive, so many people are not motivated to buy sets. Soviet television has become increasingly sophisticated and does pay some attention to popular tastes, but it is far more serious and less varied than American television.

MEDIALAB

Classifying Media

writing
drawing/painting
speech
song and music
gestures and sign
  language
printed matter (such
  as books and
  newspapers)
sheet music
drums
smoke signals
pictographs
audio recording
television
radio
video recording
phonograph records
still photography
instant photography
movies
magazines
telephone
telegraph
facsimile
photocopy
computer modems
satellite
  transmission
compact disc
digital audio tape

um and approximately how long you spent with each. Include both personal media and mass media in your inventory.

Next, multiply the three longest times on your list by 52 to approximate the maximum time you spend with those media each year. Using these times, estimate how many years of your lifetime will be spent in the company of each medium. For comparison, a 1988 survey of 6,000 people found that, in a lifetime, the average American will spend

6 months sitting at stoplights

1 year looking for "lost" objects

4 years doing housework

5 years waiting in line

6 years eating

1. Above is a list of various communications media. Which media on the list are mass media? Which are considered personal communication media but could be the content of broadcasting? Which mass media are broadcast media?

2. Imagine you discover a time machine in good working order. You want to make an impact on the past, so you dial a ride for one thousand years ago. You take along a printed book, a Walkman ™, and a battery-powered television set. What kind of impact would you make on folks one thousand years ago? Fifty years ago?

3. Keep a written record for one week of all the media you use. Make a list showing each medi-

4. Select one country other than the United States and present a picture of its ratio and television broadcasting. Use library research or talk to people who have lived in that country. Describe the types of programs on TV and radio and how they differ from those in the United States.

5. You are the ruler of an island paradise of several thousand people. A group of these people ask your permission to start a radio station. You realize that a radio station in a small, isolated country is a powerful means of persuasion. How would you want to control the station?

WHAT DO MASS MEDIA PRODUCE?

The auto industry produces automobiles, the paper industry produces paper, and the chemical industry produces plastics. But what is the product of mass media? The best one-word answer is celebrities. Celebrities are the product of the mass media industry.

Mass media start with the raw product of unknowns and refines them into famous people—celebrities. These unknowns are shaped in every possible way; they are manufactured just like autos, papers, and plastics.

The celebrity industry is not limited to athletes or movie stars. Today, unknowns can achieve high visibility in business, religion, the arts, politics, law, medicine, and fashion. Agents, publicists, and lawyers can shape the unknown person into a celebrity using mass media. In order to become a celebrity, a person often has to be willing to change to fit the image designed by the fame-makers.

Celebrity makeovers may require a change of name (especially in the entertainment industry) or, possibly, changes in appearance—through strict diet, workout routines, or plastic surgery.

The aspiring celebrity may have to submit his or her life to the control of the celebrity makers, who determine what the unknown does while in public and even with whom he or she is seen.

Talent makers make the future celebrity visible, for this is the key ingredient of a celebrity. A celebrity is known for being well known, a celebrity is a name or face recognized by the general public, a celebrity is in demand for personal or media appearances, a celebrity is visible to the public eye. The *Celebrity Register* suggests "a celebrity is a name which, once made by news, now makes news by itself."

A potential celebrity might require some talent development and take lessons in speech, voice, or "charisma." But talent does not necessarily make a celebrity. For example, if you could devise a national test to determine the most talented classical pianist, the most talented rock guitarist, the most talented actor, the best writer, or the best dancer, the winners might be relative unknowns. Certainly many celebrities (especially in entertainment and sports) have considerable talent, but the list of celebrities includes musicians with little musical talent, actors of very limited emotional range, and artists with questionable skill. In any industry, the highest quality product, while often successful, is often not the most profitable. In mass media the most talented individuals are often not the most visible celebrities. Since we identify with celebrities, the lack of talent can actually help. The unspoken thought is that if a person with limited talent can become rich and famous so can I.

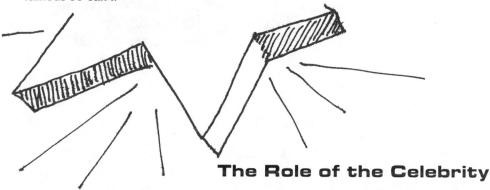

The Role of the Celebrity

Today the highly visible, the celebrities, the famous are everywhere. They are manufactured by the celebrity industry, just as cars, clothes, and computers are manufactured.

The concept of celebrity was expanded when technology in mass media made possible the duplication and distribution of images. Hollywood became a birthplace of celebrity as soon as it adopted the star system and popularized the close-up. The large screen made actors recognizable in public. But industries supply products that people need. What need do celebrities fill?

Celebrities fill the public need for fantasy. Audiences can identify with celebrities who seem to live out fantasies. Stars are presented as people who are different—but not too different—from their fans. This enables the fans to fantasize the celebrity as a more glamorous version of themselves.

As Hollywood developed, it learned that the public demanded its stars lead glamourous lives. If the real life story was not sufficiently interesting or acceptable to the public, then a new one had to be manufactured. Hollywood studies mastered the creation of pseudo events and pseudo stories. A pseudo event is one staged solely for the purpose of attracting public attention.

The recording industry also discovered it could manufacture stars. Exactly which of its products will sell best is never known for sure, but enough new acts are introduced to ensure that the next big star will be under studio contract. Motown Records has been one of the most successful star-makers. Talent was often recruited out of high school. The singer or group was sometimes put through a six-month "finishing school." Motown celebrity and later top executive Smokey Robinson explained, "We taught our artists everything from hygiene to doing interviews, even what to say to people on the street." All aspects of the potential celebrities' images were carefully shaped—repertoire, sounds, clothes, styles, work schedules, and dance routines.

A celebrity is a name which, once made by news, now makes news by itself.
—*Celebrity Register*

Before mass media, those who were well-known were known for their actions or achievements. The public knew and admired heroes, not celebrities. Heroes performed deeds worthy of admiration and imitation. Today's celebrities need not be heroes. In fact, many social critics claim that celebrities have replaced heroes in the public eye. Heroes are defined by achievement, the celebrity by a manufactured image. As historian Daniel Boorstin explains, "The hero created himself; the celebrity is created by the media. The hero was a big man; the celebrity is a big name."

The celebrity industry has branch offices throughout the mass media. These include newspaper gossip and entertainment columns, TV and radio talk shows, "infotainment" programs such as "Entertainment Tonight," fan magazines, entertainment magazines such as *People,* tabloids such as the *National Enquirer*, press conferences, and staged (pseudo) events designed for media coverage. Entertainers who find their "Q Rating" (recognition by the general public) slipping can boost it by getting their name and face in the news. Celebrityhood has been restored (if only for a

few days or months) by a marriage, divorce, carefully leaked story of a fight, an altercation with the law, or nearly any outrageous behavior.

Celebrities have become somewhat like a national extended family. If a major rock star is arrested on a drug charge, millions are shocked or dismayed. If a hot young actor marries an equally well-known actress, the marriage is a topic of conversation in millions of households. Some fans feel they really know celebrities well enough to call or write them with advice on personal problems. The nation mourns the death of celebrities, talks endlessly about their latest plastic surgery or alcohol dependency cure, and sends congratulation cards on the birth of a child.

Many viewers develop imaginary romantic relationships with media personalities. Many dress, talk, and behave in imitation of real or fictional celebrities such as James Bond, Cher, Elvis, Madonna, or Rambo. Sometimes these fictional relationships interfere with reality, occasionally with unfortunate results.

Audiences embrace celebrities and make them part of their social relationships. They dream that since in America "all men are created equal," they too might become famous. Mass media can touch the ordinary person and make him or her famous for a day. As artist Andy Warhol observed, "In the future everyone will be famous for 15 minutes." We dream of becoming rich and famous, but if we cannot actually do so, then at least we can watch those who are.

> In the future everyone will be famous for 15 minutes.
>
> — ANDY WARHOL

MEDIALAB

Thinking About Celebrity

1. To become a celebrity sometimes requires a change in name or appearance. Name some current celebrities who are known to have changed their names or undergone plastic surgery to improve their appearance.

2. Celebrities are often given "story lines" to live in order to capture public admiration. Sometimes the story line is true, sometimes not. Listed below are some commonly used story lines. Can you name celebrities who match each story?

   Poor boy or girl makes good
   Celebrity overcomes personal disaster
     and misfortune
   First of a kind
   Following mom's or dad's footsteps
   The great rivalry
   Gentle giant
   Superhuman abilities

3. The text suggests that having talent and becoming famous do not necessarily go together. This is not the same as saying celebrities do not have talent. In your opinion, which current celebrities best illustrate that celebrities do not need special talent?

4. How does a celebrity differ from a hero? Can you name heroes who have been in the news recently?

5. Record the number of times you read about, see, or hear about celebrities through mass media during one week. Specify the medium and the celebrity. Find examples of pseudo events and other star-making activities of the celebrity-manufacturing business.

6. In what ways has politics been influenced by the celebrity industry? In particular, think about political candidates' commercials you have seen or heard.

7. Stage a debate or write a paper to prove or disprove this statement: "Top rock groups become successful because they record the best music. They become celebrities because people like them."

8. In what ways are athletes subject to the same process of manufactured fame as other entertainers? Remember that the skill level separating professional athletes in most sports is very small. Explain why some athletes become household names while others, equally talented, are known only to fans of the sport.

9. What are the drawbacks of fame? Can a celebrity lead a "normal" life? Would you want to be a famous celebrity?

Team Projects

Form teams of three or four students to prepare presentations of mass media topics. These presentations will be given to the class during the course. Each report should last about thirty minutes or as determined by your teacher. Use audio or visual aids, demonstrations, or other methods to present the results of your work. Form the teams now to allow sufficient time to prepare your reports. Your team or your teacher may want to set up a schedule to make sure the projects are completed on time.

Topics

1. Research any topic about mass media that your group chooses and present your results to the class. Teacher or class approval might be required.

2. Study the role of women or men as portrayed on television, both in shows and in commercials.

3. Study the role of women or men as presented in newspaper and magazine advertisements.

4. Select and order some short films for use in the chapter on film. This team should work with the teacher or school media director. As the class goes through the chapter on film, the team members should present the short films for review. Team members may wish to work out a film review system, using the knowledge gained throughout the chapter and present it when the class finishes the chapter.

5. Research one heavily advertised product category (e.g., mouthwash, headache remedies, toothpaste). Find out the main competing brands; write down the advertising claims for those products; find out who makes the products and what they contain. Run tests where possible to see if the products satisfy their advertised claims.

6. Demonstrate a piece of video equipment.

7. Study the image of law enforcement officers on television. Analyze how they are presented on TV and compare this with reality.

8. Study the image of any of the following as presented on television: doctors, the elderly, teenagers, or criminals.

9. Call a local television or radio station or a local newspaper and request an interview with an announcer, station manager, editorial director, or reporter. Prepare questions ahead of time about the nature of the person's job and the impact of that particular medium as he or she sees it. Working with your teacher and school office, you may be able to arrange for the person to visit your class or you may be able to arrange a tour.

10. Present a history of the comic book. Use the local library as an information source. Perhaps a local comic book collector or shop will provide some examples of old comic books. The presentation should show the changes in comics over the years, relating them to changing tastes and events in American history.

11. Present a report on television as a means of two-way communication. The report should explain how television is being used in some communities as a means of polling public opinion or shopping.

12. Present a report on cable television in your area. If your area does not yet have cable, report on plans in progress and what decisions must be made before your area can be wired for cable.

13. As an experiment, deprive yourself of all contact with electronic media—no radio, television, stereo, or tape/compact disc player—for a week. As a group, discuss your experiences and report your findings to the class.

WRAP-UP

The development of mass media was prompted by the human desire to conquer time and distance. In this chapter a mass medium is defined as a means of communication to a mass of people. You have learned about the distinction between a personal medium, such as your telephone, and a mass medium, such as radio. The concept of broadcasting as a source of power, as well as entertainment, has been introduced, along with a discussion of the celebrity industry. As you explore television, film, newspapers, magazines, radio, and recordings in the following chapters, you will gain a new understanding of mass media and their impact on your everyday life.

CHAPTER 2

Television

The mass medium of television is discussed
in this chapter—from its introduction
at the 1939 World's Fair and an overview
of programming to current technology
and views on the value of television.
Think about what role TV plays in your life.

Taking a Look at TV

You will spend nine years of your life watching shadowy images moving in a glass tube. These figures you invite daily into your home look like tiny people. They talk, dance, get into trouble, and even die. They live for 30 or 60 minutes a week and then disappear like the genie of Aladdin's famous lamp, waiting for your remote control to bring them to life again.

These patterns of dancing phosphors try to make you laugh or cry, or at least feel entertained. Sometimes they ask for your love, and often get it. You become attached to some of these images and invite them back more often than your closest relatives. You become best friends with some of these electronic genies and visit them often for years. These genies of the picture tube have the power to change lives. They tell stories, teach you how the world works, show wonders you would see only in picture books; they try to sell you what they say you need, from deodorant to fast cars. Of course, you don't think of them as ghosts or genies; you call them television personalities or celebrities.

These tiny creatures that live in every household were unleashed around 1939. No one person is credited with inventing television, but it was introduced to the masses at the New York World's Fair. Hundreds of curious people crowded around a television screen not much bigger than this page to view fuzzy black-and-white images. Most thought the invention a clever novelty. The newspapers dismissed the gadget as a toy the masses had little time to support.

These creatures, however, have changed the world. They have served well as messengers of news. And they turned out

A television from the early forties

to be wonderful storytellers. You often talk about them with your friends.

The stories they tell on the tube are the myths that shape our society. If Shakespeare lived today, he would probably write for television. If Beethoven were a contemporary composer, his themes might trumpet the network news.

However, as sometimes happens with a large group we invite home, some behave rudely. Some are violent. Others tell stories that may be embarrassing. Many speak incessantly of bodily functions and dentures and panty hose and headaches as they sell their wares. But we are patient in the face of their rudeness. Television is now in its fifties.

Some say television is the greatest invention of the twentieth century, while others see it as a "vast wasteland" that steals time. Some blame television for teaching violence, while others claim TV turns viewers into couch potatoes. Still others see television as history's most effective educator, bringing knowledge of the universe to even the poorest citizens. Such education, they point out, was once available only to the wealthy who could afford to travel and to attend the best schools. Children today seem to know more about the world than their parents or grandparents did at the same age.

When asked for an opinion of television, some describe it as a harmless pastime that provides escape from the troubles of daily life. Others argue that it presents a dangerously unreal picture of the world. For every convincing statement about the

What discovery has made the greatest difference in human history? Fire? The wheel? Printing? Could it be television?

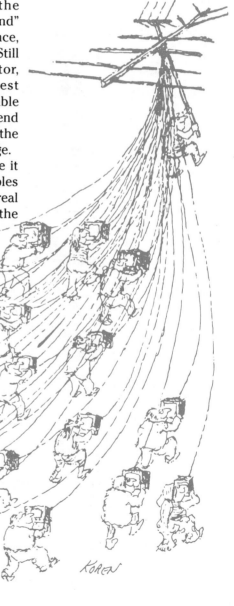

KOREN

dangers of television, there seems to be an equally compelling argument about its benefits. To watch or not to watch— that is the decision. Each time you make that decision, you reveal values.

Clearly, we have long since decided that watching television is an important activity. Ninety-nine percent of homes in the United States have at least one television and most have multiple sets. The average set is turned on (but not always watched) nearly seven hours daily. The typical sixteen-year-old will spend at least as much time in front of the TV as in school. That means those imaginary beings who live behind the glass may spend more time with you than your parents or friends.

I think Television is...!

Take some time now and write your opinion in about fifty words. Begin with "I think television is. . . ." Do not give your opinion of any particular program on television; rather, evaluate television as a mass medium. When you hand in your paper, make sure your name is on it. You will need to refer to your paper later in the chapter.

After the opinions are written and collected, discuss the advantages and disadvantages of watching television. You might do this by constructing two lists: "Benefits of TV" and "Possible Harm Caused by TV."

After the discussion of existing opinions, continue with this chapter. It deals with five important questions:

1. How does the television system work?

2. What kinds of programs succeed?

3. How would life change without television?

4. What does television teach?

5. Who should have access to television time?

TV QUIZ

Here is a test you can take to see how much you already know about the television industry in the United States. The correct answers can be found on the following pages. Take the test before reading beyond this page. Note your answers on a separate piece of paper, and check them as you read on.

1.	TRUE FALSE	Some large cities have as many as ten VHF stations from which to choose.
2.	TRUE FALSE	The three networks (CBS, ABC, NBC) own most but not all of the TV stations in the country.
3.	TRUE FALSE	Television stations are subject to more government control than are newspapers.
4.	TRUE FALSE	Newspapers are public servants; however, television stations are established mainly to provide entertainment.
5.	TRUE FALSE	One television network is supported, in part, by taxpayers' money.
6.	TRUE FALSE	Television stations are owned by the Federal Communications Commission (FCC) but operated as private businesses for a profit.
7.	TRUE FALSE	There are more newspapers than television stations in the United States.
8.	TRUE FALSE	Cable television has existed for over forty years.
9.	TRUE FALSE	A zapper is a person who doesn't want to watch commercials.
10.	TRUE FALSE	The VCR has changed the nature of commercial television.

There are currently about 1,400 television stations in the United States, about equal to the number of daily newspapers. Television stations operate on channels 2–13 (VHF) and channels 14–83 (UHF). Adjacent VHF channels (2 and 3, or 7 and 8, for example) in the same city could interfere with each other and so are usually separated by an unused channel. This means that even large metropolitan areas have only about five VHF (*Very High Frequency*) stations. UHF (*the Ultrahigh Frequency*) has many more channels available. UHF stations have a smaller coverage area than VHF stations because of the higher frequencies on which they operate. Since they reach fewer people, such stations are not as attractive to advertisers. Currently they tend to be smaller stations with smaller audiences than VHF.

VHF stations operate on frequencies similar to those of FM radio stations (in fact, TV sound is FM) and can therefore reach only an area in a 50–100-mile radius from the transmitting tower. If you had a television set that could tune between channels 6 and 7, you could listen to local FM radio stations on the TV set; FM radio could be considered channel 6 1/2.

Unlike UHF and VHF television stations, cable TV operates like a telephone. Almost 60 percent of the homes in the United States are wired for cable at this time. Cable TV will be discussed in detail later in this chapter. This section focuses on broadcast television.

Television stations are privately owned businesses just like newspapers, radio stations, or publishing companies. Unlike these other communications industries, however, television

stations are licensed by the Federal Communications Commission (FCC) to serve the "public interest." Every three years a station's license must be renewed, and to keep its license, the station must prove that it has served the public.

According to court-supported decisions, the channels belong to the people. Television stations are licensed to use those channels only to serve the public in their viewing area. If any person or group can prove that a station has not served the viewing public, then that station could lose its license. In theory, a TV station that broadcasts only network shows and old movies could lose its license for failure to treat local issues. In practice, the FCC has refused license renewals only a few times since the beginning of television.

Nearly 85 percent of all television stations are affiliated with (but not owned by) one of three major networks — Columbia Broadcasting System (CBS), American Broadcasting Company (ABC), and National Broadcasting Company (NBC). The most profitable stations are generally those affiliated with these three commercial networks. A TV station that does not belong to a major network is either an independent or a member of the Public Broadcasting Service (PBS). Independent stations program movies, local sports, and syndicated TV shows (often reruns of TV series originally run on major networks). PBS stations, sometimes called educational TV, generally carry cultural and educational programming. PBS is supported by government grants, donations from foundations and corporations, and contributions from individuals and groups. PBS is not dependent on advertisers as commercial television networks are. However, PBS stations do occasionally present

In some households TV serves a function similar to Muzak in stores, a role reserved for radio in past years. The set is turned on upon awakening and left on until bedtime.

messages about their underwriters or supporters. Messages about businesses shown on PBS are intended to present corporate images; they do not sell products as commercials do on network television.

Networks are not television stations; they do not broadcast programs. They supply programs to the local television affiliate by using telephones or satellite feeds. Each local TV station is ultimately responsible for its own programming. A station can choose not to broadcast a network-supplied program but such refusals are rare. Networks supply local stations with morning news, game shows, daytime drama or "soap operas" (so called because they were originally sponsored by soap companies), evening news, and nighttime programs. Local stations must fill in with their own programming (usually movies, local news, or reruns) when the networks do not supply programming.

The networks provide programs to the affiliates free and are paid for the advertising time they can sell during the program. A 30-second "spot" commercial in network "prime time" (the desirable evening hours) sent to all the network affiliates in the country costs an advertiser between 50 and 90 dollars. A 30-second spot on the first TV showing of a major movie can cost well over $400,000. The exact cost depends on the popularity of the program: the more viewers, the higher the cost.

According to a 1989 Gallup poll, only 50 percent of adults had read a book from cover to cover sometime in the past month.

A small amount of time during each program is left for the local station to sell to local advertisers. This advertising constitutes the main source of income for local stations. Local stations also receive some of the money their network is paid for national commercials.

Networks obtain their programs either by making them (news and documentaries), by covering live events (special news events, sports), or by purchasing the programs from producers. Most prime-time programs and weekly programs are supplied to the networks by producers. The producers (or sponsors of an event such as the National Basketball Association or the National Football League) receive money from the networks; the networks receive money from national advertisers; local stations receive money from local advertisers.

The three major networks compete with each other to attract the most viewers. The number of people who watch each program is measured by rating systems, particularly the one developed by Nielsen Media Research. Nielsen ratings are used to determine advertising rates and can spell life or death for programs or series.

What Kinds of Programs Succeed?

Television programs serve to gather an audience for the commercials. For this reason there has been surprisingly little change in programming since the beginning of television. Networks tend to stick with what has worked in the past.

When a certain type of program proves successful on one network, the others often rush to produce a similar one. This "success copying" accounts for the waves of popularity of certain types of shows from season to season. One season medical shows may be popular; the next, ethnic humor or dramas about rural families; the next, police stories or westerns.

Most commercial TV programming can be placed in one of the following categories listed in the margin.

- ☐ News and documentaries
- ☐ Sports
- ☐ Movies
- ☐ Music/Variety shows
- ☐ Westerns
- ☐ Police/Adventure series
- ☐ Talk shows
- ☐ Quiz and game shows
- ☐ Daytime drama (soap operas)
- ☐ Situation comedies
- ☐ Dramatic series/ Miniseries

MEDIALAB

Televiewing

1. How does the amount of television watched by people in your class compare with the national average? Determine some method to measure accurately the TV viewing of class members, such as keeping a log.

2. With which major networks are your local channels affiliated?

3. Why do you think newspapers are not licensed by the government but radio and television stations are?

4. Form a team to inspect the "public file for license renewal" at a local TV station and report on what that file contains.

5. Report on the history of television broadcasting in the United States.

6. Look at the TV listings in a local newspaper or in a magazine such as *TV Guide* and determine whether a program is provided by a network or by the local station.

7. Find out how much advertising time costs on local television stations. Your library may be able to supply a copy of the Standard Rate and Data Service book giving spot TV information.

8. Either by yourself or in a group prepare a report on the rating systems used to determine which programs are watched the most. Write to the local Nielsen Media Research office and ask for their literature on the rating system. Be sure to report on "people meters."

9. Which category of programming listed on page 27 is currently the most popular? Are any obsolete? What other types are available?

10. Identify some current examples of "success copying."

11. Sports programs are among the most successful and profitable television presentations. Discuss how television has influenced sports in the United States. Consider how television has helped sports; whether television encourages or discourages adults from participating in sports; whether watching sports on TV might replace watching them in person (football games in the future may be played in empty stadiums and videotaped for later broadcast just like any other TV show); and which sports are most and least successful on television.

POPULAR PROGRAMS

No one knows before a television show is broadcast how many viewers it will attract. Very few series last more than three years; many are cancelled during their first year. One dependable type of program is the daytime TV drama, popularly known as the soap opera because it originated on radio shows and soap companies were often sponsors. Another dependable type of program is the police tale or crime show.

The following article reveals much about television in its behind-the-scene examination of the world of the soap opera. It is revealing for the student of television to look at typical programming, and nothing is more typical than the soap opera.

R E A D I N G

The Allure of Daytime Television Drama

by **Stephen West**

Adapted from an article originally published in *Popular Psychology* magazine

Daytime TV drama, or soap operas, have large, devoted audiences. It is profitable, dependable broadcasting. Why do so many people watch? Here are some answers.

Every weekday morning at 11:00, the first of about a dozen daytime TV dramas, or soap operas, are broadcast daily by three major networks. About five percent (or about five million) of the homes in the United States are being filled with the sights and sounds of this particular form of entertainment.

Why is this so? Why do the networks broadcast programs which almost everyone, including the viewers, seems to think are so terrible? And, more to the point, why do so many people go ahead and watch these shows anyway? The most obvious answer is that there's not much else on the air during the daytime, except for the game shows. But this can hardly be the complete answer; for in spite of the fact that it's hard to find someone who will admit to watching daytime dramas regularly, much less enjoying them, there is a good deal of evidence that we have millions of covert "soap opera" freaks living in our midst.

These people may say they would rather watch something else, something "better." It is, after all, a common assumption that soap operas are trivial, silly and a waste of time. But I'm not convinced. I do not believe that anything which can command such religious devotion from so many people is a trivial phenomenon. That quality of addiction, of some need which must be satisfied, deserves a serious examination.

The networks' reason for offering these programs is quite simple: they make a lot of money at it. Along with the game shows, the other main program format for daytime broadcasting, the soap operas are the most profitable part of the television business. Although audience size—and thus, advertising income—is perhaps one-third the size of a nighttime show, the production costs of games and soaps may run only one-tenth as much as the expensive prime-time offerings. According to one industry source, "On the average soap opera today, we make back the production expenses for the whole week on the first day, Monday. So Tuesday through Friday's advertising is pure profit for the network. Or to put it more dramatically: for every dollar of profit which CBS makes at night, they make seven dollars of profit in the daytime. If there were no daytime, there would be no network."

. . . But this need to keep production costs low has important limiting effects on daytime television. The number of hours to be filled with *something* is more than twice as great as during the evening. For the 9:00 a.m. to 6:00 p.m. period, each network must come up with 45 hours of material every week, not counting Saturday and Sunday. Every year, the number of daytime half-hour slots to be filled approaches 4,700. No wonder the networks resort to formula programming.

Daytime TV drama series, or soap operas, are cheap because you can produce one everyday with the same basic personnel and facilities. On "As the World Turns," for example, everything is shot in one studio, on four sets erected from a total pool of 29. Every day, the cast comes in early in the morning for several hours of rehearsals and technical preparations. Blocking, camera angles, cutting, sound, pacing—everything is finalized, so that when 12:30 rolls around, this four-act playlet is ready to be broadcast live to an audience of almost ten million people. Unlike "As the World Turns," however, most soap operas are not, in fact, broadcast live, but are produced by a method known [as] "live on tape." In this case, the episode which is recorded on videotape today will be broadcast a few days from now. The pressure of a live performance still remains, though, because "you don't stop that tape and waste money by starting over unless an actor literally drops dead on the set," according to one technician.

After the day's performance, the crew begins work on erecting a new group of sets, while the actors and director spend the afternoon reading through the next day's script. That evening, the cast must memorize their lines for a new half-hour or hour episode, since the whole cycle starts again the next morning. With this kind of production schedule—compared to the week required to make an evening program, or several months for a two-hour movie—the mere fact that a coherent, reasonably polished performance can be pulled off every day is an awesome feat.

Because of these technical constraints, soap operas resemble the legitimate theater more than nighttime television or films: they are rougher, more spontaneous, more uncertain. Most are produced in New York, because Broadway has an unending supply of actors trained to memorize large sections of dialogue and to cover mistakes by improvisation in an ongoing performance, while Hollywood does not. Without background music and with relatively little cutting from scene to scene within an "act," soap operas project an intimate, almost documentary feeling, as if you're observing a few minutes of real time in some real people's lives. Somehow the clanking of forks against plates comes through much more clearly in an eating scene; the pauses, the coughs, the uncertain glances aside, all the seams in an interaction remain unclosed in these programs. They have a flatness, a looseness which resemble the tone of everyday life and which is very different from the more frenetic, tight, "flawless" productions on prime time.

Around the studio for a soap opera, everyone is concerned with only two things: maintaining a reasonable level of technical polish and keeping the Nielsen ratings high. They simply have no time to consider the broader implications of what they're doing, beyond delivering a certain number of viewers to the sponsor and thus earning a living for themselves. A question about how they think their program may be influencing its viewers will be met by a blank, puzzled stare. Hopefully, they think, the viewer will be influenced to buy the sponsor's products and to tune in the program again tomorrow; but beyond that, who cares what the viewer thinks?

The actors, director, and technical crew for a soap opera are the implementors of the script, and the pace of their job is so relentless they can hope for little more than avoiding disaster. Their chances of improving the script, of creatively enlarging its meaning through their craft, seems to be rather limited, except insofar as an actor is able to clarify the personality of his character, bit by bit, over a period of months or years. And even here the opportunities are limited. There just isn't enough time to do much more than learn your lines.

The scriptwriter himself, the creator of what seems to be the substantive core of the series, is also plagued by many of these same problems of time pressure. The language of the script is no more smooth or coherent than the acting, but the scriptwriter is responsible (along with the producer) for making choices about the plot as well as the dialogue. And it is the plot—the concrete actions which the characters make, the incredible problems which they

A set from "Santa Barbara," a popular soap opera

must confront—which keeps the viewer hooked to the program.

According to Robert Shaw, a soap opera scriptwriter for over 20 years and a man who probably knows as much about the genre as anyone in the business, there are basically two parts to writing a successful series: creating major characters—especially including the heroine—for whom the viewer can feel empathy, and working out a complex, disaster-laden, but finally optimistic plot. Soap opera viewers . . . are overwhelmingly female; men who watch daytime television, on the other hand, greatly prefer the game shows. (Eight of the top ten programs watched by women are soaps, while nine of the top ten watched by men are games).

Thus, Mr. Shaw explains, the key to daytime serials is empathy, If we can't build empathy in a character, we haven't got a show. Empathy means, in a way, identifiability, likability . . . and this hasn't changed since the first ones on the radio 45 years ago. There is a theory—which I believe, to a considerable extent—that

women tune in soap operas to watch someone who has more misery than she does. It makes you feel good to discover that somebody else has it worse. We have found, by trial and error over the years, that one of the things that's almost impossible to do is to make a sympathetic character out of a rich woman . . . ."

The leading women, for this purpose of building empathy, are generally young, attractive, and stylish, but they still retain a good bit of that small town Protestant modesty which is so much a part of almost every soap opera series. (Consider the typical names of towns where action normally takes place: Shadyside, Sunnyview, Oakville, etc.) "The ideal soap opera heroine," Shaw says, "is a woman's image of herself, which is not necessarily the truth. It's how she thinks of herself."

In Shadyside, moreover, it is the women who are running the show, according to their own domestic set of values. It is a world of weak men and strong women, a world in which the housewife heroines know that the important things in life are interpersonal, not material and certainly not political. . . .

The implicit message of all soaps, both during the show and during the commercials as well, is that any problem can be solved. Things may be pretty messed up these days, but the system is basically sound. . . . I hardly need to add that the sponsors of these programs have enormous vested interests in the *status quo*, in the maintenance of American housewives' optimism.

The problems which beset a soap opera heroine, and they are many and varied, basically fall into two overlapping categories: the disruption of health and the disruption of social/sexual relations. According to Robert Shaw, cancer . . . is probably the single best problem a writer has at his disposal for beefing up his ratings. "Of course, murder is always good, provided you murder someone the viewer cares about," Shaw says. "It has to be one of the main characters' favorite brother or sister or uncle, somebody who can hold the viewer's attention for quite a while. And, of course, this is a good way to write out an actor who's leaving the show, Then there's infidelity, which is almost basic to *all* serials."

Disease is a common problem in the soaps because it's something everyone can identify with, an irrational threat beyond one's control. In Shadyside, if not in the rest of the world, disease is democratic: it can strike anyone, regardless of position. The doctor is held in great esteem here because, unlike most other professions, he is intimately connected to the domestic world of bedrooms, children, house calls.

(Where else, except on television, do doctors still make house calls?)

Various kinds of psychological problems have recently become standard themes for these programs. Child psychology and the problems of the "disturbed child" are especially big these days, along with runaway children, amnesia, . . . drug addiction, you name it. In the social/sexual disruption category, there are still more possible disasters. . . . And finally, says Shaw, "If you're really stuck, you can always bring in the Bad Sister, the one nobody's heard from for years. That's tried and true, along with the in-laws as heavies, and what to do with your invalid parents. There's really no end to the possibilities."

Through all of these problems, of course, the heroine maintains her basic optimism. She lives in a totally uncertain world, but her faith in the idea that her problems will eventually be solved is never in doubt. For the viewer, this one certain feature of the program changes its entire character, it becomes like a mystery story, . . . in the sense that the final outcome is never in doubt. The interest in the story exists in means, not in ends, and this is why the viewer's appetite for more and more can never be satiated. A soap opera is an open-ended narrative form, like folk legends or our experience of our own lives. Were it to end, it would cease existing entirely.

By definition, there is no end to a soap opera, unless it gets taken off the air. "As the World Turns" has been churning along now for over 30 years, and it's just as superficially uncertain and basically predictable as it ever was. "I am absolutely convinced,"

Robert Shaw says, "that there is some relief in watching these serials. I think the viewer feels better after having watched, for the very reason that she's seen someone more miserable than she is. Also, our women *do* solve their problems: cancer *is* curable, husbands *do* come back. . . . We're selling hope, really, and it's not much more specific than that. We stay away from the problems of the country, we'd never mention a depression or the stock market." Then he adds, wistfully, "They live apart from it, really."

Finally, in spite of all the personal problems which living in Shadyside inevitably entails, most viewers would probably be glad to exchange their own lives for those of the soap opera's characters. There may be a lot of problems, yes; but boredom and loneliness are not among them, and these are clearly what the viewers suffer from most. At lease the characters in a soap opera have engaging, crucial problems in their lives, not an endless stream of minor frustrations and indignities, like broken washing machines, dirty dishes, and screaming kids.

The soaps open up the viewer to another world where things seem to matter. At least they provide the viewers with gossip material for times when they run short on other subjects. I have a feeling there are millions of little networks of friendships in this country based on arguing the merits of a soap opera heroine's latest move, on filling each other in on the details of a missed episode, on trying to second-guess what the scriptwriter will do next week. And given the viewer's entrapment, this is probably better than nothing.

MEDIALAB

Analyzing the Soaps

1. Discuss daytime TV dramas, or soap operas, class members have seen. Possibly your teacher will allow a taped episode (using a VCR) to be shown in class. Focus on the similarities between the daytime drama and live theater, and the differences between daytime drama and prime time TV.

2. In 1971 and 1972, M. L. Ramsdell and other researchers at Rollins College watched 600 hours of daytime TV drama and concluded that one of the messages the dramas teach is that "the good life can be achieved by anybody who is a white male professional or a white female who marries the professional and subsequently becomes a mommy." Is this message still being taught by daytime TV drama today?

3. Why do you think this genre is so popular?

4. Explain in your own words how the acting, camera work, and sets of daytime TV drama are different from those in nighttime dramatic shows.

5. What would happen if these dramas were shown at nighttime instead of during the day? In answering this question consider how the daytime and nighttime audiences differ.

6. Talk with someone who watches daytime dramas regularly. Try to find out why that person watches them and why certain ones are favorites.

7. Why do daytime series rely so much on tragedy and disaster in their plots? Are the plot and characterizations believable and realistic?

8. Stephen West, author of the article on daytime TV dramatic series, says that "A soap opera is an open-ended narrative form, like folk legends or our experience of our own lives." Explain this in your own words.

9. Daytime TV dramas can easily be criticized by those looking for high dramatic art, but they are a unique form of drama. What do they offer in terms of plot and character that no other plays, movies, or books supply?

10. Stephen West quotes scriptwriter Robert Shaw as saying, "The key to daytime serials is empathy." Explain empathy and why it is so important to the success of soap operas.

11. What prime-time shows might be considered "nighttime soaps"? In what ways do they borrow from the soap-opera formula and in what ways are they different?

THE MESSAGE
of the
POLICE TALE

by **Stuart Kaminsky** with **Mark Walker**

You watch a TV show with a police officer or detective as the main character for entertainment. Did you ever consider the educational value of such programs? What does the police tale teach about society? This reading is another behind-the-scenes look at a popular type of program—the police tale.

Unlike other popular forms such as the western, the melodrama, or the horror story, police tales have a relatively brief history, with roots in the nineteenth century. For the most part the police did not exist as a separate profession until the nineteenth century. Those who apprehended criminals before this time were soldiers, as they still are in Italy and some other countries, or extensions of the judicial system, as in contemporary Soviet Russia. In England, a police force was established when the judges started to pay people—usually "reformed" criminals—out of their own budgets to go out and catch criminals.

GENE SMITH:
A Little Visit to the Lower Depths via
The NATIONAL
POLICE GAZETTE
THE LEADING ILLUSTRATED SPORTING IN AMERICA JOURNAL
NEW YORK, SATURDAY, SEPTEMBER 27, 1890.

Novels and stories about the police officer came slightly after the rise of the police force in nineteenth-century Europe. In France, such stories predated this slightly, because the police force was established as a separate entity from the army after the French Revolution. A transitional tale, Victor Hugo's *Les Misérables* (a public domain story that was the inspiration for one of the most successful series in television history, "The Fugitive"), began the pattern. Initially police tales—and many existed in the previous century—were presented as true-crime reports and not as fiction, in spite of the latitude authors often gave themselves. Alan Pinkerton,

A scene from "Dragnet"

The most recent half hour police tale was "Sledge Hammer," which might more reasonably be categorized as a comedy/police tale.

Critical attention to these and current police tales on television has tended to focus on whether or not the series or particular episodes are accurate in their depiction of police work and whether they are too violent.

The problem for the writer who gets caught up in the realist argument is that while viewers do want the illusion of reality, the same illusion we try to capture in dialogue, they probably do not want the actuality of police procedure and routine as regular weekly fare. A friend and I conceived a pilot for the most realistic police tale ever done. We were sure it would fail, and it did. The treatment for the first episode read as follows.

Real Police

Patrolman Watkins and Patrolwoman Ennis are in their car on a hot summer day. They cruise the streets of the city, listening to calls on their radio and looking out for suspicious characters or incidents. Generally, they talk about their families, financial problems, where they are going to take their coffee break and have lunch. They get two calls: a domestic disturbance that proves to be a false alarm and a possible breaking and entering that proves to be a window accidentally broken by kids playing baseball. They stop one driver, an old woman, for having a dragging muffler, and they are called upon to direct traffic at a busy intersection where the traffic light goes out. On the way in

who founded the Pinkerton Detective Agency (which still exists), promoted his own exploits as true police tales in books and periodicals with great success.

Almost from the inception of storytelling in the medium, police tales became a staple of television.

"Dragnet" may have been one of the first, but it was far from the only example ("Racket Squad," "M Squad," "Highway Patrol," and "Rocky King" are all early examples) of the genre in its half-hour format. Today's television police tales are all one hour long.

from their shift they see a suspicious-looking man hurrying into an alley. They follow and find that he is dumping a bag of garbage illegally. They decide to warn him instead of giving him a ticket. Back at the station they report that their patrol car needs some minor work.

There are some possibilities for mild comedy here, but when treated as pure realism, normal police work does not translate into exciting adventure. Police stories on television are more about the fantasy life of the audience than the experience of the police.

Several kinds of police tales have been shown on television: those that involve an individual investigator or pair of investigators, such as "Columbo" and "Hunter"; those that involve uniformed officers, and those that concentrate on an ensemble effort by the police, such as "Hill Street Blues" and "Crime Story."

Characteristics of Television Police

In plain clothes or uniform, the central character in a television police series has an inevitable commitment to the norm, to the status quo, to keeping things the way they are. Related to this is the convention that the police detective is not usually highly intelligent. He or she may not be a fool, but with rare exceptions intelligence is not a part of television's heroic definition of the police officer. "Columbo," obviously, was one of those exceptions. "Sledge Hammer" is a comic recognition of this element of the genre.

The virtue and possible defect of the television police detective is his commitment to the rule of law

and the protection of the populace, which can often become obsessive. If, for example, the police officer has a family, the police officer's commitment to the job may threaten the family situation. That familial tension is often the basis for the second problem in an episode of a police series.

In some ways the police tale on television has become an urban substitute for the western, which is no longer a popular television form. As in the western, the hero in early police shows was inevitably male. In recent years, police tales have offered female protagonists within what was once an exclusively male community. Potentially interesting series ideas and episodes exploring the differences between television's male and female police remain to be done.

Another characteristic of both uniformed and nonuniform police tales is the importance of partnership. One does not work alone. One is part of a social group. Again, this is quite different from the private forms. Private detectives may have, but usually do not need, partners. On television they traditionally work alone or with helpers who are not equal to them. "Simon and Simon," obviously, is an exception. The exploration of male/female relationships, a combining of comedy/romance/private-detective genres has been explored in such series as "Remington Steele" and "Moonlighting." Frequently, people supposedly helping the private detective prove to be more impediment than aid. But the police officer is dependent on other people. There is a primary relationship with a partner or team.

The work situation becomes the primary social support for the television police officer. The police officer tends to live within his or her job.

Again, domestic tension becomes the basis for antagonism or even secondary plot. The neglected spouse who says, "You spend more time with your partner than you do with me," is familiar in the police genre. It may, in fact, reflect at an exaggerated level the viewer's tension as a worker or spouse in terms of time spent on the job and at home.

Work in the television tale is a way of living. The partnership is established as one of dependent parts. The police tend to be successful only when they get along and work together. When one is removed or made vulnerable, the others are endangered.

Criminals

The officer's relationship to the police force seems to depend on the nature of the criminal. Much of the criticism of police tales on television has stressed that, with the exception of some uniformed-police tales, the shows do not deal with the real nature of most crime. The criticism is, in one sense, quite true. The overwhelming majority of criminal cases in actuality are domestic, people harming people they know. This, coupled with routine and petty crime, takes up most police time. However, the police tales we see on television are not about real crime and seldom have been. They present, instead, a mythology about crimes that are symbolically important to the viewer.

A scene from "Hill Street Blues"

In television, the overwhelming majority of crimes fall into two categories that may be mythically important but exist only in small numbers in reality. The two kinds of criminals predominantly presented on television are individual lunatics and organized crime figures (Mafia, street gangs, drug gangs, terrorists). Organized crime and individual madness are opposites. Each represents something the police officers (and, obviously, the writer) must handle in a different way. When the television show defines the criminal as insane, the individual police officer assigned to the case tends to grow more and more alienated from his or her partner and other officers. The central detective becomes obsessed with catching the mad killer. Since the detective team represents a unified whole, the existence of the lunatic, who is a fragmented personality, mocks the existence of the team and the social response to the threat he or she poses. The hero, in dealing with a lunatic, comes more and more to see that lunatic as a disease to be wiped out and often as a reflection of the officer's own dark side. The hero is impelled to operate the way the lunatic operates and moves outside the law toward emotionalism and violence . . .

On the other end of the spectrum, when the criminal is a member of organized crime, the police officer tends to work more closely with the members of his or her group. The criminal organization is presented as paralleling the police organization so that there are two institutionalized forces opposing each other. What usually leads to the downfall of organized crime in a police tale is the criminal body's need for direction from above. If the police can get the key figure, the leader, the organization crumbles. That is not necessarily the way gangs or organized crime really work, but, mythically, it functions that way in television episodes because organized crime is presented as a patriarchy (and, rarely, as a matriarchy). We watch the crumbling of one family (criminal, distorted) in the face of another, the police family.

The police, in contrast to organized criminals on television, are well trained and can function without a hierarchy. The criminals are totally dependent on their rules, their parental figures. The police can be hampered by the rules of law, but unlike the criminals, they are not dependent on their hierarchy. There is no single person a criminal can "get" in the police force to stop an investigation . . .

The Structure of the Police Show

While you do have the option of altering the pattern, the narrative pattern of police tales exists for a reason. It is familiar, fulfills the functions I have outlined, and provides the framework for the particular kind of moral tale that characterizes the police show.

The pattern, which provides a model for treatments for a police episode, is as follows.

1. The tale begins with the *commission of a crime*. This immediately gives us information the police do not have, which places us in a position superior to the hero's.

2. An officer, *the hero, is assigned to the case by chance*. The cop has no personal ties to the case. Obviously, variations can be played in which there is an immediate personal tie, but these are rare. The second problem, usually involving the central figure's partner, is introduced. The problem often reflects the central figure's problem. For example, if Cagney is involved in trying to deal with a criminal who tried to kill her and who she fears will escape punishment in his trial,

Lacey may be involved in what proves to be an unfounded fear of a recently released criminal who threatened her years earlier at his trial.

3. *The destruction widens*. The lunatic kills another apparently random victim, or organized criminals blow up one more Vietnamese restaurant. The villain always commits at least two crimes. Whatever the specific nature of the acts, the crimes become more personal to the hero. Perhaps the hero knows the random victim or a relative of the victim, or the random victim bears a painful resemblance to someone the hero knows, or in questioning a relative of the victim the hero begins to identify with the victim. As the crimes continue, they start happening to people who represent something particular and personal to the police officer. In a made-for-television movie or a miniseries and sometimes in an individual one-hour episode, the officer will begin to neglect his or her personal life and relationships.

4. *The quest becomes more and more obsessive*, and the hero behaves less and less rationally.

5. *The hero meets the criminal.* Sometimes this takes place a bit earlier or later, but it is usually in step 5. Sometimes it is a chance meeting. The hero doesn't know the criminal is the one who committed the crime and, possibly, the criminal doesn't know the hero is the person pursuing him or her. Sometimes the police officer does know but does not have the evidence to hold the culprit. But there is some meeting, perhaps a confrontation, and then the criminal

gets away. This usually involves a chase either immediately before the face-to-face confrontation or after it.

6. *The warning*. Someone—spouse, partner, superior—warns the police officer about obsession and the danger of loss of balance. The cliche´d line, which exists because it is meaningful, is, "Don't lose your perspective. You're a cop. You have a responsibility to the law, the public." The warning is, of course, ignored.

7. *Following the trail*. The hero has to work his or her way through a cross section of society in an attempt to find or retrieve the criminal. The rich, the poor, bartenders, taxi drivers, rooming-house owners, bums, and company presidents provide a chain of information that leads to . . .

8. *The second confrontation*. A direct, open, physical confrontation between the hero and the villain takes place in a hostile or an unfamiliar environment.

9. *The police officer destroys or captures the villain*. The strong tendency in television is not to destroy, however, but to capture, contain, and control the symbol of evil.

10. *The epilogue*. The second problem, that of the partner, is resolved. If the central problem is resolved violently, the secondary problem is usually resolved nonviolently. The resolution of the second problem can also take place during step 8. The criminal dealt with, the hero is either alone and shaken, or, more often, taking the first steps toward returning to the partnership and balance.

MEDIALAB

Real Life vs TV Crime Shows

1. One of the most common criticisms of television is that it does not reflect the real world. The reading can be used to answer this objection. Explain why police (and doctors, lawyers, private investigators, or just about any professional) may not always be presented in a realistic way.

2. Discuss this sentence from the reading: "Police stories on television are more about the fantasy life of the audience than the experience of the police." Do you agree or disagree?

3. How does television crime differ from real crime?

4. Watch one or more police tales currently available on TV.

   Evaluate the characters and criminals according to the article.

   Do the police have a "commitment to the status quo"?

   Is the hero possessed of an obsessive commitment to the rule of the law?

   Is there tension between job and family responsibilities?

   What is the relationship between male and female police officers?

   Is the importance of partnership shown? Remember, police have equal partners. Private investigators are often loners.

   Is there a paternal or maternal figure within the police department?

5. Compare the structure of a current police show with the ten-point structure in the article.

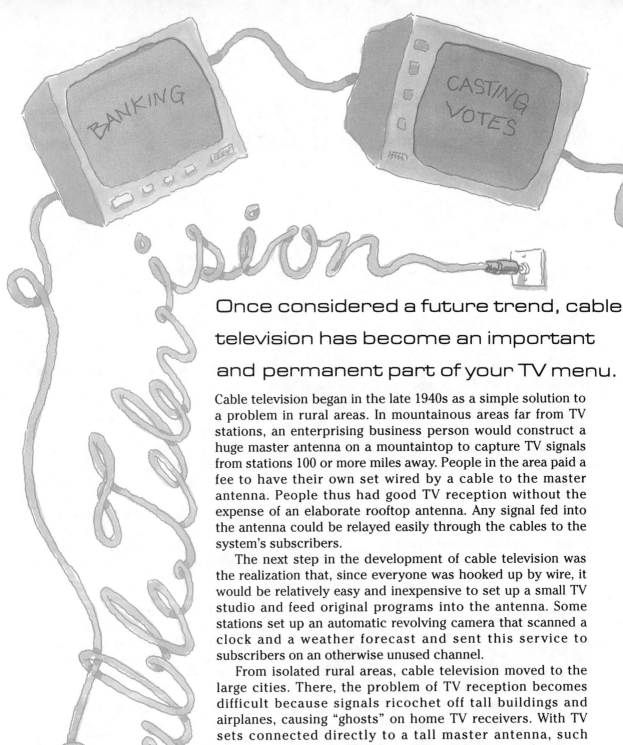

Once considered a future trend, cable television has become an important and permanent part of your TV menu.

Cable television began in the late 1940s as a simple solution to a problem in rural areas. In mountainous areas far from TV stations, an enterprising business person would construct a huge master antenna on a mountaintop to capture TV signals from stations 100 or more miles away. People in the area paid a fee to have their own set wired by a cable to the master antenna. People thus had good TV reception without the expense of an elaborate rooftop antenna. Any signal fed into the antenna could be relayed easily through the cables to the system's subscribers.

The next step in the development of cable television was the realization that, since everyone was hooked up by wire, it would be relatively easy and inexpensive to set up a small TV studio and feed original programs into the antenna. Some stations set up an automatic revolving camera that scanned a clock and a weather forecast and sent this service to subscribers on an otherwise unused channel.

From isolated rural areas, cable television moved to the large cities. There, the problem of TV reception becomes difficult because signals ricochet off tall buildings and airplanes, causing "ghosts" on home TV receivers. With TV sets connected directly to a tall master antenna, such problems were eliminated, so cable television moved to some cities. A few cable systems offered subscribers additional channels brought in from nearby cities as an added service.

The cables used to connect the TV antenna to the set can transmit hundreds, some say thousands, of channels of information. Cable television opens the possibility of more TV channels than are possible with broadcast television. The

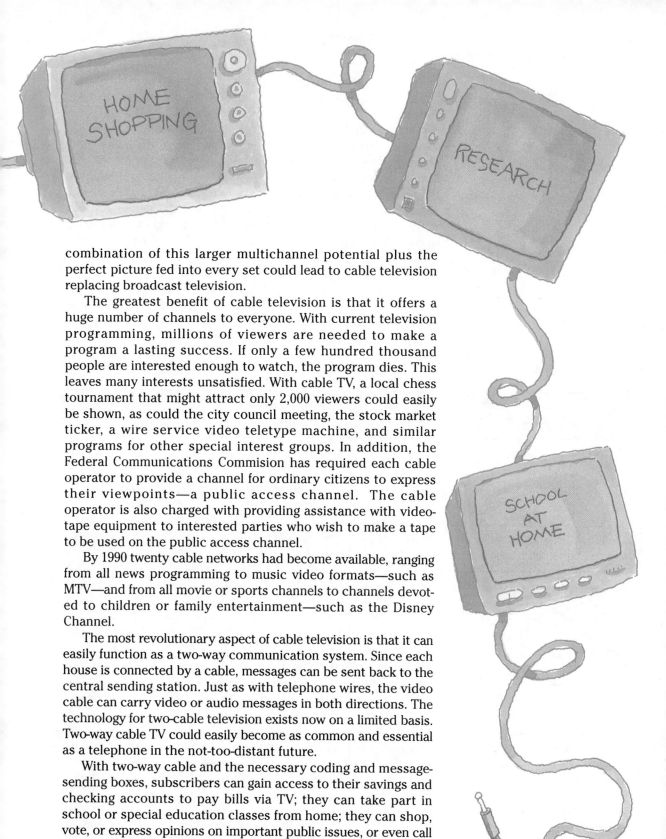

combination of this larger multichannel potential plus the perfect picture fed into every set could lead to cable television replacing broadcast television.

The greatest benefit of cable television is that it offers a huge number of channels to everyone. With current television programming, millions of viewers are needed to make a program a lasting success. If only a few hundred thousand people are interested enough to watch, the program dies. This leaves many interests unsatisfied. With cable TV, a local chess tournament that might attract only 2,000 viewers could easily be shown, as could the city council meeting, the stock market ticker, a wire service video teletype machine, and similar programs for other special interest groups. In addition, the Federal Communications Commision has required each cable operator to provide a channel for ordinary citizens to express their viewpoints—a public access channel. The cable operator is also charged with providing assistance with video-tape equipment to interested parties who wish to make a tape to be used on the public access channel.

By 1990 twenty cable networks had become available, ranging from all news programming to music video formats—such as MTV—and from all movie or sports channels to channels devoted to children or family entertainment—such as the Disney Channel.

The most revolutionary aspect of cable television is that it can easily function as a two-way communication system. Since each house is connected by a cable, messages can be sent back to the central sending station. Just as with telephone wires, the video cable can carry video or audio messages in both directions. The technology for two-cable television exists now on a limited basis. Two-way cable TV could easily become as common and essential as a telephone in the not-too-distant future.

With two-way cable and the necessary coding and message-sending boxes, subscribers can gain access to their savings and checking accounts to pay bills via TV; they can take part in school or special education classes from home; they can shop, vote, or express opinions on important public issues, or even call up research information from the local library computer.

Most of the cable systems now in existence in the United States are still one-way systems. But FCC regulations require two-way capacity in all newly constructed systems.

One possible far-reaching effect of cable television is to make movie theaters a thing of the past. Attendance at films declined enormously with the invention of television. More people went to films more often in 1940 than they do today. To attend a movie requires an auto or bus trip somewhere, a $3.00-$7.00 admission fee, maybe parking or babysitting costs, perhaps standing in line and putting up with a noisy crowd, and tolerating overcooled or overheated movie theaters and over-priced popcorn and candy, not to mention finding a seat only to have a 6-foot-8-inch basketball player sit in front of you.

Some cable networks produce full-length movies strictly for cable channels. In the future, first-run movies may open at movie theaters and on cable television at the same time. If that happens, the future of movie theaters will be affected.

Comparing Over-the-Air and Cable TV

OVER-THE-AIR	CABLE
Quality of signal varies with location of set and with weather.	Consistent high quality of transmission for everyone.
Number of channels available is limited. Even a large city such as Chicago has only ten channels.	Over 20 cable networks available plus commercial networks.
Currently reaches about 98 percent of all households.	Currently reaches about 60 percent of all households with TV sets.
Requires a TV set and sometimes a rooftop antenna.	Requires that the house be wired to the cable operator. The hook-up charge ranges from nothing to $100.
Free. No monthly bills.	Those wired to the system pay an average monthly fee of $25.
One-way system.	Has the potential for two-way communication.
Needs many viewers to interest advertisers.	Needs far fewer viewers than over-the-air transmission to be economically workable.
Few individuals can obtain TV time to state their opinions.	Each cable franchise is required to have at least one channel for citizen access.

MEDIALAB

Cable Viewing

1. Find out what sort of cable systems exist in your area. If none exist currently, do some research to find out what applications for cable franchises exist. Who has made the applications and what have they promised?

2. If a new cable television system with 50 channels began operation tomorrow, what sorts of programs would you like to see carried? Remember that the ideas would have to be inexpensive to produce (to put a camera in a city council room is easy, but to produce a weekly filmed TV show is much too expensive for such an operation).

3. If you received an offer for free cable installation tomorrow, would you subscribe? Find out what factors influence people's decisions about whether to subscribe.

4. Do you think first-run movies on cable television would bring about the end of movie theaters?

5. Prepare a report on two-way cable television as it exists today. Be sure to find out about the Qube system, a two-way cable service developed in Columbus, Ohio, by Warner Cable.

6. Brainstorm, as a class, for possible uses of two-way cable television.

7. How has cable television changed television?

8. Many predictions of the future turn out to be little more than wishful thinking. Do you think two-way cable TV is a significant social invention or merely a fad?

9. Could two-way cable in any way change schooling?

10. Two-way radio has never made a major impact on society. Amateur radio is for hobbyists and citizen's band is used more for companionship than for important communication that would allow people to work or shop at home. Why should two-way video be any more important?

FLIPPERS, ZAPPERS, and ZIPPERS

or

How TV Is Changing

Television viewing today has been effected by several developments: the VCR, the dethroning of the three major networks, and the remote control. In the following section you'll read of flippers, zappers, and zippers, but first take a look at the VCR—TV's time machine.

The VCR

The home VCR (videocassette recorder) is an electronic teenager who won't celebrate its twenty-first birthday as a consumer product until 1997. Back in 1976, when Sony introduced the first consumer version of a VCR, most thought it a toy for the wealthy. As recently as 1984, only 12 per cent of households owned a VCR; today this rapidly maturing invention sits in nearly three-fourths of all American households. The videotape machine has changed our entertainment habits and is now changing the nature of commercial television.

The VCR introduced the concept of "time shifting," meaning viewers could view what they want when they want. No longer does a household member have to turn down a social invitation just to be able to stay home and watch a favorite series or the final installment of a made-for-TV miniseries. No one knows how many prime-time TV shows or sports events are taped and watched the next day, but millions of machines turn themselves on every night in obedience to preset directions.

Sports fans now enjoy the security of knowing they will be able to view Sunday's "big game" even if they are not at home when it's played. Of course, they also learn just how difficult it is to avoid hearing or reading about the final score until they watch the tape.

The VCR is threatening to TV because it gives viewers some control over commercials. The millions who watch a network broadcast on tape often fast-forward right through the commercials. Should TV sponsors receive a rebate from the networks for all the lost commercial time? VCRs threaten the network's schedules, carefully prepared to capture audiences.

VCRs also mean viewers can watch shows aired simultaneously on competing networks. VCRs play havoc with network rating systems, making old concepts of "audience-share" obsolete. Before 1976, using the TV set at night meant watching either ABC, CBS, NBC, or public TV. Today a VCR and videocassette tapes can provide a whole week's TV viewing without a single program from a national network.

VCRs have revolutionized the movie industry as well. Going out to the movies today means a social night out to see what's new. No theater can survive on reruns and old movies. But older movies can live for years on the shelves of video stores instead of silently vanishing when their run in local theaters ends. People might go to the movie theater less often today than in years past, but they spend more time watching movies on television.

Consider how videotape has changed living patterns:

Before 1976, there were no video stores. Today, video rental outlets are as commonplace as gas stations and fast-food franchises. In fact, many supermarkets rent videotapes right next to the bakery and produce departments.

The camcorder has almost completely replaced super-8 home movies as a way to document the life of a family. A family album of the future is as likely to be on videocassettes as on slides or in photographs.

Disasters, such as tornados, plane crashes, and other news events often reported but rarely seen live, are now seen more often captured on a bystander's home camcorder.

Many high schools offer videotape versions of the school year-book.

Instructional videos, from aerobics to how to improve your golf score or fix a leaky faucet, now teach difficult-to-explain subjects even to those not highly literate.

Last wills and testaments are now sometimes done on videotape and accepted because the image of the person, along with his or her voice, is clear and difficult to forge. Videotape has the potential to replace legal documents and other written records.

The Dethroning of the Networks

A major trend that has effected network TV is that the three major networks are losing their monopoly on our viewing time. Cable television, satellite dishes, independent "superstations," and alternative networks mean the average household can now see almost thirty TV channels. Television networks now have more competition and find fewer viewers in prime time, especially on Friday and Saturday nights. In prime time, the three networks used to count on capturing 90 per cent of all TV viewers; last year that figure was closer to 75 per cent.

In the 1970s, the major networks' share of the audience was nearly 100 per cent, minus a few points for public broadcasting. The accompanying chart shows the loss of network (ABC, CBS, NBC) share since 1980.

Competition for viewers now comes from cable TV networks; independent superstations, such as Turner Broadcasting's WTBS in Atlanta, WOR-TV in New York, and the Chicago Tribune's WGN; public television; Spanish-language television; home video software; home shopping stations; radio networks; and pay-per-view cable services.

Advertisers are spending more money on cable stations, since they can deliver a more controlled audience. This reflects a move away from "bigger is better" in audiences to capturing the loyalty

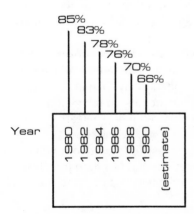

Network Share

85%
83%
78%
76%
70%
66%

Year   1980 1982 1984 1986 1988 1990 (estimate)

of defined segments of the public. Some network executives see a two-level future for television. They see network television (which they call "free" TV) much like a basic car with no options. They see a second level controlled by cable networks that deliver the best movies first and the most important sporting events. Of course, this second level will cost more than free TV.

Flipping, Zapping, and Zipping

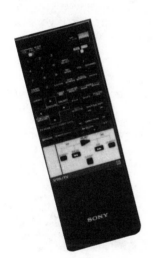

Another innocent-looking invention that changed television is the remote control. If you use remote control, you know it as a convenience. However, those who make TV schedules and keep a pulse on what the public watches know it has changed the way we use television. Remote control has created new types of viewers—the flippers, zappers, and zippers.

One-third of all TV viewers are "flippers." They change channels instead of watching a program from beginning to end. Younger viewers are more likely to be flippers. According to a J. Walter Thompson survey, over 50 per cent of 18 to 24-year-old viewers are flippers. But only 9 per cent are "zappers"—they zap out ads, changing the channel when one comes on. Zappers treat television the way some handle a pushbutton car radio looking for music and avoiding ads. Nearly 20 per cent of viewers are "zippers," who avoid commercials by fast-forwarding through them while watching on a VCR.

Why are flippers, zappers, and zippers a problem for television? Television depends on delivering a measured number of viewers to advertisers. Measurement systems have not yet caught up with those who graze from channel to channel instead of watching single programs when broadcast. These new viewing patterns suggest television is following the pattern of radio.

When radio was a young medium, people listened to entire programs from beginning to end. The shows were listed in radio guides and broadcast weekly much as television schedules are today. In fact, a radio schedule from the 1920s bears a surprising resemblance to today's evening TV schedules. But television changed radio. Today, people listen to "the radio:; they rarely tune in specific programs at a set time. Radio is part of the electronic environment and is often listened to while doing other tasks. Television, in years to come, will be a more constant part of the electronic environment—on all the time—serving sometimes as a background and other times as a foreground. Cable, VCR, and increased program choices are changing the nature of television. Today, we still watch the news or a sportscast or the "Cosby Show" or some other favorite program. Increasingly, however, we just watch television.

MEDIALAB

Flippers, Zappers, and Zippers

1. In what ways do cable, VCRs, and remote control threaten the three major networks?

2. Do you think cable and VCRs will have an influence on attendance at live events, such as football games? What about live theater? Movies in theaters? Live music concerts? Examine attendance not only in terms of numbers of people but also their behavior. For example, do people today behave differently at a baseball or football game than they did ten or fifteen years ago? Has the VCR changed the way we behave in a movie theater?

3. How does the VCR influence your movie attendance? How do you decide if you want to see a movie at a theater or wait until it is out on videotape?

4. How does your household use time shifting?

5. Take an informal survey of class members to identify flippers, zappers, and zippers. Compare how you select and change stations on the radio with your television viewing.

Life Without Television

Television is like a drug. Habitual viewers are addicted to television and need their daily fix in order to get along. When television is not available, the addicted become nervous, restless, and irritable.

One way to measure how television influences the way we live would be to find a community (perhaps a town of at least 1,000) where people are *not* exposed to television. We could watch these people very closely to see how their lives differ because they lack television. But finding such a community is nearly impossible, for there is hardly a place in the United States that is without television. Even in the most remote and mountainous areas at least 90 percent of the households have television. Since there is no city that would suit our experiment in tubelessness, perhaps we could look for 1,000 average people who don't watch television. But since these people are such a minority, they can hardly be considered average. To measure the effect of television is indeed difficult precisely because television has become so much a part of ordinary life in America.

One experiment on the absence of television was conducted in Germany, where 184 volunteer television viewers were paid to give up TV for one year. At first the volunteers reported that they spent more time with their children, went to movies more frequently, read and played more games, and visited friends and relatives more than they did before they gave up television.

But within a few weeks things began to change. Even though the people were paid not to watch, one man dropped out after only three weeks. No one lasted more than five months. Why? Tension, fighting, and quarreling increased among families without television. When the experiment was over and the television sets were back on, these effects disappeared.

For some television is like a drug. Habitual viewers are addicted to television and need their daily fix in order to get along . When television is not available, the addicted become nervous, restless, and irritable.

MEDIALAB

How TV Influences Us

1. The experiment described on the preceding page took place in Germany. Do you think the results would be any different if it were conducted in the United States?

2. How do you think your family would react to such an experiment?

3. What positive aspects of television did this experiment reveal?

4. Why did tension, fighting, and quarreling increase within the TV-less families? The psychologists who conducted the experiment made an educated guess at the answer. Stop and think of your own reasons before reading any further.

One of the psychologists who conducted the experiment believes that watching television tends to cover up conflicts and disagreements between habitual viewers. That is, instead of working out problems, people avoid them by watching television. Television works as a sort of buffer between people, helping them to be together without having to work out their conflicts. Take away the TV set and the rough edges begin to show.

5. Write a very short fictional story entitled "The Day Television Disappeared." Base your story on the unexpected occurrence of huge sunspots or some other phenomenon that wipes out all television reception in the world. Your story should tell what might happen when people discover the event and then how things might change without television. You might want to include in your account some of the effects of television on the following: family life, movie attendance, library use, newspaper and book reading, sports, advertising, radio programming.

6. Occasionally, newspapers carry a story about parents who pay their kids to give up TV for a period of time, sometimes a year. Usually the payment is substantial, sometimes five hundred or a thousand dollars. Why would a parent make such an offer? What would your price be to give up television for a year?

7. Find someone in the class who either does not have a television set or who lives in a family where someone almost never watches television. Find out from that person why he or she does not watch television. What is the extra time spent on instead?

8. One of the undeniable effects of television is that it takes up a lot of time. The average person watches TV for six to eight years during a lifetime. If TV were to vanish, a lot of extra time would be available to do other things. How might people be different if they had this extra time to fill? How would you spend your time if you had no TV?

9. Talk to one or two people who remember the days before television. Ask them how they think television has changed family life and the way people spend their time.

10. Television is a rather recent invention. Imagine an invention that could capture the public's interest and time as much as television has. Would it be like television or something very different? How would it change people's lives?

HAVING A FEW LAUGHS

Another view of the effects of television is sometimes seen in satirical cartoons. Take a look at the cartoons on these pages and discuss what statements about television they make. Do you agree or disagree with each viewpoint? Make a cartoon of your own that shows your opinion of television.

"KID'S ESPECIALLY LIKE THIS MODEL... IT DOESN'T HAVE AN 'OFF' SWITCH!"

Animal Crackers

Calvin and Hobbes ® 1988. UNIVERSAL PRESS SYNDICATE

LOOKING AT THE STATISTICS

The following charts from the Nielsen report on television show TV viewing habits of the average household in the United States.

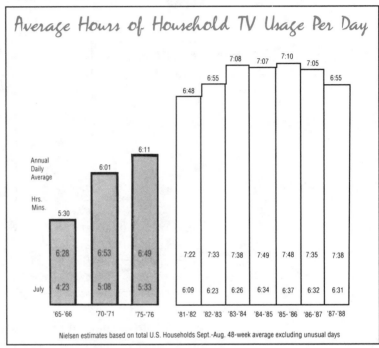

Average Hours of Household TV Usage Per Day

Nielsen estimates based on total U.S. Households Sept.-Aug. 48-week average excluding unusual days

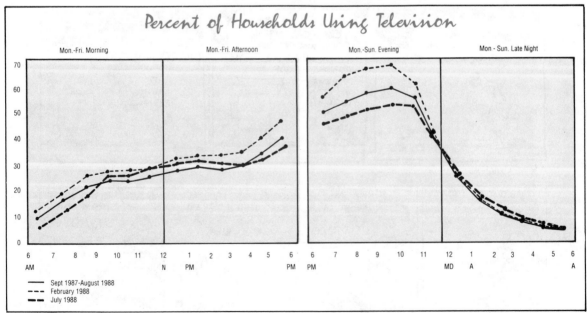

Percent of Households Using Television

Reprinted by permission of Nielsen Media Research from the **1989 Report on Television**.

MEDIALAB

Cartoons and Nielsen Charts

1. What opinion about television is expressed in each of the cartoons?

2. Why are more cartoons published that criticize television rather than praise its benefits?

3. Use the cartoon format to make a statement about television. If you don't want to draw, use cutouts or photographs.

4. The top chart on page 52 shows average hours of household television use per day. The numbers for each year show how many hours and minutes the set is on in a household. This does not mean any one member of the average household watches television for six or seven hours a day. What conclusions can you draw from the chart about how viewing habits change with the seasons, how viewing habits have changed since 1965, and how your household compares to the national average?

5. The bottom chart on page 52 shows the percentage of households using television. What conclusion can you make about the national tele-vision audience in the course of a day? At what time of the day are the most TV sets on? What conclusion can you make about seasonal viewing and time of day?

Reprinted by permission of Nielsen Media Research

THE VIOLENCE QUESTION

The critics of television often point an accusing finger at television's role in teaching about violence. Perhaps you already have an opinion on the question of whether television encourages violent behavior.

How much violence is presented on television programs? Perhaps you believe that the make-believe violence does not affect viewers. The slam-bang fights and wild chases that take place in cartoons may seen harmless, but researchers have found various effects on children. On the following pages, one person presents a strong argument that TV violence is harmful.

" IT'S BLOOD!! "

TV VIOLENCE *IS* HARMFUL

by **Jesse L. Steinfeld, M.D.**

Dr. Jesse L. Steinfeld has been a professor of medicine at the University of Southern California and an official of the National Institute of Health. He has also served as Surgeon General of the United States.

Every day some 40 million American children ages two through eleven tune into their family television sets for an average of 3 1/2 hours of watching. By age 12, the total an estimated average viewing time of 13,500 hours apiece—far more than double the time they spend in the schoolroom. In the process, they will have watched 101,000 violent episodes, including an estimated 13,400 deaths.

What is the effect of all this television mayhem on our young people? Consider these recent findings:

• At the University of North Carolina Child Development Center, researchers recently paired ten preschoolers who had similar television and play habits. Then, over an 11-day period, one child was shown a violent Saturday-morning television offering, while his partner watched a nonaggressive show. The five exposed to violent programming became remarkably more aggressive, some even tripling their violent acts (kicking, choking, hitting, pushing), while their mates' scores remained largely unchanged.

• Two Penn State researchers carefully recorded the level of physical and verbal attacks among 92 kindergartners, then divided them into three groups to watch different half-hour television films over a four-week period. One group saw "Superman" and "Batman" shows, each containing several physical and verbal assaults. A second group saw "Mister Rogers' Neighborhood," whose puppet vignettes teach youngsters how to cope with anger, jealousy, fear, and frustration. As a control, the third group saw neutral shows. Among children who had measured initially low in aggression there wasn't a significant response one way or another. Children from the lower socioeconomic backgrounds who saw "Mister Rogers" improved strikingly in cooperation, obedience to rules, and daily relations with others. However, among those who were above average in aggressiveness—fully half the total—exposure to the violent films caused a sharp increase in their attacks on playmates.

• In 1959, New York Department of Mental Hygiene researchers evaluated both television-violence viewing and aggressive behavior of 184 third-grade boys. In a follow-up study of the same group ten years later, they discovered an astonishing long-term effect. "Regardless of whether the individual's behavior at age eight was combative or nonaggressive, if he watched high levels of television violence he was likely to rank high in aggression ten years later," concludes Dr. Monroe Lefkowitz, the senior researcher.

• Survey teams studied 2,900 junior- and senior-high-schoolers and 1,500 graduates from almost 100 schools throughout the nation. In each group the researchers found a correlation between television-violence viewing and a wide range of troublemaking behavior.

Research Proves the Point.

These studies—and scores of similar ones—make it clear to me that the relationship between televised vio-

> The debate over the effects of violence on television watchers is like the debate over cigarette smoking and cancer.
> —ARNOLD KAHN, American Psychological Association

lence and antisocial behavior is sufficiently proved to warrant immediate remedial action. Indeed, the time has come to be blunt: We can no longer tolerate the present high level of televised violence that is put before children in American homes. Many citizens and parents have long fretted over the impact of television on our youth. Therefore, in March 1969, Sen. John O. Pastore (D., R.I.), chairman of the Senate communications subcommittee, asked that the Surgeon General create a Scientific Advisory Committee on Television and Social Behavior to determine "what harmful effects, if any, these programs have on children." Three years later, the work of hundreds of scientific investigators, spelled out in 2,500 pages of studies, left no doubt that televised violence adversely affects our younger generation. Dr. Robert M. Liebert, State University of New York expert in imitative learning and child development, best summarizes the researchers' findings: "We have impressive evidence that watching television violence causes a significant increase in aggressive behavior. It is not the only or even the most significant cause of antisocial behavior, but it certainly is one of the major contributors. It also happens to be one cause we can change."

The high level of violence is truly appalling. For six years, Dean George Gerbner, of the University of Pennsylvania's Annenberg School of Communications, studied violence levels on all three networks. The combined output contained incidents of physical force intended to hurt or kill at a rate of about eight per hour.

And cartoons—the mainstay of children's programming—averaged 22 such incidents hourly.

Indifference to Harm.

Gerbner's study is supported by Boston University Prof. F. Earle Barcus. In 1971, Barcus monitored all the children's programs of his city's three network stations and one UHF independent. He found 71 percent of the stories had at least one instance of human injury or killing, and about a third of the dramatic segments were "saturated" with violence.

Why? To find out, Prof. Muriel G. Cantor of American University interviewed 24 Los Angeles producers and scriptwriters—a group responsible for nearly all the cartoons and live-action programs aimed at the Saturday-morning children's market. None had any specific academic background for preparing children's programs. Over half had been in entertainment,advertising, promotion, or publicity. Most displayed an appalling indifference to possible harmful effects of their output on children. "As long as we are on the air," said one producer, "I don't care." Always, the ruling consideration seems to be audience size.

Yet the violence-equals-ratings-equals-profits formula is not infallible. A survey in England showed that children overwhelmingly prefer humor to "action" or "adventure." Could this be true also in the United States? We don't know. Our commercial broadcasters have never bothered to conduct extensive research, and thus American audiences simply have had little choice.

MEDIALAB

Researching the Violence Question

1. Your class can conduct a study to measure the amount of violence currently shown on television. The class can be divided so that a group of students is assigned to each local TV channel. Each group should divide viewing time among its members so that the entire prime time schedule of its station can be monitored during one week. In addition to evening hours, someone can be assigned to monitor the Saturday morning childrens shows. Each student should keep a written record of all the televised violence. Be sure to include the date, time, channel, and name of program or programs viewed. Note each act of violence committed during viewing and write down a description of each act in a few words. Also note why the violent act was committed (for example, self-defense or to escape the police). List each weapon seen and keep track of the number of people wounded and killed.

After one week of watching for TV violence, each group should gather its data and compile a record of that channel's "violence report" for the entire week. Once these are compiled, compare the local stations and programs to determine which is the most and which the least violent.

2. Judging from your statistics in the study above, estimate how many killings appear on television in an average year. Which programs seem to depend the most on stories in which killing is involved?

The article by Jesse Steinfeld quoted a study that found an average of eight incidents per hour on TV of "physical force intended to hurt or kill." How does this compare with your more recent findings?

3. What kind of violence is most common on Saturday mornings? Is there more or less than on prime time?

4. What are the most common reasons for the violent acts shown on television?

5. Reach some conclusion from your violence study.

6. Think of at least one good argument in favor of the opinion that "TV violence is not harmful." Discuss these arguments in class. If you cannot think of one reason, do some library research using the *Reader's Guide to Periodical Literature* under the heading . . . television.

7. The article tells of experiments by "two Penn State researchers." Read this section (fourth paragraph of the article) carefully and discuss their findings.

8. What studies mentioned in the article conclude simply, "Watching television makes children more violent"?

9. Is there any kind of control on your television watching or on that of your younger brothers or sisters in regard to violent programs?

10. Write a short essay in which you state your own opinions about violence on television.

TV or Not TV

Frozen dinners in a tray were introduced in 1954. They were called "TV Dinners" and sold for about one dollar. Ten million TV Dinners were sold the first year.

Let's look at some of the arguments for television and at some of the criticisms commonly aimed at it.

The first article, written by the author of this textbook, reminds us that addiction to television is not uncommon. A belief that life's problems can be solved or, at least, avoided by changing channels is pervasive and disturbing.

The second article stresses the value of the common collective experiences we have shared by watching live televised events, such as the manned space shuttle launches or the Olympic Games. These shared experiences are seen as important in an era when a sense of community seems to be slipping away.

Television is probably somewhere between the most wonderful gift ever bestowed on humanity and the source of all evil. Let's look at the two views of television that follow.

An Attack on TV

Most arguments against television concern possible
harmful effects of certain types of programming.
Here are some ideas about the
negative effects of television as a medium.

By the time a typical person reaches the deathbed (very likely placed beneath a TV set in a hospital room), he or she will have spent almost nine years watching television. Without television, nine years would be added to the average person's "activity life." It is difficult to believe we have freely chosen to spend so much of a lifetime watching dancing phosphors on a glass screen.

For millions of regular viewers, television is no longer one choice among many to occupy a weekday night. The option has become which programs to watch, not if the set should be on. On any given weekday night, year after year, no matter what programs are presented, there is a fairly constant TV audience of one hundred million people.

People do not watch television because of certain shows they find exciting. If the show they claim to enjoy is not on, they watch some other show. Paul Klein, former vice-president for audience measurement at NBC, claims that viewer choice is based on the L.O.P. theory—the least objectionable program.

The L.O.P. theory states that people don't watch particular programs—they watch television. The set is turned on for the same reason people climb mountains—it's there. The program viewed at the time is the one that is considered least objectionable. To garner high ratings, all a show has to do is be less objectionable than its competition. A show does not have to be well written, well acted, or lavishly produced. Network programmers know that some well-received programs are stupid, but they also know that a program doesn't have to be good, it only has to be less objectionable.

Our language further supports Klein's L.O.P. theory in that we read THE newspaper, listen to THE radio, read A book or A magazine, but simply watch television. There is truth buried in this linguistic habit, for we do watch the medium of television, and that is significant no matter if the program is about culture or crooks.

Many people watch television simply because they are addicted to the tube. Addiction, normally thought of in terms of drugs, has two neccesary components—tolerance and a withdrawal illness or abstinence syndrome. Tolerance means the body gradually adapts to the drug so that constantly larger doses are required to produce the same effect. A withdrawal illness is a negative physical reaction to a lack of the drug. In other words, without the drug, a person becomes very ill. Abstinence syndrome refers to usually minor ailments (running nose, sweating, tremors, irritability, etc.) when the normal dosage is delayed or missed.

Both these elements of addiction can be seen in viewing habits. The component of tolerance can be seen in the gradual increase of the "average daily dose" self-prescribed by viewers over the years. In 1963, the average household had the set on for five hours and twelve minutes daily; by 1974 that figure had increased to six hours and fourteen minutes; and by 1989 the daily dose had increased to almost seven hours.

Television's power to addict might spring from its ability to involve us emotionally.

We have all experienced deep emotions in front of TV screens; we have all learned about the world we will never visit in person or experience "live." We watch television in order to be manipulated into feeling. We want

"George, one of these days you're going to turn into a vegetable from all that TV."

cases our heart throbs, the pulse quickens, and the body sensations are real. The feelings are real, only the televised stimulus is lacking a third dimension.

People have always sought out games and theater to experience feelings normally missing from daily life. But when the seeking takes six to eight hours a day, it is a sign of an absence of a rich emotional life based on reality. The shadows become substitutes for reality. A Los Angeles soap opera addict explains: "Without these programs going on, I wonder if I would go on. People seem to forget me. . . . These people are my company. My real friends. I have it (TV) on because I feel people are talking to me."

This woman is an extreme case of TV-as-reality-substitute, but her symptoms are common to millions. By watching television, the feelings and sense of companionship can be enjoyed

without responsibility, without the need to share these feelings with others or express them in public or even to "own" them as ours. These TV-generated feelings come from skilled writers and producers and not from within ourselves—they are safe and nonthreatening. Television encourages habitual viewers to avoid responsibility for their own recreation and feelings of aliveness. Responsibility slips into the willing hands of corporations who control TV content as well as the supply of goods presented as means to "come alive."

A professional polling organization conducted a survey of the attitude of readers of the *National Enquirer*. Of the responders, 76 percent agreed that "TV makes me feel tired," 75 percent agreed that it "makes me eat more," and 56 percent claimed that TV causes them to "sleep more." Less than half rated entertainment programs as

"satisfactory." Yet this box that shows mainly unsatisfactory programs and makes viewers hungry and sleepy is one of the few those images on the screen to be frightening, to make us cry or howl with laughter, to help us feel vicarious thrills and excitement, to stimulate awe at the ability of others. Our nervous systems do not distinguish between the fear of a mugger lurking ahead on the deserted street at three in the morning or the fear aroused by the midnight creature feature. In both experiences we as a nation have in common.

The medium itself teaches values, regardless of the programs. Children who grow up on "Sesame Street" learn early to be regular consumers of TV programming. They also learn to accept as normal the fast cutting of "Sesame Street" and fail to learn the value of watching any one scene or visual for more than a few seconds. Television in general teaches the value of frequent change. Images chage constantly, programs change, and there is always that knob to change the channel.

Some psychologists believe TV may be partly to blame for the belief that life's problems can be solved by changing the channel. Los Angeles psychiatrist Dr. Lawrence Friedman explains one tendency of the channel-changing personality. "I'm convinced that at least fifty percent of all divorces in this country are unnecessary. And it's all because TV teaches us simple solutions to complex problems. People tell me, 'If only I could get rid of this marriage, everything would be all right.' Nonsense!"

MEDIALAB

Responding to the Attack

1. Summarize each of the following "attacks" against television as given in the article:
> TV as a time-stealer
> TV as an addiction
> TV as an emotional substitute for reality
> TV as a passive medium
> TV as a teacher of simple solutions

2. The article points out that saying "TV is addictive" is more than a figure of speech. In what way is the "addiction" to television like the addiction to drugs? Be sure to discuss tolerance, withdrawal, illness, and abstinence syndrome.

3. One of the reasons we watch television is to feel a wide range of emotions through others' experiences. This is often called vicarious experience. In what main way is vicarious experience from television different from that gained from theater or books? What danger does the article point out in regard to television as a supplier of emotions?

4. How are the emotions you experience while watching television (or movies) different from emotions in "real" life? How are they the same?

5. Explain the L.O.P. theory in your own words.

6. How do you explain surveys that show many viewers find television unsatisfying coupled with constant increases in the time spent watching television?

7. The TV program "Sesame Street" is often given as an example of helpful educational programming. What "hidden teaching" of the show is pointed out in the article? Do you think television shows in general have such "hidden lessons"?

8. As a television viewer, notice how often a serious program is presented back-to-back with a comedy. How do you react when commercials interrupt a serious, moving drama? Discuss how today's viewers have been conditioned to this kind of programming.

9. In a policy statement issued in April of 1990, the American Academy of Pediatrics said that long-term television viewing not only is a cause of violent or aggressive behavior in children, but also contributes substantially to childhood obesity. Discuss these findings and what, in your opinion, should or should not be done.

In Defense of Television

by **Peggy Charren** and **Martin W. Sandler**

Shared experiences are one of the most important aspects of television viewing. Here are some ideas about the benefits and opportunities of television.

In March 1939 a New York *Times* reporter, assigned to the World's Fair, at which television was introduced, offered a prediction about the new invention. "The problem with television," he wrote, "is that the people must sit and keep their eyes glued to a screen: the average American family hasn't time for it. Therefore . . . for this reason, if no other, television will never be a serious competitor of broadcasting."

The reporter was one of the first of a long line of people who predicted that, as the novelty of television wore off, TV-watching would decline. They could not have been more wrong. Since 1948, when television first became widely available to the American public, TV-viewing has risen so steadily that today Americans spend more time watching television than doing anything else except sleeping. Television has become such an important part of our lives that by the age of 65 the average American will have spent 9 full years watching TV.

Television is this nation's common denominator, its shared experience. Millions watch the same programs every night, laughing at the same jokes, absorbing the same information, being subjected to the same points of view. And chances are that the next day at school or the office or the factory much of the talk will center around the characters and stories of television dramas and situation comedies, the antics of Howard Cosell or Johnny Carson, or one of the many "specials" that appear throughout the year. Wherever we go in the nation we take this experience with us. If we begin watching a week-long miniseries in Chicago one night and we need to make a business trip, we turn on our set in Boston or Los Angeles or New Orleans the next night and tune in Part Two. For millions of people, not to watch television is to be out of the flow of American life. More than one set of parents in this country, after years of forbidding certain

TV programs in their home, have relaxed their rules, concluding that they could not continue to keep their children out of touch with what their classmates talked about.

Television's unique strengths lie in the way it is able to present people with interesting topics of conversation and in its ability to transmit pictures of events to all parts of the world at the moment they are happening. Someone once said that the best thing on television is golf—because no one can write a script for the ball. Television thus far has been most effective when it has gone outside the studio. The highest ratings throughout television history have not gone to situation comedies, soap operas, miniseries, or even lavishly promoted network spectaculars. They have gone to what Israeli sociologist Elihu Katz calls the "live broadcasting of history" or "the high holidays of mass communication." Time and again in the last two decades the activities of the entire nation have come practically to a halt as we have shared a common collective experience by watching a live televised event.

Some of these events have been awe-inspiring—the moon landings, the manned space shuttle flights, the victory of the underdog United States hockey team at the 1980 Olympics. Televised events of this type take on the quality of holidays. In an era when a sense of community seems to be slipping steadily, these occasions have given us the opportunity to share together, rejoice together, and exult in our accomplishments as a nation and as human beings.

This shared experience is one of the most important aspects of the televised event. Just as television has allowed us to share our joy and pride, witnessing triumphs and discoveries, so have we found collective solace in viewing together the tragedies of the nation. Somehow—by sharing the experience of the Kennedy and Sadat funerals, the plight of the Iranian hostages, the assassination attempts on our Presidents—we have been able to comfort ourselves, renew our commitment to democracy, and carry on.

If television binds us in joy and sorrow, it also unites us as creatures dependent on an electronic box for many human needs. In less than four decades, television has become educator, comforter, entertainer, babysitter, titillator, salesperson, patriot, investigator, *paterfamilias* to the nation, and psychiatrist to the individual. We watch television when we are bored and when we are anxious, alone and together, to laugh and to cry, to learn and to avoid learning. Even so, watching television is like sex in Victorian England. Almost everybody does it, but few brag about it. As one critic has said, "Disparagement of television is second only to watching television as a national pastime."

Television, like comic books and the movies before it, has been blamed for all the ills of society—from the quality of our candidates to crime in the streets. This is not a particularly happy time in history. Populations are growing so quickly, resources are being used up so rapidly, and poverty is such a significant problem that the very survival of the human race is in question. Yet, terrorism and crime are probably no more commonplace and pervasive than in certain other times in history. The difference is that with TV, the world now has a messenger that brings the actual sights and sounds of these disruptions into living rooms night after night. Our tendency is to place the blame for these disruptions not on their complex causes but instead on the messenger.

If television is not entirely to blame, neither is it the innocent messenger. The truth is that television both reflects and affects behavior, and it does neither perfectly. TV does not cause poverty, but it does affect our attitudes toward the poor and their condition. It does not cause crime, but it affects our attitudes toward the role of violence in our society. To say that television didn't invent the most serious problems and isn't responsible for most of them is not to say however, that this infant medium has not presented us with a myriad of significant problems of its own.

. . . In an age when, as a nation, we have come to regard TV as one of the essentials of life, it is vital for us to learn how to make the most of it. Television is here to stay. And today more than at any other time in its history, it is growing and expanding. . . .

Celebrities Speak Out About TV

"Once I thought the most important political statement we could make about television was to turn it off. But television can instruct, inform, and inspire, as well as distract, distort, and demean. And turning it off rejects the good with the bad. My family wants its voice added to the summons for quality, and I urge you to speak up, too, in every way possible. This marvelous medium, with all its potential for laughter, and light, is worth fighting for."

BILL MOYERS,
TV commentator and interviewer

"Television has had a wonderful impact on social change throughout the world, but I believe television has indirectly contributed to our country's growing illiteracy. Why read the book when you can watch the movie?"

PATRICK COYNE, Editor,
Communication Art

"Television is one of the greatest engines in terms of disseminating information . . . that's the television we hope to use and be effective in reaching people."
PAUL JUNGER WITT, executive co-producer,
ABC Earth Day TV special, 1990

"There are times, and today was one of those times, when television approaches the truly magical, when it becomes the sort of instrument that, 50 or 60 years ago, would have been regarded as supernatural....This has been, without question, one of the more memorable days in our nation's history; and television, much maligned television, which frequently does numb the brain and dull the senses, today produced a technological miracle. Never has any generation of Americans had greater reason to claim they were eyewitness to history."
TED KOPPEL, "Nightline" January 20, 1980,
on the occasion of the
1980 Winter Olympics

MEDIALAB

Responding to the Defense

1. Notice that "In Defense of Television" does not deal with specific programs on television. It treats television as a mass medium. What is the main benefit of the medium of television, as explained in the article?

2. What does it mean to say that television is this nation's "common denominator, its shared experience"?

3. What kind of programming does the article claim is the strength of television?

4. Every few years there is some event that seems to unite the country, an event shared by television. The event could be an Olympic celebration, a funeral or tragedy, or even a televised miniseries. What event in your memory has been a nationwide emotional experience shared through the medium of television?

5. When asked, "Why do you watch television?" you would probably respond with a simple, "Because I like some of the shows." But there are deeper reasons for watching. The article points to the following uses for television:
   educator
   comforter
   entertainer
   baby sitter
   titillator
   salesperson
   patriot
   investigator/reporter
   paterfamilias (Latin for "head of the household")
   psychiatrist

Discuss each of these roles and give examples of how television is used for each.

Some Questions to Ask Yourself About Watching TV

adapted from an article by
Peggy Charren and **Martin W. Sandler**

TV programs, like an addictive drug, have a built-in failure to satisfy. They provide only enough pleasure to bring viewers back for more. What does television teach? Television teaches you to watch more TV.

Are you upset with the amount of time you spend in front of the TV set? How much time do you spend with TV? How does this compare with national viewing statistics? (The average American watches 6 hours and 55 minutes per day.)

• What kinds of things have you stopped doing because of your TV watching?

• Do you find yourself watching selected programs that you look forward to, or do you simply watch whatever is on?

• Has television affected your life positively? Negatively?

• Do you find that your buying decisions in the supermarket or the department store are helped by TV commercials? Hindered?

• Do you automatically turn on the television set when you walk into your home? Is the TV set on in your bedroom right up until the time you fall asleep? When else do you automatically turn on TV? For example, as soon as you enter a hotel room? Whenever you're home alone with a couple of hours alone with a couple of hours to kill?

• For the most part, do you watch TV alone or with other people? When you watch with others do you ever discuss what you have seen with them? When you have finished watching a program alone do you ever ask yourself what you liked or did not like about it?

• Has television affected the quality of time you spend with your family? Do you do less together because of televised weekend sports? What about mealtimes? How many meals do you eat in front of the tube?

• Is television a major irritant in our home? Do you fight about what to watch, about turning it off?

• Do you have cable or a video recorder? If you do, do you find that you're watching even more television than you did before? Have the increased options made your TV viewing more enjoyable?

MEDIALAB

TV Detective Work

1. Imagine you own an experimental TV station and design a TV schedule for one day of programming. The schedule should reflect the prime purpose of every station to "serve the public interest of those in the viewing area." Your schedule should run for one 24-hour day, should contain only programming that cannot be found on other TV stations in the area (no movies, reruns, or network shows allowed), and should reflect an active imagination. Here is an example, a part of one such experimental TV schedule.

Evening
5:30-6:00
30-Minute Meal. Turn the TV on in the kitchen, follow the direction of the TV chef, and 30 minutes later you have dinner. Necessary ingredients are listed in the newspaper each day.

6:00-7:00
Newsmakers in the City. While other stations are having news reported by announcers, this station has a one-hour news program in which there is no announcer. If a robbery is in the news, the entire report will consist of the person robbed telling the story of what happened. All-film presentation.

7:00-10:00
Citizen Access. Groups and individuals with some thing important to say will be given free time to speak. Videotape equipment will be provided along with instructions on how to make the presentation interesting.

Detailed contents of the program will be listed each day in the newspaper.

10:00-10:30
The Local Consumer Guide. Guide to where to get the best prices in the city on various products. This show will name names and give prices. Also it will give warnings about shoddy merchandise or unethical salespeople working in the city.

10:30-11:30
On the Job. Portable camera will ride along in a local police squad car or follow detectives while they work. Other weeks this show will follow people in other occupations to give an idea of what it is like to be, for example, a computer programmer, radio disc jockey, or a construction worker.

11:30-1:30
Night Life. Portable cameras visit city night life (night clubs or popular hangouts) to show what happens at night.

1:30-3:00
Insomniac's Special. Soothing music and hypnotic visuals especially designed to induce sleep.

2. Take a survey of the class to find out which current TV program is watched by the most class members. Discuss why that program is the most popular and what it teaches.

3. Write a critical review of a television program that you have watched. Point out

both the weak and strong points of the program.

4. Arrange to have in class as many TV sets as there are local stations (or as many as possible). Turn all the TV sets on at once (each tuned to a different station), with the sound off. Watch the sets during class. Be able to tell the difference between a live or videotaped program and a film program. What part of the programs has the fastest visual pace, the most changes of picture angle per minute? How is the effect of TV without sound different from that with sound? How is televiewing different when multiple sets are used?

5. The project teams formed at the beginning of the course should now present their reports on the image of various groups as television portrays them. Allow plenty of time for each report and for questions from the class. Teams include those on the images of law enforcement personnel, doctors, elderly people, teenagers, women, men, criminals, or any topic chosen by a project team.

6. Attempt to group television programs by type: situation comedy, daytime drama, quiz show, talk show. First draw up a list of as many types of programs as you think exist. Next test your list of types by attempting to classify all TV programs according to the list. Use the daily newspapers or a TV schedule magazine such as *TV Guide* to provide program names.

7. Select one TV show to watch during prime time (evenings). On a sheet of paper make two columns: "How the Program is Realistic" and "How the Program is Unrealistic." Fill in both columns as you watch and then report or discuss your findings with the class. This project can also be done by having the entire class watch the same program (or programs) and compare and discuss their lists.

8. Watch some TV programming intended for young children and make a written or an oral report. Select either entertainment-type programs, such as those seen on Saturday mornings, or educational programs, such as "Sesame Street" or "3-2-1 Contact" or watch both kinds and compare them.

9. Prepare a report on how televised sports programs affect family life.

10. Prepare a report on television censorship. Use *The Readers' Guide to Periodical Literature* to find material on recent censorship cases. General books on the history of television would be better sources of information on past cases.

11. Find out how much time in each television hour is given to commercials. Note how many different commercials are given in one time period. The percentage of time devoted to advertising will vary according to the time of day—daytime, prime time, and late night. Keep track of these differences.

12. Prepare an information sheet on all your local TV stations. List (a) the channel and call letters of all TV stations in your area; (b) the network each belongs to if any; (c) the location of the station's studio and transmitting tower; and (d) the owner of the station.

13. The Standard Rate and Data Service books (found in the reference section of many libraries) give information about media advertising rates. Check in the book on TV spot advertising to find out how much each local TV station charges for advertising. Report the findings to the class.

14. If you enjoy and understand electronics, report on how television works. What makes color in a TV picture, and how does a picture travel from a TV studio to the home TV set?

15. Have a class discussion/poll and select the three worst programs on television. Explain and defend your choices.

16. Examine the opinion about television you wrote at the beginning of this chapter, and rewrite it based on what you have learned in this chapter. You do not have to change your opinion.

INDIVIDUAL STUDENT PRESENTATIONS

Following is a list of forty research topics or readings about television. Select one and prepare a three-to-five-minute oral report or a short essay summarizing and reacting to that topic or reading. This list cites material from novels, short stories, movies, newspapers, nonfiction books, magazines, and journals. A trip to the library is necessary with most of these suggested presentation topics.

Books/Short Stories/Movies

1. Television as presented in *Fahrenheit 451* by Ray Bradbury.

2. Television as presented in the novel *1984* by George Orwell.

3. Television as seen in *Brave New World* by Aldous Huxley.

4. The role of television in *Being There* by Jerzy Kosinski.

5. The role of an advanced version of television in the short story "The Veldt" by Ray Bradbury.

6. Compare movies, books, or stories you have seen or read in which an alien or foreigner learns about our culture from watching television.

7. "How To Make TV Commercials That Sell," chapter eight of *Ogilvy on Advertising* by David Ogilvy.

8. A chapter of your choice from the book *The Plug-In Drug* by Marie Winn.

9. A chapter of your choice from *The Show and Tell Machine* by Rose K. Goldsen.

10. A chapter of your choice from *Television: The Business Behind the Box* by Les Brown.

11. A chapter of your choice from *The Crowd-Catchers* by Robert Lewis Shayon.

12. A chapter of your choice from *Watching Television,* edited by Todd Gitlin.

13. A chapter of your choice from *Tube of Plenty: The Evolution of American Television* by Erik Barnouw.

Articles from Periodicals

14. The report on television at the 1939 World's Fair in the March 19, 1939, edition of the *New York Times*, sometimes available on microfilm in the reference section of large community and school libraries. The article contains the following judgment: "The problem with television is that the people must sit and keep their eyes glued on a screen; the average American family hasn't time for it."

15. "To Grab Viewers' Attention, TV Ads Aim for the Eardrum" by John Koten in *The Wall Street Journal,* January 26, 1984.

16. "The Videophobes," *Time* (November 8, 1968).

17. "The Structure of Televised Football" by Brian R. Williams, *Journal of Communications* volume 27, no. 3 (Summer 1977).

18. "Media Mentors" by John L. Caughey, *Psychology Today* (September 1978).

19. "What TV Recommends Most" by Clark Norton, *Hippocrates* (January-February 1989).

20. "Advertising in Disguise" *Consumer Reports* (March 1986).

21. "Cutting to Smithereens" *New York Times Magazine* (October 19, 1986).

22. "Prime Time Cereal" *The New Republic* (December 22, 1986).

23. The interview with Neil Postman, *U.S. News and World Report* (December 23, 1985): page 58.

24. "TV Versus Me," *Weight Watchers Magazine* (November 1985), an article on the image of beauty in television commercials.

25. "What TV Does To Kids" by Neala Schwartzberg, *Parents' Magazine* (June 1987).

26. "What Television Does Best" *Life* (March 1989).

27. The article about Hispanics on television by Geraldo Rivera, *TV Guide* (April 18, 1987).

28. "How On-Screen Violence Hurts Your Kids" by Benjamin Spock, *Redbook* (November 1987).

29. "Why Only Patty Duke Can Have It All" by Anna Quindlen, *New York Times* (November 17, 1988).

30. "MTV's Message" by Eric Gelman, *Newsweek* (December 30, 1985).

31. "The Huxtables: Fact or Fantasy?" by Alvin Poussaint, *Ebony* (October 1988).

32. "TV and the Ethics of Television" by Michael Ignatieff, *Harper's Magazine* (February 1986).

33. "Caught in Fantasyland: Electronic Media's Hold on Society" by Jay Martin, *USA Today* (July 1988).

34. "What Is Television Doing To Us," *New York Times Magazine* (June 12, 1949).

35. "Don't Blame TV for Society's Ills" by Jeff Greenfield, *TV Guide* (January 18, 1986).

36. "The Age of Abundance for Television Worldwide" by James H. Rosenfield, *Vital Speeches* (January 15, 1986).

37. "What Makes Some Kids More Vulnerable to the Worst of TV?" by Robert Coles, *TV Guide* (June 21, 1986).

38. "Overextending the Family: Replaced by Surrogates, Mom and Dad Have Lost Control of the TV Home" by Harry Waters, *Newsweek* (November 24, 1986).

39. "Too Rich and Too Thin" by Roger Simon, *Vogue* (February 1985).

40. "Where the Media Critics Went Wrong" by Walter Karp, *American Heritage* (March 1988).

WRAP-UP

Since its introduction at the 1939 World's Fair, television has established itself as a mass medium in 99 percent of American households. There are differing opinions as to the value of television, but the truth is many of us depend on it for entertainment and education. Television ties us together as a community, acting as a common denominator. Developments in technology, such as the VCR and cable television, have given us many viewing options. The word *couch potato* has become part of our language. Do we watch too much TV? Throughout Chapter 2 you have read and thought about TV programming, current statistics, and TV habits. Have you become a better, more discerning, more critical TV viewer?

SONY

Getting the L.A. Marathon off the ground.

Perception.

CHAPTER 3
Advertising

MY VIEW

Advertising is the fuel that powers mass media. Broadcast television is free for the viewing audience— while advertisers gladly pay thousands of dollars a second to reach those who are watching. Newspapers, magazines, and radio and TV stations would cease to exist if advertisers deserted them.

THE HISTORY OF ADVERTISING

Advertising exists to create a demand.

No one knows who was the first advertiser. Perhaps thousands of years ago one of our ancestors carved a sign in a rock announcing a fire restarting service for the reasonable fee of one carved ax handle. But mass advertising didn't exist in prehistoric days simply because there was no need for it.

Advertising exists to solve a problem: the presence of more goods than are needed. In a society of scarcity, where there is not enough to go around, there is no need for ads. Everything that is grown or made is put to immediate use. Advertising requires a surplus of goods or services. It exists to create a demand. There is no need for advertising if the demand already exists far beyond the supply.

As long as goods were supplied locally, handmade as needed, there was little need for advertising beyond an occasional announcement or sign. A shoemaker would hang a sign outside his house (which was also his workshop), but had no need to advertise. All he could do was make a few pairs of shoes a week. Each shoe was custom-made for a specific person—there was no back room filled with inventory; there was no surplus of shoes to be moved before the new fashions could be introduced.

Even if our humble shoemaker could hire workers to turn out a surplus of shoes, how would he advertise? The technology of printing was not a mass medium until after the year 1500. Only with printing could the shoemaker make handbills to pass around the village. Before printing he would have to rely on a town crier or perhaps a strolling minstrel to sing a jingle about his shoes.

Modern advertising had to wait for a surplus of goods. And a surplus of goods came about only with machines that could turn out more than one item at a time—not until the Industrial Revolution. Only after the Industrial Revolution were there enough products and money to support mass advertising.

Mass advertising thus required the technology of printing and the Industrial Revolution. But there was a third requirement—literate customers. During the 1800s laws were passed both in England and the United States requiring children to attend school. These laws were important to advertising since they raised the literacy level of the general population to the point at which printed advertisements could be understood.

Printers were quick to see that handbills were a profitable source of business. By combining handbills with news, printers produced what would eventually become the modern newspaper and magazine. Printers realized they could make money both by selling their paper to readers and by charging merchants to print advertisements.

But printers found they spent too much time soliciting ads from merchants, so they hired agents to sell advertising space. These agents were not paid a salary; they were paid a commission on each ad they sold. The size of the commission became standardized at 15 percent of the cost of the ad and often remains that today.

As more newspapers, newsletters, and magazines were printed, merchants were besieged by advertising agents. "Which publication is best for my goods?" each wondered. The agent knew the most about advertising and so became a kind of selling consultant. In 1870, two competing agents, J. Walter Thompson and N. W. Ayer, realized that they could best serve their clients by writing effective selling copy and by planning an advertising campaign. These agents created the age of modern advertising.

Advertising changed as new media became available—color posters, radio, and television. Advertisements transmitted via broadcast media are called commercials. The purpose of advertising, both print ads and commercials, changed as well. Advertising went through a series of refinements, each representing a new approach to selling. At first, advertising was only information. Next, advertisers saw the value of capturing reader attention before presenting the information. In general, advertising progressed through eight stages.

These eight stages did not follow in orderly steps, and a new step did not completely replace the previous step. Tracing these eight steps or approaches gives a clear picture of the role of advertising today.

Advertising Approaches

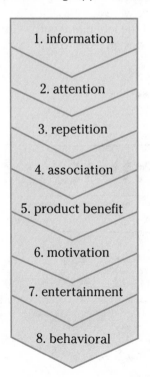

1. information
2. attention
3. repetition
4. association
5. product benefit
6. motivation
7. entertainment
8. behavioral

Information Approach

Before the nineteenth century most advertising was merely informative. It consisted of price lists, signs on walls, printed announcements, and even the calls of the town crier. Supply and demand were in balance and there was no need to produce new products. People bought what they needed and needed what they bought. There was limited competition among merchants.

Attention Approach

By the start of the nineteenth century, factories were turning out goods that needed public attention to sell. The goods had to be sold in markets away from the factory. Manufacturers found it necessary to use various devices to attract attention.

To call attention to the "advertisement," devices such as borders, headline type, and increased white space were used. Today, we take these devices for granted, but remember, the earliest ads were considered news. "A shipment of tea arrived by ship yesterday and is available for sale at dockside" is both news and an ad. In fact, the word *advertise* originally meant "to announce." Many early newspapers (and some today) were named the "Advertiser" not because they carried ads but because to advertise meant to announce.

Consider page one of Boston's *Daily Evening Transcript* of April 9, 1840. On its front page were three-line notices for Italian cravats, money to loan, potatoes, two teens who wanted work in a "Publik House," and shares of bank stock. The page was a solid mass of small type, broken only by a large capital letter here and there. Ads and news were not separated, nor were ads classified according to type of merchandise. Not until the late nineteenth century were large sizes of type and graphic design used to gain readers' attention.

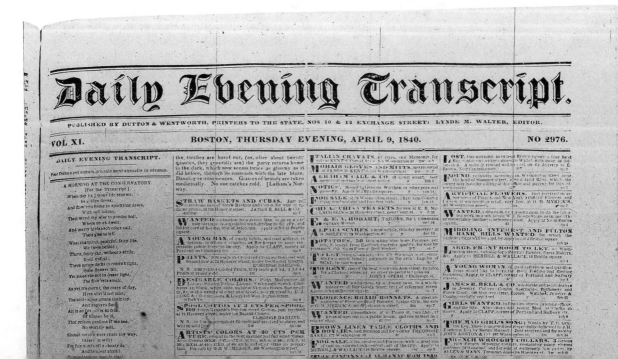

Repetition Approach

Many influential large city newspapers objected to large-sized type for some announcements. They felt it would be unfair to others. The "agate rule" stated that all announcements had to be set in agate type. On this page you see a typical 1800s newspaper advertisement, announcing a cure for rickets—a disease once common in children, caused by a lack of vitamin D. Note that the ad is set according to the agate rule.

> SMALL BAGGS to hang about Children's necks, which are excellent both for the *prevention and cure* of the *Rickets,* and to ease Children in breeding of Teeth, are prepared by Mr. Edmund Buckworth, and constantly to be had at Mr. Philip Clark's, Keeper of the Library in the Fleet, and nowhere else, at 5 shillings a bagge.

Repetition as an advertising device was created to get around the "agate rule."

If the type could not be made larger, it could be repeated to attract attention. Repetition as an advertising device was created to get around the "agate rule." It is still used today as perhaps the most common of all persuasive devices.

Robert Bonner, an early publisher, took a whole page of the *New York Herald* in 1856 and repeated his message 600 times. P. T. Barnum was a master of the art of repetition. An ad Barnum ran in a newspaper in 1841, promoting his museum of Americana, is reproduced on this page. Notice the use of line duplication.

The reader of a newspaper does not see the first insertion of an ordinary advertisement; the second insertion he sees, but does not read; the third insertion he reads; the fifth insertion, he speaks of it to his wife; the sixth insertion, he is ready to purchase; and the seventh insertion, he purchases.

—P. T. BARNUM

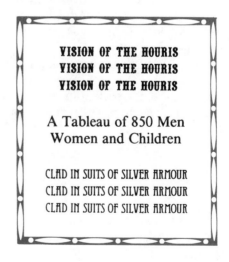

VISION OF THE HOURIS
VISION OF THE HOURIS
VISION OF THE HOURIS

A Tableau of 850 Men
Women and Children

CLAD IN SUITS OF SILVER ARMOUR
CLAD IN SUITS OF SILVER ARMOUR
CLAD IN SUITS OF SILVER ARMOUR

While Bonner and Barnum were practicing repetition, technology made it possible to sell food in glass containers or tin cans. Prior to this time, merchants scooped food from huge bins or barrels. There was little room for the development of a name brand. But cans and bottles made possible the sale of small quantities of food under a brand name. The method of repetition was ideally suited to making the public aware of brand names.

Repetition as a means of persuasion still thrives today. It received a boost from the scientific work of Ivan Pavlov and J.B. Watson in the 1920s. Pavlov and Watson introduced the idea of the "conditioned reflex." The theory held that learning involved the association of a response with a stimulus. A response to the specific stimulus was learned if the stimulus was repeated often enough. Pavlov demonstrated that a dog learned to lift its paw at the sound of a bell if the dog was repeatedly rewarded for doing so.

J. B. Watson was hired by the J. Walter Thompson Advertising Agency to apply this theory to advertising. Advertising quickly learned to repeat often and to treat the purchase as a reward for the consumer's correct response.

By the 1930s repetition meant using a catchy phrase or jingle on the radio that was repeated over and over again. A classic example is the famous Pepsi jingle on this page. Pepsi-Cola set this jingle to the tune of an old English hunting song and used it in their advertising for decades.

The repetition approach thrives today—and not only for products. Celebrities also know that keeping a name before the public breeds familiarity and acceptance.

Pepsi-Cola hits the spot.
Twelve full ounces, that's a lot.
Twice as much for a nickel, too.
Pepsi-Cola is the drink for you!
Nickel, nickel, nickel,nickel,
Trickle, trickle, trickle, trickle,
Nickel, nickel, nickel, nickel.

Association Approach

By the end of the nineteenth century, advertisers began to suspect that pure repetition was not enough. Advances in color printing and techniques developed by French poster artists led to the next phase in advertising—association.

Artists such as Aubrey Beardsley, Toulouse-Lautrec, and Edward Penfield showed that paintings of attractive people in poster ads created pleasant associations for the product. Even today, pleasing graphics and appealing pictures lead to favorable product associations.

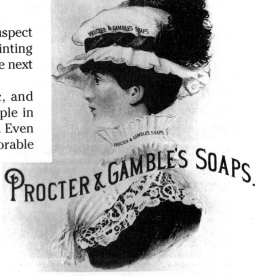

In the early 1900s Hudson River steamboats turned on searchlights at night so passengers could read the billboards that lined the banks.

Product-Benefit Approach

As products became more complex, advertisers found it necessary to explain what the products were and why the consumer would benefit from their use. In the 1950s, Rosser Reeves developed the phrase "unique selling proposition" (USP) to show that every ad must present the product as unique. The USP had to be a product benefit that no other brand could offer.

Reeves agency took Colgate toothpaste and coined the word *Gardol* for its decay-fighting ingredient. It didn't matter if the ingredient was unique to Colgate; it was sufficient that the name *Gardol* be unique. Colgate was unique because it alone had Gardol; and it alone had Gardol because its ad agency made up the word.

Motivation Approach

By the end of the 1930s, the fledgling science of motivational research was discovered by ad agencies. Products were seen to have psychological meanings. Advertisers realized that people bought goods not only because they needed them but also because of various and often hidden psychological needs.

"In the laboratory I make cosmetics, in the stores I sell dreams."
CHARLES REVSON
founder of Revlon

During this time the work of Sigmund Freud was recognized in the United States. Although few advertisers completely understood his theories, they realized that people often bought products for unconscious motives. In other words, before this time advertisers assumed that people bought a certain brand of soap because it cleaned best or cost less. From Freud's work they realized that a brand may be bought because the buyers feel the brand makes them more powerful, more loved, or more socially acceptable.

Motivational research learned, for example, that women would not pay more than a dollar for a bar of soap to make them clean. But they would pay many dollars for a "cream" that promised to make them beautiful. In other words, don't sell soap- sell dreams. Don't sell oranges—sell health and vitality. Don't sell automobiles sell prestige and power.

Ernest Dichter became the leading proponent of motivational research, and his ideas still exert a strong influence on advertising. One of the most popular books on advertising, *The Hidden Persuaders* by Vance Packard, became a best-seller in the late

1950s. The book "exposed" motivational techniques and promised to explain

Why your wife buys 35 percent more in the supermarket than she intends to.

Why your children like cereals that crackle and crunch.

Why men wouldn't give up shaving even if they could.

But even with the techniques exposed in a best-seller, they are still used today to create new products and repackage old products.

Entertainment Approach

In the middle of the 1950s, the Doyle Dane Bernbach agency realized that advertising could also be entertaining. The history of advertising so far assumed ads were to be informative. But the Doyle Dane Bernbach television commercials entertained. Television commercials today take entertainment value for granted, but keep in mind that the only good commercial is one that sells.

Behavioral Approach

By the 1980s consumers were more critical and better educated. They were becoming increasingly skeptical about commercials.

Behavioral research studied consumer needs and buying patterns to present a product image that would be seen as satisfying a real consumer need. An example of the behavioral approach can be seen in the long-running Virginia Slims (You've Come a Long Way, Baby) cigarette campaign. The campaign seemed to illustrate an understanding of the changing role of women in society and presented a product that fit this changing self-image. Another example of this approach is the ads for reduced-calorie soft drinks as products produced for active, weight-conscious people.

MEDIALAB

The History of Advertising

1. What type of society is needed before mass advertising can become commonplace?

2. What three conditions are needed for mass advertising?

3. Explain how the first advertising agencies were formed.

4. Discuss each of the eight stages or approaches of advertising. Explain them in your own words.

5. Find advertisements (newspaper or magazine ads) that illustrate each of the eight stages of advertising. You do not have to find eight separate ads; many ads contain illustrations of more than one stage.

6. Repetition is one of the most effective persuasion devices. Examine the power of persuasion in a different medium-music. Argue both sides of this statement: Certain songs become "hits" not because they are the best songs but because they are played so much by radio stations. The constant repetition of a song "persuades" listeners of its value. In other words, hits are not played so often because they're popular; they're popular because they're played so often.

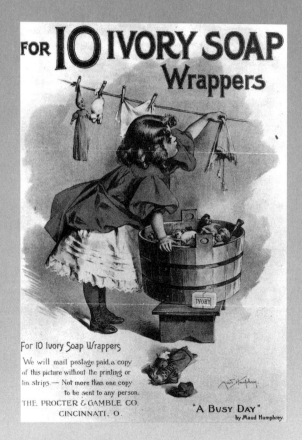

For 10 Ivory Soap Wrappers

We will mail postage paid, a copy of this picture without the printing or tin strips. — Not more than one copy to be sent to any person.

THE PROCTER & GAMBLE CO.
CINCINNATI, O.

"A BUSY DAY"
by Maud Humphrey.

7. Imagine what the ninth stage of advertising will be in the 1990s. The eight stages are still at the heart of advertising, but current ad campaigns point to new methods of persuasion. What new approach(es) do you see?

The Fine Art of Deception Detection

By the time you are 60 years old, you will have seen and heard over 50 million advertising messages. Most will be ignored, some will help, but others will mislead.

Advertising can help you discover new products or show where to buy goods at the lowest price. But it can also mislead you into buying what you don't want or into believing a particular brand is better than it really is. To be able to tell the difference, you need to become a skilled reader of ads.

You must learn to determine exactly what facts are presented in an ad. You must also recognize how the ad strives to make the product appealing. These may seem two simple skills, but advertising experts spend millions to make the job difficult.

Looking for facts in ads and commercials requires the mind of a Sherlock Holmes and the logic of a computer. Almost every advertisement makes what is called a *product claim*. The claim is simply what the ad says about the product. For example, "Jumbo pens write longer than any other ballpoint pen" *claims* very clearly that the Jumbo pen writes longer than any other pen. That sounds simple, yet claims are rarely that plain.

aDVERTISING CLAIMS

There are two basic kinds of claims—one that provides information useful in making a purchase decision, and one that tells little or nothing factual. Here are some advertising claims similar to ones that have been used repeatedly on radio and television and in print advertising.

Look at each ad claim and then write (on a separate piece of paper) what you think the commercial claims about the product. Rate each claim as either (a) one that provides useful information or (b) one that gives little or no useful information. After you have done this with each of the four ads, go on and read the comments made by a skilled ad reader.

CLAIM 1
"Everbright toothpaste helps get your teeth whiter and cleaner. Its special ingredient XT-40 fights tooth decay."

CLAIM 2
"Brushing with Goodteeth toothpaste helps fight tooth decay. Nine out of ten dentists interviewed agreed that brushing with Goodteeth is effective in combating decay."

CLAIM 3
"New improved Blubbers bubble gum now has twice as many sticks of gum. New Green Blubbers is chewed by more professional football players than any other bubble gum. Look for Blubbers in the bright green package wherever good gum is sold."

CLAIM 4
"Strictly controlled scientific tests by an independent testing laboratory show that Imperial gasoline with PowerTane® outperforms any gasoline made without PowerTane. Get Imperial gasoline with PowerTane to help your car run quieter, smoother, and get more miles per gallon."

[Do not read this until you have made your
own comments about the four fictional ads.]

COMMENTS OF A SKILLED AD READER

CLAIM 1

This ad contains no useful information. Many ads make use of
comparative adjectives, such as *whiter*, *cleaner*, or *quieter*, without
saying whiter or cleaner than what. Cleaner than if you used mus-
tard as toothpaste? Whiter than if you used licorice paste? The ad
doesn't say. Perhaps the ad means only that brushing teeth is better than not brushing. The claim invites the reader to supply the
missing comparison by saying "cleaner and whiter than any other
toothpaste." But the ad does not say this, and to believe it does
is a misunderstanding. The ad can be misleading unless it is read
very carefully.

*Whiter or
Cleaner than
what?*

Another claim made in the ad is that Everbright contains a special ingredient-XT-40-to fight tooth decay. What is XT-40? It could
be something that has always been in the toothpaste; it could be
something that all toothpastes contain.

The claim "fights tooth decay" is very carefully worded. It
doesn't say "stops" tooth decay. If Everbright could stop tooth
decay, the ad would say that. Brushing with water also "fights
tooth decay"; so does using toothpicks.

CLAIM 2

The word *helps* is used constantly in advertising. Remember that
"helps" does not mean "does"—it means "helps." It would be perfectly accurate to say that "a bucket of water helps fight forest
fires." But that is not the same as saying that a bucket of water can
put out a forest fire.

"Nine out of ten dentists" (or doctors, athletes, or whomever)
means simply that the company was able to find nine who agreed.
Note that dentists would agree that brushing with anything would
help fight decay; brushing is more important than what is put on

the brush. Dentists know that the proper brushing technique is more important than the brand of toothpaste. The statement doesn't say that Goodteeth itself stops or fights decay—it says that *brushing* with Goodteeth "helps" (remember that word) fight decay.

Help does not mean "does."

CLAIM 3

The word *new* (or *revolutionary*, or *improved*, or *all new*) is another of the advertiser's favorites. "New" does not necessarily mean better—it simply means different.

The fact that Blubbers has twice as many sticks is not the same as saying twice as much gum. They simply may have cut up the same amount of gum into smaller pieces. If the amount of gum had doubled, the ad would probably state that very clearly.

The claim that pro football players chew Blubbers means little. Perhaps each player was mailed a case at the beginning of the season. It would be a very hard claim to either prove or disprove. Also, there is no real connection between chewing gum and playing football.

New does not necessarily mean better.

CLAIM 4

Be careful with this claim. Begin with the knowledge that gasolines are all pretty much the same. The claim here sounds good, but if you read carefully you can see that you never find out exactly what PowerTane is (remember XT-40). If PowerTane is simply a trademark for some common ingredient, then it would certainly be honest to say that "Imperial gasoline outperforms any gasoline made *without* PowerTane." All gas has the same ingredient that Imperial calls PowerTane. But Imperial has registered the name "PowerTane" so no other company can use it—this is called a registered trademark. The claim amounts only to saying that "our car with wheels rides smoother than any car made without wheels."

The ad encourages the unskilled reader to think that Imperial outperforms any other gasoline. But the ad does not actually say that. If Imperial did indeed outperform all others, you can be sure the ad would say so very clearly. Notice that the ad never uses untruth. Also notice that the final sentence again contains comparisons without an ending. Quieter, smoother, and more miles per gallon than what?

Our Cars with round wheels ride smoother than any other car made with square wheels.

A Short Course in Advertising

If your analysis of the four fictional claims was not as perceptive as that of the advertising expert, you need at least a short course in advertising analysis.

One basic rule to remember in analyzing ads is that if any product is truly superior, the ad will say so very clearly and will offer some kind of convincing evidence of its superiority. If an ad hedges at all about a product's superiority, you can suspect that it is not really superior. You will never hear Standard Oil (or any other brand) say "Standard gasoline in your car gives you four miles per gallon more than any other brand." Standard would love to make such a claim, but it simply isn't true. Various brands of gasoline are more alike than different. Although there were some clever and deceptive gasoline ads a few years ago, no one has yet made an outright claim that one brand of gasoline is better than any other.

To create the illusion of superiority, advertisers often resort to one or more of the following eleven basic techniques. Each is common and easy to identify.

1. The Unfinished Claim

The unfinished claim is one in which the ad claims that the product is better or has more of something but does not finish the comparison.
Examples:

> **"Magnaflux gives you more."** (More what?)
>
> **"Supergloss does it with more color, more shine, more sizzle, more!"**
>
> **"Twice as much of the pain reliever doctors recommend most."** (Twice as much as what?)
>
> **"You can be sure if it's Westinghouse."**
>
> **"Scott makes it better for you."**
>
> **"Turbo Glide —700% quieter."**

2. The Weasel Word Claim

Weasel word is a modifier that makes what follows nearly meaningless. The term *weasel word* comes from the habit of weasels of sucking out the inside of a raw egg through a tiny hole. An unsuspecting person picks up what looks like a whole egg only to find it is empty. Weasel word claims sound convincing at first, but upon closer examination turn out to be empty claims.

better

more

helps

The most common weasel words include *helps* (perhaps the most used), *virtual* or *virtually*, *like* (used in a comparative sense), *acts* or *works*, *can be*, *up to*, *as much as*, *refreshes*, *comforts*, *fights*, *the feel of* (also *the look of*), *tastes*, *fortified*, *enriched*, *strengthened*.

Examples:

"Helps control dandruff symptoms with regular use." (This claim is an accurate statement about the product. A consumer would be wrong to think that the claim is the same as "cures dandruff.")

"Leaves dishes virtually spotless." (An unskilled ad reader will remember the claim as being spotless and not *almost* ["virtually"] spotless. We hear so many weasel words that we tend to tune them out which is exactly what advertisers want.)

"Only half the price of many color sets." ("Many" is the weasel here. The ad does not claim that this set is inexpensive, only that others cost twice as much.)

"Fights bad breath." (This is much like "helps control dandruff"; it does not say "stops bad breath.")

"Lots of things have changed, but our chocolate's goodness hasn't." (This claim does not say that their chocolate has not changed.)

"Bacorenos, the crispy garnish that tastes just like its name." (This does not say that Bacorenos taste the same as bacon.)

A special weasel—"better" and "best"

virtually

fortified

The reason so many ads need to use weasel words and the other techniques described here is that they are *parity products*. A parity product is one in which most of the brands are nearly identical. Since no one superior product exists, advertising is used to create an illusion of superiority. The largest advertising budgets are devoted to such parity products as beer and soft drinks, cigarettes, soaps, and various drugstore pain remedies.

In parity claims, the words *better* and *best* take on unique meanings. In such claims, *better* means "best" and *best* means "as good as." Here's how this word game works: Let's say that in a given product category there are a number of brands that are alike. Legally this means that each can claim to be best—they are

best

fresher

all "superior." Since they are all equal, they must all be best. So "best" means that the product is as good as all the other superior products in its category. If one orange juice says "the best there is," this means only that it is as good as (not better than) any other orange juice on the market.

On the other hand, the word *better* has been legally interpreted as being comparative and therefore becomes a clear claim of superiority. That orange juice ad could not legally have claimed "better than any other brand." The only times "better" can be used are (a) if the product is indeed better than anything else; (b) if "better" is actually used to compare the product with something else ("our orange juice is better than powdered drinks"); or (c) if "better" is part of an unfinished claim ("the better breakfast drink").

Examples of "better" and "best" weasels:

"Better Shopper brand cocoa is the very best."

"Tests confirm Fresh mouthwash is better against mouth odor."

3. The "We're Different and Unique" Claim

This kind of claim states simply that there is nothing else quite like the product advertised. For example, if a lemonade manufacturer added blue food coloring to its product, it could advertise, "There's nothing like new blue Tarttaste." The uniqueness claim is supposed to be interpreted by readers as an indication of superiority.

Examples:

"There's no other mascara like it."

"Only Inca has this unique filter system."

"Panther is like nobody else's car."

"Either way, liquid or spray, there's nothing else like it."

"If it doesn't say Goodyear, it can't be Polyglas®."
("Polyglas" is a trade name that was copyrighted by Goodyear.
Other tire manufacturers could make a tire identical to the
Polyglas tire Goodyear marketed; yet they couldn't call it
"Polyglas"—a registered trademark for fiberglass belts.)

4. The "Water Is Wet" Claim

"Water is wet" claims say something about the product that is true
for any brand in that product category, such as, "Schrank's water
is really wet." The claim is usually a statement of fact but not a
real advantage over the competition though it is made to sound
like one.

Examples:

"The Detergent Gasoline" (true of any gas)

"Brasilia: The 100% Brazilian Coffee" (Most American brands
import coffee from Brazil.)

"Super Lash greatly increases the diameter of every lash."
(Any mascara does.)

**"Friendly Persuasion Perfume smells differently on every
one."** (as does all perfume)

5. The "So What" Claim

This is the kind of claim to which the careful reader will react by saying "So what?" A claim is made that is true but gives no real advantage to the product. This technique is similar to the "water is wet" claim, except that it does claim an advantage that is not shared by most of the other brands in the product category.

Examples:

- **"Hearty Time chicken soup gives you tasty pieces of chicken and not one but two chicken stocks."** (What good are two stocks?)
- **"More than twice the iron of ordinary supplements"** (But is twice as much any better?)
- **"Strong enough for a man but made for a woman"** (This deodorant claim says only that the product is aimed at the female market.)

Strong enough for a man but made for a woman

6. The Vague Claim

The vague claim is simply not clear; this category often overlaps others. The key to the vague claim is the use of words that are colorful but meaningless as well as the use of subjective and emotional opinions that defy verification. Most of these claims contain weasels.

Lips have never looked so luscious.

Examples:

- **"Lips have never looked so luscious."** (Can you imagine trying to either prove or disprove such a claim?)
- **"Lipslicks are fun—they taste good, smell good, and feel good."**
- **"Its deep rich lather makes hair feel new again."**
- **"For skin like peaches and cream."**
- **"The end of meatloaf boredom."**
- **"Take a bite and you'll think you're eating on the Champs Elysées."**

7. The Endorsement or Testimonial
This technique uses a celebrity or authority in an ad to lend his or her stellar qualities to the product. Sometimes the people actually claim to use the product, but sometimes they don't. Some agencies survive by providing "names" for testimonials.

Examples:

> **"Don't leave home without it."** (Karl Malden for American Express Travelers' Checks)
>
> A picture of an athlete on a Wheaties box
>
> Michael Jackson for L.A. Gear
>
> Michael Jordan for Nike
>
> Sheena Easton for Chicago Health Club

A variation on this technique is the "John or Jane Doe" testimonial, where an average person endorses a product. This approach can be used to convince potential customers that people "just like them" use the product.

33% more cleaning power...

8. The Scientific or Statistical Claim
This kind of ad refers to some sort of scientific proof or experiments, to very specific numbers, or to an impressive-sounding mystery ingredient.

Examples:

> **"—Bread helps build strong bodies 12 ways."**
> (Even the weasel "helps" did not prevent the Federal Trade Commission from demanding that this actual advertisement be withdrawn. But note that the use of the number *12* makes the claim far more believable than if it were replaced by—for example—"many ways.")
>
> **"Mrs. Molly's Oven Cleaner has 33% more cleaning power than another popular brand."**
> ("Another popular brand" translates simply as some other kind of oven cleaner sold somewhere. What the claim probably means is that Mrs. Molly's Oven Cleaner comes in a can $1/3$ larger than the can used by another brand.)
>
> **"Special Morning—33% more nutrition"** (also an unfinished claim)
>
> **"Certs contains a sparkling drop of Retsyn."**
>
> **"Sinarest. Created by a research scientist who actually gets sinus headaches."**

9. The "Compliment the Consumer" Claim

This type of claim flatters the consumer.

Examples:

"You've come a long way, baby."

"You pride yourself on your good home cooking. . ."

"The lady has taste."

"If what you do is right for you, no matter what the others do, then RC Cola is right for you."

10. The Rhetorical Question

This technique demands a response from the audience. A question is worded so that the viewer's or listener's answer affirms the product's goodness.

Examples:

"Plymouth—isn't that the kind of car America wants?"

"Shouldn't your family be drinking Hawaiian Punch?"

"What do you want most from coffee? That's what you get most from Hills."

"Touch of Sweden: Could your hands use a small miracle?"

"Wouldn't you really rather have a Buick?"

11. Incomplete Information

The ad can make some claim that is accurate but incomplete. Some important bit of information is withheld from the consumer, thus increasing the chances for misunderstanding.

Examples:

"Made with wool" (This claim does not mean "made entirely out of wool" or "100% wool." It means only there is some wool in the garment.)

"BINGO cereal is part of a nutritious breakfast."
(This claim does not mean BINGO is nutritious. If you serve pure junk food with milk and fruit, you could still claim it is "part of" a nutritious meal.)

MEDIALAB

Advertising Claims

1 As a class, go through the list of claims below and note for each (a) what a casual or nonexpert reader might believe each ad says, and (b) what an expert ad analyst would say about the claim:

"Built better, not cheaper."

"You're not getting older. You're getting better."

The taste of extra freshness."

"Five of these six top shipping pros are more than satisfied with the new Pony Express Shipping System."

"New lemony Woodwright gives you the look of hand-rubbed wood beauy instantly."

"Hair Beauty shampoo is enriched with pro tein and conditioners to make hair look healthy."

"Custom Blend Coffee lets me be different."

"If you care enough to serve the very best, you serve Crystal Springs natural water."

"Super-Clean works to eliminate unwanted odors. It works faster and smells fresh."

"Give an acne pimple something to worry about. Use Wipeout medicated soap. Fortified with AR-2."

2. Find examples of each of the 11 advertising claims or techniques explained in this section.

Write down or photocopy the ads from magazines or newspapers or quote directly from TV or radio commercials.

3. Select one or more products and devise a way to compare the advertising claims made for that product with the product itself. Construct a test (or a series of tests) to verify or disprove the advertised claims.

4. Rewrite some ads so that they change from ads presenting little or no information to ads that are genuinely helpful to consumers.

5. What kinds of products do you believe have the most useful and honest advertising? Which have the least useful? Is it possible to generalize?

6. Write letters to the manufacturers of some products whose advertising you believe is deceptive. Explain your case in writing in rough draft form. As a class, decide on the best letters and mail them. Report any responses.

7. Write advertising copy that accurately describes a product you believe to be of high quality. Make your ad useful to consumers and completely honest—but at the same time make it one that will sell the product.

UNDERSTANDING EMOTIONAL APPEAL

Once you are able to evaluate ad claims so that they don't mislead, you are ready for the second important skill needed to deal with advertising. You need to see how the ads appeal to you, involve your feelings, wishes, and dreams. Ads attempt to make products look luxurious, sexy, grown-up, modern, happy, patriotic, or any of dozens of other desirable qualities.

Nearly every ad (except purely factual advertising, such as that of a grocery store listing its prices) attempts to give the impression that the product advertised will make the user one or more of the following: Popular, Powerful, Happy, Free, Successful, More Grown Up, Younger, A Real Woman, A Real Man, Important, Creative, WITH IT, or "in", SAFE, SECURE.

Of course, toothpaste, shampoo, soap, or deodorant will *not* make their users any of these things. But the advertiser tries to say that the user will *feel* loved or popular or whatever if he or she uses the product.

A product claim is an attempt to convince potential buyers that a certain product is better than any other and that it works. The ad appeals to feelings and emotions. Many studies have shown that a person's choice of a specific product and brand is more often based on feelings than on specific product claims. Most ads have both a reasonable-sounding claim and an appeal to feelings. The careful viewer or listener should be able to see in any ad not only what claim is being made but also what emotional appeal is being used.

Here are some descriptions of ads or portions of commercial outlines or storyboards. Read each and determine what feelings the ad implies the product will give its users. After you have done this, read the comments of a skilled ad reader that follow.

APPEAL #1:
Automobile ad: the auto is parked in front of a huge mansion. A uniformed chauffeur stands nearby as a man in a tuxedo and woman in a formal gown exit the car.

APPEAL #3:
Razor ad: a football player in uniform holds a package of Quik-Shave razor blades, saying, "If Quik-Shave can shave me close, it can shave anybody."

APPEAL #2:
Ad for any one of many possible products: picture of a handsome man and a beautiful woman hugging each other while looking over a lush green valley.

APPEAL #4:
Soap ad: picture of a beautiful rose with fresh dewdrops on its petals. The rose grows out of a sink filled with soapsuds. Somewhere on the ad are the words "For hands soft as roses use Rosebud."

Man with dandruff on his coat.

Man looking at his dandruff.
MAN: Billy, why don't you use . . .

Man and woman
MAN: Jeanie, I don't know what I
would do without you.

Family in living room. Father
taking pictures.

Camera with chromakeyed sunset.

Film and logo. Chromakey of sunset.
Music over.

APPEAL #5:

TV commercial: a man is unable to get a date
with a woman he likes. A friend tells him that he
has bad breath (or dandruff, body odor, acne,
messy hair, the wrong kind of clothes, or any
one of countless evils). He takes the advice of
his friend, switches to the product advertised,
and in the end he and the woman are together.

APPEAL #6:

TV commercial for a certain kind of film: a
happy family is together in front of a fireplace.
The father is taking a picture of the rest of the
happy family.

The Ad Reader's Comments

APPEAL #1:

In looking for the emotional or feeling hook in an ad, always notice the setting in which the product is placed. Placing the automobile by the mansion with a chauffeur and people in expensive-looking clothing says that this is a car for wealthy people: If you want to feel wealthy or be considered wealthy by others, buy this car. Such an ad never states directly, "Buy this car and people will think you're rich," but that is what the picture implies. Always look for the setting in which the product is placed for a clue to the feeling hook.

APPEAL #2:

This picture could be used for hundreds of different products. Probably the ad would show a bit of ad copy (written claims) at the bottom and a picture of the product. The picture suggests love, beautiful people, freedom, the beauty of nature, and even a certain "naturalness" and youth. The picture could be used in an ad for shampoo, deodorant, clothes, hair spray, or even cigarettes or jewelry. The emotional appeal of the ad is that, by using the product advertised, you will somehow be associated with the feelings the picture suggests. At the very least, the picture creates a good mood, so the reader will experience a pleasant feeling when seeing the product's name.

APPEAL #3:

Celebrities are paid huge sums to appear in advertisements holding, sitting in, or wearing, eating, or drinking certain products. If you view such ads carefully, you will see that the celebrity rarely says he or she uses the product all the time. Advertisers pay famous people to endorse their products. They select according to the feeling the person communicates—a feeling the advertiser wants associated with the product. In the Quik-Shave ad, the maker assumes that men like to think of themselves as rough and

tough, and the football player is an excellent choice to suggest such a person.

The idea behind endorsements is that some of the heroics and fame of the star "rub off" on the product and on the users of that product. The ad suggests that you, too, can be like this famous person by using Quik-Shave.

APPEAL #4:
The rose suggests softness, beauty, and delicacy. By placing the rose in the soapsuds, the ad suggests that your hands will feel as soft as rose petals if you use Rosebud. The picture says this far more appealingly than words could.

APPEAL #5:
This is a very common kind of commercial. It suggests that the product will make the user popular and will instantly solve a personal problem. The commercial appeals to people who feel left out or unpopular. People who are popular know that their popularity has nothing to do with which brands they use.

APPEAL #6:
This commercial creates good feelings by showing the happy family around the fireplace. The suggestion is that, by using the kind of film being advertised, you too can achieve such family joy.

MEDIALAB

Advertising Analysis

1. Make a portfolio of ads from magazines illustrating the various types of emotional appeals. Write an explanation of each ad's appeal.

2. Pick either a print ad or a TV or radio commercial that best fits each of the following categories:

The World's Most Honest Ad

The Forked-Tongue Award—for skill in sneaky, misleading, and deceptive use of language.

The At-Least-It's-Fun Award—to the most entertaining ad.

The Foot-in-the-Door Award—to the most persuasive ad

The World's Worst Advertisement

My Favorite Ad

3. Write or draw an ad you consider to be honest, helpful, and important. The ad may be for some service or quality— peace, the elimination of poverty, love, better education, ecology, or justice. You may pick your own topic for the ad or use one of the following:

A horse is better than a car.

Garbage is valuable—save your garbage.

A toothpick

A button is better than a zipper.

No one over 21 should hold public office.

The legal age to vote should be 14 years.

Water

A machine that dispenses a whiff of fresh air for 25¢

An automatic watermelon deseeder

A new concept—black-and-white television

Old, warped phonograph records

4. Find some old advertisements—either in magazines at least ten years old or in books that reprint old ads. Photocopy some ads and bring them to class. Examine how advertising has changed yet remained the same over the years. Also discuss whether the changes in ads mirror changes in society.

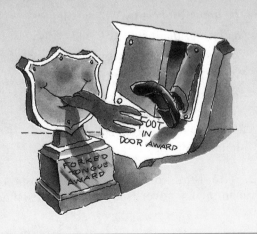

5. In some European countries with commercial television, ads are shown together at the beginning of a program segment. If a one-hour program is shown, the first eight or so minutes contain all the ads, and the program then runs uninterrupted for the next 52 minutes. What do you think of this system? How might it change the nature of ads? Would such a system work in the United States?

6. In many countries the television and radio stations are run by the government. They contain no advertising at all. Do you think such a system (one in which the government provides all the money) has any advantages over a system in which advertisers provide the money? Are there disadvantages?

7. What kinds of ads are most commonly found in comic books? Why do you think advertisers choose these books?

8. One of the most important selling techniques in advertising is repetition. Repetition is used within an ad, and ads themselves are repeated frequently. A common technique is to repeat the selling message several times within each ad. Commercials on TV and ads in magazines are used dozens or even hundreds of times. Do you think this repetition irritates people or increases the likelihood of the ad's being successful? How is repetition used in a similar way in school?

9. Which of these do you think benefits most from good advertising: a product truly superior to its competition? A product no better and no worse than its competition? A product obviously worse than its competitors?

10. What would happen if all advertising were abolished?

11. Read and report on one chapter from any of the following books:

Thirty Seconds by Michael Arlen
The Want Makers by Eric Clark
Motivating Human Behavior by Ernest Dichter
The Image Makers by William Meyers
Ogilvy on Advertising by David Ogilvy
The Hidden Persuaders by Vance Packard
Reality in Advertising by Rosser Reeves
Advertising: The Uneasy Persuasion by Michael Schudson
Why They Buy by Robert Settle and Pamela Alreck

12. The team project on the image of women/men in advertising could be presented now.

The Appeal of Television Commercials

The images in television commercials often are so bright, so wonderful, and so exciting that we fail to find out just how they are created. We want to believe that people and products are as clean and shining as the images we see. The following article shows the ways in which highly skilled directors give us gorgeous scenes full of action and excitement to whet our dreams and appetites. The images in commercials often appear almost magical. A cucumber slice appears as a UFO and a bar of soap seems as majestic as the Grand Canyon. How does a television commercial make the genuinely artificial food substitute look deliciously real? Here's how.

R E A D I N G

OF DIRECTORS, MAGIC AND WATERFALLS OF SALAD DRESSING

by **Jonathan Price**

The art of making consumer products appeal to the casual television viewer is part of the skill of TV commercial directors.

In primitive times Celtic kings hired sorcerers to cast a "glamour" over a hill to make the enemy imagine a fortress where there was only a hut. Nowadays the strategists of commercials seek such magical interference with our vision from a director. For approximately $2,000 a day a director is expected to add a glow to the idea. The director sets up bright-bright lights and brings wraparound lenses in for giant closeups of superactive scenes, featuring realer than real consumers. The best directors hypo the hype.

Unlike a real movie director, the director of a commercial does not work with the writer during the process of writing; he is not consulted about a script before it is submitted to him for a bid; and often he does not meet the cast until the day of the shoot. He may not change the basic

story, or the characters, during the shoot. And although he may have the right to try his own editing, he almost never controls the final version, since the ad agency steps in, choosing the shots they like and ordering those shots the way they like.

Because his control is cramped in so many important ways, a director of commercials has a limited range of decisions to make (lights, camera, acting, sets), but even in this restricted field a good director can make the difference between humdrum and startling appearance. Directors add gloss. Directors work in film, which still provides slightly sharper images, clearer depth of field, stronger colors than videotape, because it is fast, cheap, and relatively easy to edit, these commercials *look* better than the shows . . . .

The personality of a director tends to show up in his choice of specialization. You might not think it, but each major product category has its conventions (wine ads are misty;

shampoos require brilliantly back-lit showers), and some directors polish those conventions to a slick gleam. One director excels at food, another at cars; a third can handle animals and kids well; still another actually works with grown-up human actors to get a strong performance. (This is known as "people-directing.")

Tony Ficalora, for instance, shows us food the way it might appear to a baby rolling in it or to a starving man hallucinating in the desert. Ficalora can make a salad dressing seem like a waterfall and a salad like a jungle. In one spot we move through the lettuce leaves slowly—as moisture from above drips into the camera—nosing our way to the heart of the greenery. Only when red dressing slops down onto these giant bushes do we realize that our sense of scale has been fooled and we are actually in the bowl. In another spot for Kraft, giant eggs roll toward us, lumbering left and right, until one gets picked up and cracked at the end. That frame freezes motion in glistening white while the mayonnaise label appears...

Ficalora likes vast banquets. His home economist (a director who works with food has to have one) knows how to cook for looks—and how to keep the food looking luscious despite hours under the hot lights. She will bake ten chocolate cakes, a dozen chickens, in succession, bringing each out of the oven at intervals so that there will always be a fresh one in front of the camera. And in his best films, Mateus rosé comes surrounded with slippery hot lobsters and misty grapes; Celeste pizza drips oil and cheese as we lift a slice; another hand-size food becomes a basketball for Tropicana.

Such directorial exaggeration enlarges our appetite, encouraging us to dream of jumping into our food as if it were a pile of hay. When a Ficalora orange flies open, so many giant drops of juice fly out in a medium-size TV that, if they were real, we could use up a whole sheet of Bounty cleaning the screen. Surreal? He seems medieval to me, like an archetype of the Glutton, whose eye is bigger than his belly.

Andy Jenkins, by contrast, likes to work outdoors, shooting supposed "locals" and "real people," making fake scenes seem more real than any hand held documentary ever could. Following the maxim that seeing is believing, Jenkins persuades us by his attentive work with actors, generating whole lives for people who appear for only three seconds, and building a complete town or home for them, even if we see only one corner. Often these grizzled inhabitants are actors, but with Jenkins, they woof and scratch and go around looking like "jes folks." He set fire to an abandoned farm for Metropolitan Life. We see chickens run from an old-fashioned fire truck; we see geezers staring; we hear the grateful farmer hold out his thanks to the firemen—"You boys want a couple of chickens?"

Except for the fact that every shot is gorgeous and full of active detail, we might think this brief film had been shot during a real fire. Jenkins' most spectacular shot shows the misty dunes of Kitty Hawk or Cape Hatteras; we see the tan plane clearly, it comes toward us, it takes off, then we soar with it, over the first hill of sand. The mood is gentle, lovely, gray. Jenkins likes intricate construction: he built the Wright Brothers' plane for that spot; and for Owens-Corning, he built an igloo in the Mojave desert and insulated it with their Fiberglas. It did not melt.

Bob Giraldi, a popular director, costs five to ten thousand dollars more than a nonstar director, but he can give you a dreamy "look" that will glamorize your product. He once did an antique spot for Barney's, showing how the men's store started; he used forty suits from the period and shot the whole in sepia; only when we come up to the present do we enter a world of color. Giraldi shot a karate dojo in yellowish light, showing slow-motion turns and kicks, then went to a bar for the after-workout drink of Miller's; the bar is darker, crowded with reds and browns, and the beer seems to light it up. Lots of smiles, taps, and handshakes here; so we get two spaces, two moods. For Arrow shirts he re-created an upper-crust British garden party in such detail that a regular movie director would wince with envy; for Pioneer he made beautiful pictures of the interior of Carnegie Hall.

... One of the few directors who does keep the kind of total control a Hollywood pro does is Dan Nichols, and he started out as a writer ... Nichols' involvement with the writing allows him to plan the high volume of scenes in his spots; in one sixty-second McDonald's spot he showed sixty-five scenes, and in most spots he crams in fast cuts, zooms, and reverses. For one commercial about McDonald's take-out food, called *Ice Nine*, he figured out sixty-four potential snow scenes and listed them in categories; under "Down-hill Skiing," for instance, he listed these shots:

1) Aerials of skis, flip, spread eagles, layouts, crossing
2) Ski race start at timing gate
3) High-speed powder skiing
4) High-speed slalom
5) Mogul head bops
6) Kite
7) Ski jump (high speed)
8) 36-degree pole swings
9) Cross-country skiing
10) Hot dogging. . . ballet

After that ten seconds, we go on to look at ice skating, snow chores, sledding, snow romps, snow school, snow sports, picnickers in the snow eating McDonald's take-out food, and girls indoors, "nice and warm."

One McDonald's spot is titled *Quick Cuts*, and that is Nichols' style. To be seen and recognized in half a second, each scene must be clear, well-lit, and carefully planned. If we pan left in one scene, we often pan right in the next; if we are moving forward for one second, we may pull back in the next. His editing established a rhythm of movement: two stills, a move forward, a move back, a still, then the camera holds still while someone moves past it to the right, then back to the left. He uses frozen frames like dotted notes, or syncopation, holding one image for a while so that the next one is more sharply emphasized. They mark the end of one sequence of ski sports, the

beginning of ice hockey scenes; they give us a rest. In another one, each frozen frame shows us a person, the target of the song "You, you're the one." Nichols comments, "My formula is energy. You have to keep it going."

Such complex, baroque visions make McDonald's seem dense with life— lots of physical movement, lots of memorable snapshots. But ultimately such spots are as artificial as a McDonald's shake. Perhaps that very artificiality—the "madeness" of the spots—appeals to Americans at least as much as the whetted-up vitality. There are two men who disagree: David and Albert Maysles believe people want to look at reality, and they have made grimy documentary films like *Salesman*, in which they trail Bible salesmen around the country. Their films seem unrehearsed. As David Maysles says, "The viewer never really knows what's coming up next because that's the way it was shot. The photographer doesn't know what's coming up next." When they make a film, they pay for it themselves, so they keep complete control. But they pay for these feature films by making spots.

They do not charge the advertiser much because they just take their cameras out on location and talk to real people who use the product or make it. "The transition from documentaries to commercials wasn't as difficult as you'd think," says David Maysles. "The copywriters and art directors did most of the research in picking the people we were going to work with, and then we shot as we normally do." Bob Judd and Jerry Weldor of J. Walter Thompson located a Champion Spark Plug dealer who would let them film him; we see him chat with customers, go out to service a broken-down car, wave at the cam-

era. He seems friendly, at ease. Evidently it took a few hours for him to relax, but after a while he just went ahead with his work without "acting" and the results seem casual and comfortable. Nothing hard-hitting, but something fairly intimate. Then there's the spot they did for IBM in which we see one employee after another wishing us Happy New Year—it's moving because there are so many and they seem to be having such a good time with the cameraman. Advertising coffee, the Maysles shot an impromptu basketball game in a gym; as guys came off the court to relax, they were asked if they had drunk coffee for breakfast. Yes, indeed. It looks like luck, but a lot of the casual, friendly mood comes from the down-home directness of the men behind the camera.

Reality, then, is a certain "look." "You've got to give the Maysles their head, or you shouldn't hire them," says Howard Rieger of Young & Rubicam. That could apply to any of these top directors. But the Maysles lived with one family for three days just to get a picture of them eating Jell-O. "For Jell-O we wanted spontaneous, natural, believable dialogue," says Rieger. "If you're looking for reality, they're the guys."

Perhaps. But once "reality" is sliced into a commercial selling a dream of coffee as a high-energy food, we reenter the fantasy realm. Perhaps, as Aristotle suggested, we want to believe in dramas and get angry only when forced to face their open falsity. So a high premium gets put on making the lie believable, shiny, hypnotic, luscious, active, and arresting. In a commercial, it seems, the director is the person who makes the genuinely artificial food substitute look more deliciously real than steak. And Americans love it—we eat dreams.

MEDIALAB

The Magic of Images

1. In what way are some directors of television commercials like magicians?

2. Describe some current television commercials in which ordinary products (autos, soda, salad dressing, etc.) seem to glow, appear larger than life, appear in color on a black-and-white background, or perform seemingly impossible feats.

3. Debate the following proposal: "There ought to be a law forbidding advertisers to show their products in an unreal way. Advertisers are not allowed to tell lies in print or spoken words; they shouldn't be allowed to deceive in pictures either."

4. The article concerns television commercials. Much of what is said about TV commercials, however, is also true of magazine advertising. Find examples of visual persuasion in magazine advertising.

5. Discuss how people are chosen for commercials so as o be the most convincing. What special values do people with no professional acting experience possess?

6. The article talks about one sixty-second McDonald's spot containing sixty-five scenes. What current commercials use such fast-paced editing? Why?

7. Are there some products that are better presented in longer, slower moving shots?

8. Examine some television commercials and explain the various ways in which the director makes the product attractive.

9. Describe how a commercial for milk would look if directed by Tony Ficalora. How would it be different if directed by Andy Jenkins or the Maysles brothers?

10. Directors of TV commercials do not receive on-screen credits. Discuss some currently popular commercials that have similar "looks" to those discussed in the previous reading.

ADVERTISING IN THE 1990s

Viewer Fatigue

A paradox of advertising: One of the reasons advertising is so powerful is that we don't give it much attention.

How many television commercials you saw yesterday can you remember? Research shows the number of commercials on American television is up, but viewer recall is down. "Recall" measures the ability of viewers to remember a commercial the next day. It is one of the most widely used measures of success in advertising. According to research published in *Forbes* magazine from 1975 to 1979, the average recall rate was 24 percent, meaning that 24 percent of viewers could remember seeing a specific commercial the night before. From 1980 to 1984 the rate went down to 23 percent, from 1985 to 1987 the rate dropped to 22 percent, and in 1988 the recall figure was a lowly 21 percent. Another study that measured how many television commercials people recalled from the previous week found that in 1983, 1.72 commercials were recalled, but in 1988 the figure dropped to about 1.2.

Recall Rate of TV Commercials

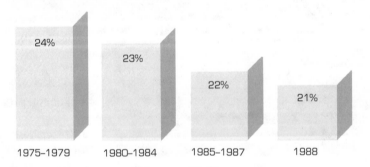

| 24% | 23% | 22% | 21% |
| 1975–1979 | 1980–1984 | 1985–1987 | 1988 |

No one knows the exact reason for the decline, but one suspect is the 15-second commercial, which began airing in 1985. In the 1960s a television commercial was often one minute in length, and throughout the 1970s and 1980s, the 30-second spot was standard. The 15-second length was introduced as an economy, but some advertisers now fear viewers are suffering from advertising overload. In spite of this fear, advertisers know that European television is now filled with 7-second commercials. Another suspect is the changing habits of television viewers.

Many viewers now use remote control to change channels at the first sight of a commercial, while others use the VCR to fast forward throught the commercials as they view prerecorded programs.

In America, advertisements play upon the brain of a man, like the musician does upon a piano.
—JACQUES OFFENBACH, after visiting America in 1876

Ads, Ads Everywhere

In a mass media society, advertising expands to fill any available space. Advertisers are not content to use traditional mass media—they seek new avenues for print ads and commercials.

Companies now pay huge sums to have their products used by stars in major motion pictures. If James Bond drives a specific brand of sports car in a 007 movie, some of the "Bond mystique" rubs off on the car. But the car is not chosen to be in the movie for its ability to outrun another model; it is probably chosen because the advertiser is willing to pay for the exposure.

Magazine readers soon might find a new gadget demanding their attention—talking advertisements. A California company is working on a voice chip and speaker system that will enable print ads to talk to a reader for up to twenty-four seconds. The chip will be bound into a magazine or book and be activated either by opening a page or pulling a tab.

Advertisers look for spaces where there are people but no ads, and fill them. Now commercials sometimes are shown before the feature film in movie theaters. You may find commercials on the film you rent on video. You often will see ads on shopping carts in grocery stores, and even on parking meters and hot air balloons. One enterprising advertising agency invented a liner for golf holes that would hold a small ad seen when a golfer reaches into the cup after sinking a putt.

Advertisers look for spaces where there are people but no ads, and fill them.

Advertisers actively seek controlled audiences rather than the vague "general public" and are rediscovering the power of billboards. They are finding billboards effective in reaching a local audience. An outdoor billboard delivers its message for about $2 per thousand viewers, compared to $17 for a prime-time network commercial. New ideas in billboards enable 3-D images and animation to catch the overloaded eyes of passers-by. A Kodak billboard features a good-enough-to-eat ear of corn dripping a pat of butter that is cleaned up by a three-dimensional mannequin. Fiber optics and holographic displays now add motion to billboards. In fact, billboards of the future might be similar to the high-density television screens used at sports stadiums. A twenty-first century innovation being developed now includes a sensor that activates a prerecorded message when someone passes the display.

Mind Games

Advertisers will continue to play mind games in the 1990s. Ads and commercials always have appealed to emotions, but researchers now find that even practical, everyday products are purchased more on emotion than on durability, ease of use, or other functional qualities.

For example, a series of ads for Betty Crocker cake mixes forgoes the traditional emphasis on ease of baking or superior results

Getting the L.A. Marathon off the ground. **TWA**

and instead shows that using the cake mix is an expression of love for one's family.

Esther Thorson, an advertising researcher at the University of Wisconsin, finds that making viewers feel *both* sad and happy during a commercial is most effective. A commercial for Hallmark cards, for example, shows a soldier waiting in the rain to pick up a letter from home, thus combining the sadness of being away from family with the joy of getting a letter. Thorson finds that "making consumers feel something is much more important than convincing them that a product is better."

For example, researchers found that some teens feel a pimple can call a halt to their social lives. That research led to a commercial in which an active teenage boy walks down a street and glimpses a pimple on his face in a store window reflection. The world stops at this discovery, but he applies Clearasil, the pimple recedes, and life continues at full speed.

No commercial works unless it first captures viewer attention. The first three seconds of a commercial are often carefully designed as an attention grabber. Researchers find that taking advantage of the brain's reflex actions works well: loud noises, sudden movements, and extreme contrast of light and dark grab attention. Other devices to capture attention include rapidly shifting scenes, the sound of a baby crying, jerking—rather than smooth—camera movements, grainy film that looks like a home movie, black-and-white instead of color, or flashing light.

MEDIALAB

Advertising in the 1990s

1. Studies show people remember fewer television commercials than in years past. What are some theories about why this is true? Can you think of any other explanations? What will happen if this trend continues? What kinds of commercials do you watch and which do you ignore?

2. Television commercials have become shorter over the years. Do you think the 7-second commercial, now common in Europe, will work here?

3. Explain the sentence, "In a mass media society advertising expands to fill any available space." Can you recall any place that was once free of ads and commercials but is now carrying selling messages? Is there a certain space or time where the existence of such advertising irritates you most?

4. The next time you watch a feature film on video or in the theatre, look for "hidden ads"; that is, products displayed with brand names as the result of fees paid to the movie's producers. You won't know for sure if the exposure is paid, but a clearly seen brand name is a good clue. Look for brand names on products, passing trucks, billboards, in scenes shot in supermarkets or stores, or in angles carefully chosen to show off a car.

5. Billboard advertising is perhaps the oldest medium to carry ads. Outdoor advertising dates back to ancient Egypt, where merchants placed stone tablets with sales messages along public roads. The 1965 Highway Beautification Act restricts outdoor signs and none are allowed on the U.S. interstate highway system. But billboards are making a comeback in the 1990s—why? Can you see any evidence of this in your town?

6. Can you find an example of print ad or commercial that makes you feel both sad and happy?

7. Find examples of ads and commercials for ordinary, everyday products that are promoted primarily by appealing to feelings rather than product features.

8. Make notes on the next ten television commercials you view. What devices are used to grab your attention (sight and sound) in the first five seconds?

WRAP-UP

Beginning with the invention of the printing press and followed by the Industrial Revolution in the 1800s, advertising became a necessity for merchants and a driving power behind mass media. Looking at advertising in general, eight stages or approaches emerge—ranging from informational to behavioral. In this chapter you have learned to analyze advertising claims. You have learned how advertisers can play "mind games" with print ads and commercials. In the 1990s you may face viewer fatigue—it seems that you are being bombarded with advertising. However, ask yourself if mass media as they are today could survive without it.

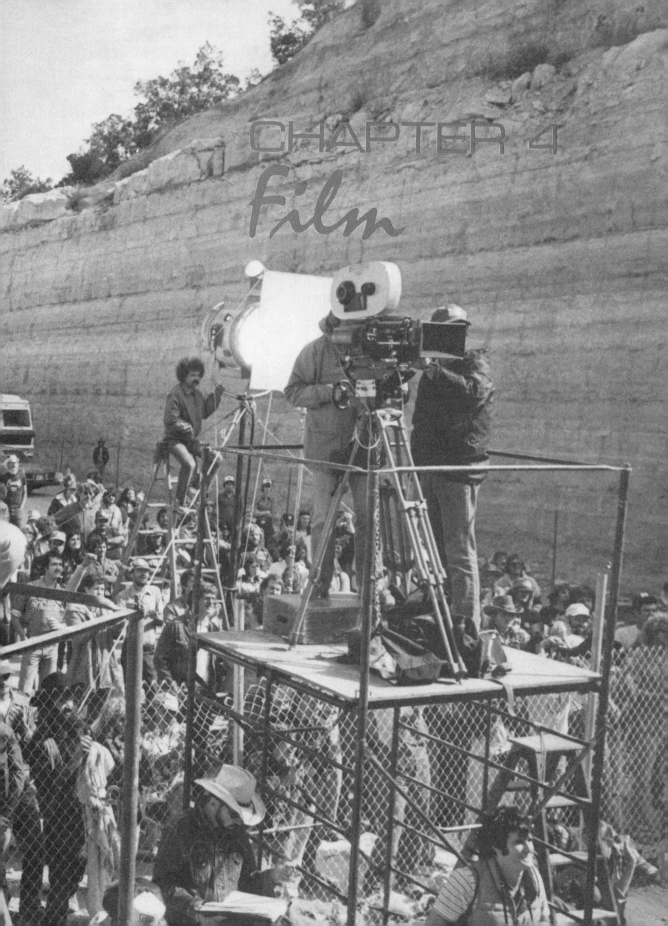

CHAPTER 4
Film

Have you seen any good movies lately?
Such a familiar question. . . Now ask
yourself how much you really know about
the mass medium of film, also known as
motion pictures, movies, or the flicks.

So you think you UNDERSTAND FILM

TEST YOUR KNOWLEDGE

If you can correctly answer six out of the following eight questions
before reading this chapter, you already know so much that you
should be making films instead of reading about them. If you cannot correctly answer at least six, read the rest of this chapter.

The questions are not the most important that can be asked
about film, but they require a firm understanding of film.

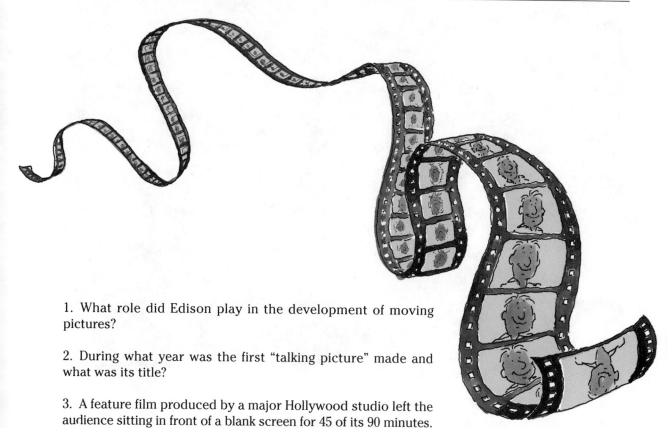

1. What role did Edison play in the development of moving pictures?

2. During what year was the first "talking picture" made and what was its title?

3. A feature film produced by a major Hollywood studio left the audience sitting in front of a blank screen for 45 of its 90 minutes. The blank screen was part of *every* showing and was not caused by equipment failure. The film was a box office success and played in your area. What was the film and why did the audience put up with the blank screen?

4. If you watch a feature film for two hours, how many separate still pictures do you see? (Assumption: You don't fall asleep or leave for popcorn.)

5. The 1971 film version of the Broadway play *Fiddler on the Roof* was filmed almost entirely with the camera lens covered by an ordinary nylon stocking purchased in a local department store. Why?

6. How many pictures does a professional movie camera take in one minute of shooting?

7. Which arts do not have "editing" as part of the creative process?

8. Define (a) a scene, (b) a cut-away, (c) an establishing shot.

AT THE MOVIES: PLAYING THE CRITIC

Take a look at these comments by film critics made after they viewed the first of the *Star Wars* trilogy.

. . . . warmed-over 'Wizard of Oz,' Flash Gordon, Jack Armstrong, and World War II dogfights all rolled into one.
—P. Rule (*America* magazine)

Lucas has rather left his audience out in the cold, with only regularly administered shots of special effects to keep them warm.
–R. Bombs (*Monthly Film Bulletin*, a British magazine)

. . . . so strong and so refreshing that it takes a crusty person indeed to resist its charms.
—K. Turan (*The Progressive*)

This is the trippiest, most convincingly technological science-fiction film ever made.
— D. Robbeloth (*Audience* magazine)

. . . . fundamentally dull and misconceived. . . an empty thing. . . the biggest exploitation movie of them all.
— *The New Statesman*

This is the kind of film in which an audience, first entertained, can later walk out feeling good all over.
—*Variety*

You might expect six professional critics to agree if a major film is a crashing bore or an exciting masterpiece. But as the excerpts from film reviews show, opinions on *Star Wars* were quite divided. Six jewelers would not disagree on whether a necklace was made of diamonds or glass. But six film critics can look at the same film and judge it anywhere between "dull" and "extraordinary."

Critical opinion of almost any film, whether by professional critics or the weekend filmgoer, will vary from those who consider it the best film they have ever seen to those who find it puts them to sleep. Often a film widely praised by critics will play only to the projectionist and empty seats, while another film generally conceded to be junk will break box office records.

One explanation for this wide range of opinions about film is that no two people "see" the same film. Each viewer enters into the world of the film and becomes part of that world. Comments made about films are often no comments about the film at all—they are comments we make about ourselves.

To help explain the special problem of discussing film, take a look at the drawing on this page and quickly (in five seconds or less) describe what you see.

Some will say the picture is an old woman, while others see a fashionable young woman. The problem is not one of disagreement about age. If you look at the picture long enough, you will see it change from young woman to old woman and back again. To see the gnarled old woman, focus on the neck band of the young woman—this is the old woman's mouth. The young woman's chin is the nose of the old woman.

The picture is no more an optical illusion than any other picture—or any movie. When looking at objects, we see selectively and are often surprised to find that others looking at the same picture or situation see something completely different.

You cannot accurately say the picture is of an old woman any more than you can say it is of a young woman. You *can* say, "I see an old woman" or "I see a young woman." Or "First I saw the young woman, then I saw the older one." In other words, you can make a statement about yourself that is accurate. The same is true in film.

Listen to an audience as it leaves the theater after watching a film. You will overhear some say the film was terrific, some, meaningless or simply bad. Some will leave the theater and have a long discussion, perhaps an argument, about whether the film was good or bad. But such a discussion is similar to an argument about whether the picture is of an old or a young woman.

Most likely the participants in such a discussion are not talking about the film at all; they are making statements about themselves but disguising the remarks as film criticism. In other words, most people do not distinguish between revealing personal reactions to film and criticizing the film itself. Let's say you watch a film and

Opinions about films vary widely. *The Old Man and the Sea* is one of the films regarded anywhere from "flawed" to "extraordinary." Copyright© Warner Bros. Inc.

later tell someone, "It was a bore." What you really mean is, "I was bored." There is a big difference between the two. Your comment is about *yourself* and not the film. Probably there were some people in the audience who were not the least bit bored. There is no commonly agreed-upon standard by which to judge whether a film is boring or not. But it is easy for you to recognize your own feeling of boredom.

In talking about films, you should be able to distinguish between comments about the film and comments about your reactions to the film. When talking to friends, you will probably stay on the level of speaking in terms of yourself—unless you want to impress someone with your knowledge of film. When attempting film criticism, especially in communicating with an audience who does not know you, making statements about yourself is of limited value. If someone tells you that a certain film is "sickening," that does not mean that you will find it "sickening"; you might enjoy the film. If you know the person well, you might be able to say, "If that person found it sickening, I wouldn't like it either." A most common error in film discussion is to confuse statements about the film with statements about oneself.

The following statements were taken from overheard remarks or from written film criticism. Each statement is presented in terms of talking about the film. Imagine you are the person who made each statement and change each comment into a personal statement about a film, using "I" (first person). Do *not* do this by adding "I think" to the beginning of the statement. For example, the statement, "It was good but too long" could be changed to "I enjoyed the film but was bored toward the end."

"It was a confused movie with a stupid and complicated plot."

"A moving work of art that will drive you to tears."

"This flick is really fantastic: you just have to see it."

"A dumb, idiotic film that didn't make any sense."

MEDIALAB

presented in

CINEMASCOPE
DOLBY STEREO
SENSAROUND

1. Explain the different feelings you have when you talk about a film in terms of yourself and when you comment in terms of the film alone. Which is most difficult? What special skills or attitudes are needed for each kind of statement?

2. Reread the critical comments about the film *Star Wars* on page 116. Which are statements about the film and which about the critic? Do you think any of them are statements about the critic "disguised" to look like statements about the film?

3. Some film critics write more about their personal reactions to films, while others attempt to be more objective and judge the film on its merits as a work of art or entertainment. Examine several film reviews by different critics (such as those in a local newspaper or a magazine you read) and

decide which approach they use most. Which do you prefer? Which would you use if you were a professional movie critic?

4. We could call those who write mainly in terms of their own reactions "subjective critics" and those who write about the film as "objective critics." Why is it not possible to be completely objective about a film? Is it possible to be completely subjective?

5. During this chapter, the team project on short films can be presented.

6. Write two film reviews of some feature film you have seen recently or a short film shown in class. Review 1 should present you, the subjective critic, providing personal reactions to the film. Review 2 should present you, the objective critic, talking mainly about "it"—the film.

HOW MOTION PICTURES BEGAN

A motion picture is a series of still pictures projected rapidly to give the illusion of smooth movement. The invention of the motion picture was not a single stroke of genius in an inventor's workshop. Rather, it resulted from a long series of smaller discoveries in optics, chemistry, and even psychology.

In the seventeenth century a German priest, Athanasius Kirscher, painted images of the saints on glass and fascinated small groups with what he called a "magic lantern show." His oil-burning lantern produced a dim light and the images were barely visible, but rumors spread that this magic was in league with the devil. It was chemistry, however, rather than the "black arts" that improved the magic lantern show.

The oil lantern was replaced with a much brighter light achieved by burning lime. This "limelight" (from which comes the expression "in the limelight") was used in stage productions as well as magic lantern shows until it was replaced by electric lights.

Until the nineteenth century all the images projected were created by hand—no one had learned how to capture images through photography. It wasn't until 1839 that artist Louis Daguerre and chemist Joseph Niepce demonstrated a clear photograph, called a daguerreotype. The image was made on a copper plate coated with silver. The plate was first exposed to iodine fumes to coat it with light-sensitive silver iodide. Next, the plate was exposed to the scene to be photographed. Finally, the image was "fixed" on the plate in chemical baths. Daguerreotypes were clear but expensive and clumsy. Creating one required a building (or at least a horse-drawn van).

> . . .film is the only art whose birthday is known to us—the beginnings of all others are lost in the fog of antiquity.
>
> — BELA BALASSA, educator

William Henry Fox Talbot invented a way to use paper coated with silver halide so that photographs could be made by anyone, not just technicians and chemists. By the 1880s George Eastman marketed a flexible celluloid film in rolls that made photography popular. His celluloid rolls also made motion pictures possible. But the jump from still photography to "movies" required an understanding of how the eye can be fooled into seeing movement where none exists.

Key to the illusion of movement is an understanding of persistence of vision. We see an image for a fraction of a second after the object has moved or changed. In other words, the image persists in our vision for an instant after it has moved. If we see images in rapid-fire order, our eyes can't keep up and the individual pictures blur into motion. If each image is the same except for a tiny movement, we

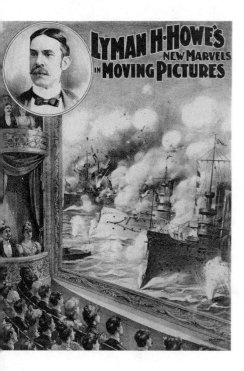

see the illusion of actual motion. This principle, first described in 1824 by Peter Mark Roget, makes movies and television possible.

Roget's discovery led to toys and gadgets that demonstrated the principle. The most important was called a "Zoetrope," or "wheel of life." Small photos or drawings were pasted inside a cylinder. The cards showed successive movements in scenes, such as a horse jumping or a person running. The cylinder was mounted on a spindle and spun. The viewer would look through slits in the cylinder and see an illusion of a person running or horse jumping. The Zoetrope was clearly a primitive forerunner of motion pictures.

Photography at this time could only make pictures of objects that remained still. You may have noticed that, in portraits from the early days of photography, no one is smiling. The likely reasons were that the pose had to be held for so long and the process of taking a picture was so torturously intricate, a smile was nearly impossible. An important advance in photographing motion was made as the result of a bet made by Governor Leland Stanford of California. The bet questioned whether a running horse ever had all four feet off the ground at once. A photographer named Eadweard Muybridge, who specialized in motion studies, was hired to prove the issue. He set up a row of twenty-four cameras along a racetrack, each shutter connected to a thread running across the track. As the horse galloped by, it broke the threads, giving a series of twenty-four pictures taken in one second. The photos proved the horse was indeed completely airborne at some point in the gallop. The next advance in motion pictures was to invent a camera that could take twenty-four pictures in one second instead of twenty-four cameras each taking one picture.

By 1895 audiences in France viewed short moving pictures produced by August and Luis Lumiére. But it was Thomas Edison and his assistants Thomas Armat and William Dickson who perfected the motion picture. Edison believed the most profitable way to show movies was in a peep-show box he called a Kinetoscope. These hand-cranked movie boxes were novel but did not catch on.

Early films ran only a few minutes. Audiences would gather just to be thrilled and amazed at the frightening sight of a railroad engine bearing down on them. Early audiences reportedly gasped in amazement and some viewers even hid behind seats for protection. Films were shown as part of vaudeville shows (live stage entertainment) between 1896 and 1906. The movies shared the stage with comedians, magicians, and trained dogs. The first rooms specifically designed to project moving pictures were called nickelodeons, because admission cost a nickel. By 1910 there were ten thousand nickelodeons showing short films continuously from early morning to late night.

Woman adjusting her train. A Muybridge motion study, 1887.

The Edison Projection Kinetoscope

In 1909 the Motion Picture Patents Company (often called simply the "Trust") was formed by nine companies in an attempt to control the film business. The Trust used tactics ranging from legal contracts to hired thugs to enforce its control. It made a fatal mistake, however, in assuming that audiences would continue to want short films lasting about ten minutes, and that few would be willing to pay more than a dime to view movies. To keep prices down the Trust paid low salaries and could ill afford film "stars."

A few upstart independents headed for remote but sunny Hollywood to form their own film-making and distribution companies. They sought good weather and outdoor locations but also freedom from Trust thugs. By 1915, the Trust was disbanded and the upstart producers discovered that the public wanted stars and glamour. The three most successful independents became Twentieth Century Fox, Universal Studios, and Paramount Studios. Today the city of Hollywood is a global symbol of movies, glamour, and the American entertainment industry.

The moviemaking industry matured in the 1930s thanks to the invention of sound tracks. Warner Brothers' 1927 film *The Jazz Singer*, starring Al Jolson, included a few lines of spoken dialogue and songs. The silent movie quickly became obsolete, but the scandalous 1920s led producers to adopt an ethics code that was almost puritanical. The code required bedroom scenes to always show twin beds and fully clad actors. Forbidden words included *broad*, *tart*, and *pansy*. Criminals had to be punished. Films in the 1930s and 1940s were wholesome and attendance soared.

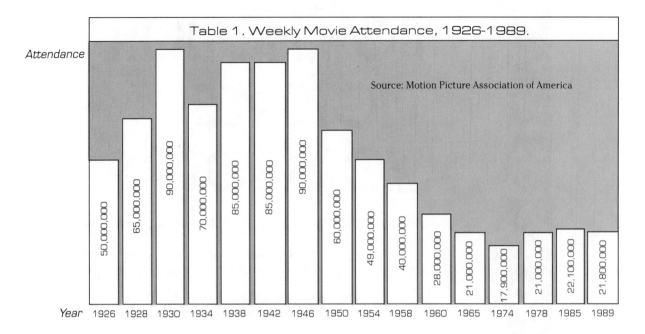

Table 1. Weekly Movie Attendance, 1926-1989.

Source: Motion Picture Association of America

Attendance

Year	Attendance
1926	50,000,000
1928	65,000,000
1930	90,000,000
1934	70,000,000
1938	85,000,000
1942	85,000,000
1946	90,000,000
1950	60,000,000
1954	49,000,000
1958	40,000,000
1960	28,000,000
1965	21,000,000
1974	17,900,000
1978	21,000,000
1985	22,100,000
1989	21,800,000

In 1930 the average American household sent three members to the movies each week—that meant 90 million people each week saw a movie. The movie industry, although still healthy today, never regained this "golden age" (1930–the late 1940s). The table below shows the national average weekly attendance at the movies. Average weekly attendance per household reached a high of three members in 1930, declined to one in 1954, and today stands at a low of .22.

The decline in the 1960s and 1970s can be attributed to the rise of television. Movie attendance is currently steady or on a slight increase; however, the audience now consists more of young people than of entire families as it did in the 1930s.

Will people in the year 2000 and beyond still go to theaters to watch films? There is a trend in movie theaters toward smaller sizes (the "cinema-six" concept means both smaller theaters and smaller screens) and an opposing trend toward larger TV sets. Will TV and videotaped movie viewing come closer to theater quality and size by the year 2000 and make theaters a relic of the past?

Currently, films are physically shipped from studios to theaters. Will an electronic delivery system using videotape and cable or satellite relays make this time honored system obsolete? If movies can be transmitted electronically, why not transmit them directly from the producing studio to the home, thus bypassing the need to pay a theater owner? Could electronically transmitted movies put an end to theaters or will a new approach to film revive the importance movies enjoyed in the 1930s?

I would say that there is no art form that has so much in common with film as music. Both affect our emotions directly, not via the intellect. And film is mainly rhythm; it is inhalation and exhalation in continuous sequence.

— INGMAR BERGMAN, Swedish filmmaker

HOW MOTION PICTURES WORK TODAY

Let's take a look at the machinery of film—at what makes movies move.

Would you go to see a movie that sounded entertaining and exciting but featured a sign at the theater entrance that read:

**"For One Hour Of This Two Hour Film The
Audience Will Look At A Blank Screen!!"**

Maybe you wouldn't, but you already have. In fact, every time you go to a film you spend half the time watching a blank screen. Perhaps an explanation is in order.

As you look at a piece of motion picture film, you see it consists of a column of tiny pictures, each divided by a thin black line. Film in movie houses is 35 millimeters—occasionally 70 millimeters wide. When you examine a piece of film, you notice that each frame is a picture of the same thing in a slightly different position each time. The illustration shown is 24 frames long and, therefore, shows movement that takes one second.

The sound track is carried on the left side of the film or, in the case of 70mm film, on both sides. Both sides of the film have holes. These holes fit the sprockets and claws of a projector that moves the frames between the projection bulb and the magnifying lens 24 times each second.

The illusion of movement in movies comes more from the projector in the theater than from the camera used to make the film. A movie camera takes only still pictures, just like a snapshot camera. The main difference is that the movie camera takes 24 "snapshots" every second while a still camera, operated by hand, takes pictures only as fast as the photographer moves. A movie camera is a rapid-fire still camera; it doesn't actually take "moving pictures," it takes still photographs.

Films become moving pictures only because our process of seeing is sluggish. The retina of the eyeball (which sends images to the brain) retains images for about 1/30 to 1/10 of a second after an object is out of sight. A most extreme example of this after-image (often called "persistence of vision" because the image "persists" for a time) is the white or blue spot you see after some-

Frames 1, 2, 3, 4, and 5 show the individual pictures that make up a film sequence. The blanks in between indicate the projector shutter is closed. This entire sequence would take less than one half a second to show on a movie projector.

one has taken a picture of you using a flashbulb. This after-image persists much longer than most images because of its intensity and brightness.

When you watch a film, you are "seeing" what was on the screen a fraction of a second ago. The movie projector has gears and claws that jerk the film in front of the lens in a stop-and-go motion. Each frame stops in front of the projector light for about 1/24 of a second. Then the projector shutter (a whirring disk with holes that alternately block light and let it through) blocks the light while the next frame is pulled into place. In the course of a film, the projector shutter blocks out the picture for about 50 percent of the time, so that the audience is really sitting in front of a blank screen. During a two-hour film, the audience will see 172,800 individual pictures (24 frames per second, 60 seconds per minute, for 120 minutes), but the projector shutter will have blocked off the light for about one hour of that time. During that time, the audience is watching the after-images.

Every film you see is, in a way, an optical illusion. The movement in movies comes from the combination of the slowness of your seeing process and the rapid movement of the film through the projector.

MEDIALAB

How Motion Pictures Began

and How They Work

1. List the inventions that made motion pictures possible and enabled film to become a mass medium.

2. Vaudeville was very popular at the beginning of the twentieth century. Motion pictures contributed toward its decline and virtual death in the early 1930s. In what way does the mass medium of film influence your attendance or interest in attending live performances, such as concerts?

3. In what way was film to vaudeville as television is to film today?

4. How would you answer a ten-year-old who asks you, "How do movies move?"

5. Demonstrate the principle of "persistence of vision," first mentioned on page 120. You may want to do some research at the library to create this experiment or demonstration.

6. If a movie projector is available, look at the inside of one and find where the light passes through the film. Also, find the magnifying lens, the claw, and the device that picks up the sound track.

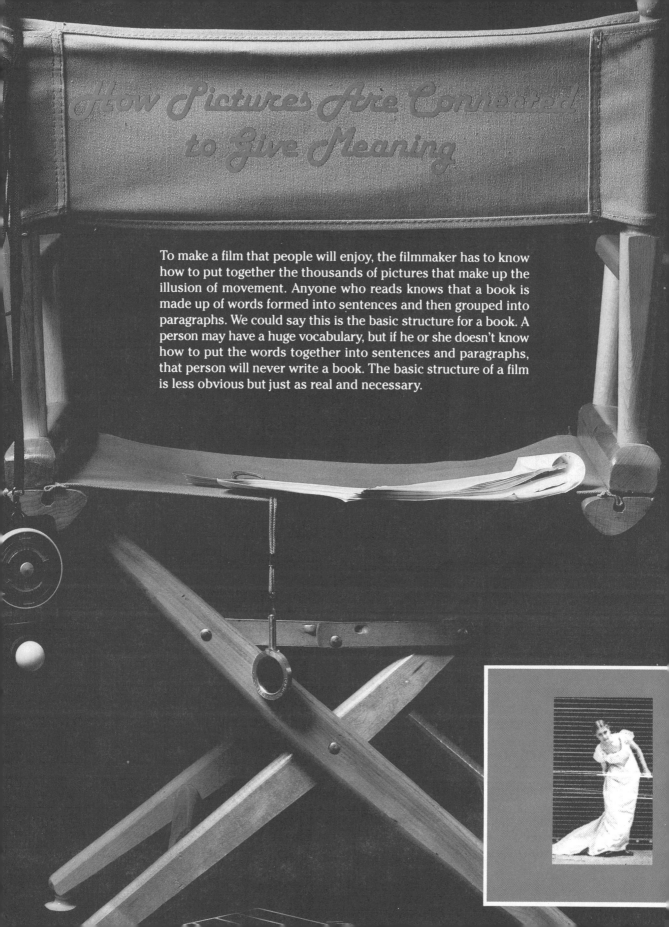

How Pictures Are Connected to Give Meaning

To make a film that people will enjoy, the filmmaker has to know how to put together the thousands of pictures that make up the illusion of movement. Anyone who reads knows that a book is made up of words formed into sentences and then grouped into paragraphs. We could say this is the basic structure for a book. A person may have a huge vocabulary, but if he or she doesn't know how to put the words together into sentences and paragraphs, that person will never write a book. The basic structure of a film is less obvious but just as real and necessary.

SHOTS AND SCENES

The basic building block of a film is the "shot." A shot is simply what happens in front of the camera from the time the camera starts until it stops. The shot is to a film as a word is to a book. Just as words are put together to make sentences, shots in a film are put together to make scenes. A scene is a single shot or a group of shots usually unified by time and place. Both a sentence and a scene are difficult to define but easy to demonstrate. Let's take a look at the making of just a few seconds of film that will eventually become part of a feature film. Here is the script for two scenes (numbers 114 and 115) from a film:

114 LONG SHOT–Bank building on busy street. Entrance to bank is clearly visible. Pedestrians pass by, uniformed guard stands on right side of door. Charley stands to the left of the revolving door.

Cut to

115 MEDIUM SHOT–Charley
Charley chews his ever-present toothpick and glances around nervously.

Cut to

CLOSE-UP–Charley
He checks his watch.

Scene 114 calls for only one shot—a long shot. A long shot is one in which the camera is set up a long way from the subject. This particular shot establishes the fact that Charley is standing in front of a bank and not just any building. A long shot that establishes a location is called an establishing shot. Establishing shots set the stage for the action to follow. The camera for scene 114 will probably be set up across the street from the bank or perhaps in a third-story window of another building across the street.

In the final film, scene 114 will last no longer than three seconds. To shoot the scene, however, the camera will be set up and as much as two to ten minutes of film will be shot. From this the director or editor will select the best footage and decide if the pace of the film requires the long shot of the bank to be shown for two seconds or five seconds or maybe not at all.

Although this scene is very short and simple, it can be used to illustrate the work, cooperation, and patience needed to make a full-length feature film.

For instance, if the ordinary people walking by the bank can be identified when the film is projected, they must give their written permission in the form of a "release" that allows their pictures to be used in the film. This is done to protect those who might find it embarrassing or somehow damaging to be recognized in a particular place by the public or those who simply wish privacy.

Most often the pedestrians and crowds you see in movies are paid to be there. They are called extras and are hired for films on a per-day basis. They are hired only to walk by a bank front, to stand on a corner, to carry a bunch of bananas through a fruit market, or to jump rope on a sidewalk. If the script called for a flock of pigeons to be on the sidewalk and to scatter when the hero approached, they, too, would be hired from an animal rental specialist.

If a film were being shot in your city, you might find an ad in the local newspaper asking for extras for crowd scenes. If you applied and were accepted, you might find yourself in a scene such as 114.

Long before actual shooting, the film's producers would have obtained the permission of the bank to film in front of it. The work would probably be done when the bank was closed. If the film is about a bank robbery, the bank might not like its name associated with the film. In this case the property department ("prop" for short) would make a fictional nameplate so the bank would not be identified in the film.

As the actual shooting of scene 114 begins, the director yells, "Quiet on the set," and an assistant holds a slate in front of the camera reading "Scene 114, Take 1." The camera runs for several seconds or several minutes and then stops at the director's order. The slate board appears on the film as identification so that when the film is edited, a particular shot can be found easily. The actual film of the slate board is discarded.

If the budget for this film is limited, the director might decide to save money by using a "stock shot" for scene 114. Film studios and special film libraries have large collections of footage of almost every conceivable situation, which they sell for use in films. If a director needs a picture of a house exploding, a ship sinking, a forest fire raging through thousands of acres, a jet taking off or landing, these stock libraries will provide the needed footage.

One of the most commonly used stock shots, especially in television films, is the jet plane landing and taking off. These shots are used to indicate the movement of characters from one city to another. Some of these stock shots are supplied by the airlines, who realize their name on the plane is free advertising.

So scene 114, which will appear on the screen for a few fleeting seconds, requires much time and effort to shoot. Selecting the right bank (which means first deciding whether the scene will be shot on a studio lot or "on location" on a public street); setting up

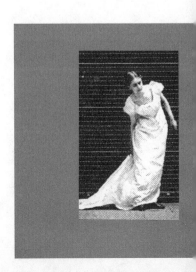

Medium Shot

CloseUp

Long Shot

the camera position; obtaining all the needed permissions; transporting the crew and actors to the right place at the right time; enlisting police permission to block off the sidewalk and perhaps the street (if the film takes place in the 1930s, the director can't have 1980s cars driving past the bank); taking the light readings and supplying any artificial light needed; planning costumes and makeup; and finally directing the scene itself—all these take hundreds of hours of labor.

For scene 115, the camera will move closer to Charley, and again the filming will begin with the slate board. The director may decide to shoot this scene from two different angles and pick the best one later while editing the film. If so, the second angle will be slated as "Scene 115, Take 2." If, during the second take, Charley sneezes or a jet roars overhead or a member of the stage crew drops a hammer with a loud clang, that take will have been ruined. It will then be started over, with the slate reading "Scene 115, Take 3." The director's quest for perfection can result in scenes being reshot four, six, or even twenty times.

After the entire film has been shot, the editing begins. The editor or the director or both working together select the best footage and make the crucial decisions of how long each shot should remain on the screen, which footage should be used and which thrown in the scrap pile, and in what order the shots should be arranged to tell the story. The three shots in scenes 114 and 115 will pass across the screen in a few seconds. Few people in the audience will appreciate the time and effort that went into those few seconds.

You can't say as much as you can in writing, but you can say what you say with great conviction.
—ROBERT FLAHERTY, Documentary filmmaker

SEQUENCE

In our description of the structure of a film, we have compared a shot to a word and a scene to a sentence. The next larger division is a "sequence," which is a grouping of scenes joined by a common purpose or setting. When people speak of the "chase scene," they really mean the chase *sequence*. The two scenes used to illustrate "shot" and "scene" were part of a sequence informally called "Charley's Arrest." The arrest sequence will run in the film for about three minutes and will have about twenty scenes.

We can use the example of a football game to illustrate these terms. Let's say a real football game is being filmed (or televised) as it happens—the director cannot control the action, so instead the cameras must be directed to cover what happens on the field. One of the sequences of the football game is the "Goal Line Stand."

SCENE 225—FIRST DOWN AND GOAL TO GO

Teams take positions with the ball on the six-yard line.

LONG SHOT of players lining up.

Cut to

MEDIUM SHOT of quarterback barking signals and receiving the ball from the center. The quarterback steps back to pass and throws the ball.

Cut to

MEDIUM SHOT of intended receiver over goal line. The ball misses his fingertips by inches.

SCENE 226—SECOND DOWN AND GOAL TO GO

LONG SHOT—team huddle.

Cut-away to

Cheerleaders.

LONG SHOT—Team breaks huddle and enters formation.

Cut-in to

EXTREME CLOSE-UP of football in center's hands.

Cut to

LONG SHOT—Ball is snapped to quarterback who is immediately tackled. Players untangle and the quarterback walks dejectedly to the huddle.

Scenes 227 and 228, we can guess, would show unsuccessful attempts at the third and fourth downs. Scene 229 would begin a new sequence, perhaps to be called "94-Yard Touchdown Drive."

Notice that scene 226 uses a shot called a cut-away and one called a cut-in. A cut-away is a shift of attention from the main action to some related action. Shots of the crowd or the cheerleaders during a sports event are cut-aways. They cut away from the main action. A cut-in directs the viewers' eyes to some very specific action or object within the main focus of attention. A close-up of a football sitting on the goal line or a close-up of a basketball hoop during a free-throw attempt are cut-ins.

Cut-ins and cut-aways are used in television sports to provide visual variety. They are also used in film because that is the way we look at things. If you attend a football game, your own eyes will spend most of the time watching the action on the field, but occasionally they will cut away to catch some of the action in the stands. In a classroom you might cut in to watch the teacher's hand as he or she picks up a piece of chalk. You might cut away to look out the window at the passing clouds.

The cut-away is also useful to the director in manipulating time in a film. Film time and real time are different. If a film were made in real time, you would almost certainly find it boring. If the character were to fly from Chicago to Washington in a real-time film, you would have to watch the plane in the air for an hour—a scene that would quickly empty any theater. In film-time, you see the plane take off and a second or two later the traveler is standing beside the White House. Because you have learned to accept film time, this causes you no problems. Time in films is both compressed and expanded.

The cut-away is used to compress time. Say, for example, a script calls for a scene of a boat steaming up a river and docking at a wharf. In real time this action takes about 20 minutes, far too long for a film. The director solves the time problem by filming a long shot of the boat out in the river, cutting away to someone walking along the wharf to meet the boat, and then cutting back to the boat, which is now in the process of docking. Viewers understand what has happened because they understand film language. Someone watching this sequence of shots who had never before seen a film would probably find it confusing and might even wonder if the boat docking is the same one that was out in the river just a second ago.

If the cut-away to the person walking were not used, the boat would be seen in one shot in the middle of the river and then would appear to jump magically to the dock. Viewers would not accept such a "jump cut." With the cut-away, the action appears smooth and logical.

REAL TIME AND FILM TIME ARE DIFFERENT

Cut-aways are used in film because they are used in real life. This reduplicating of reality is also why there is a basic shot sequence in putting together films. The basic shot order is long shot, medium shot, close-up, and reestablishing shot. This order of shots was used in the "Charley's Arrest" sequence.

The long shot, also called the establishing shot when it is used to establish where the action takes place, shows the main character or object in its general surroundings. The medium shot shows the main character or object in its immediate surroundings. A close-up includes only the main character or object or maybe only a part of it. A reestablishing shot reminds the viewer of what surrounds the main character or object. This technique is easy to see in this opening scene for a Western, which could even be used while the credits are being shown:

LONG SHOT—
Sunset over wide-open prairie land. The figure of a horse and rider trailing a cloud of dust can be seen in the distance heading toward a small town.

MEDIUM SHOT—
The man on horseback rides along a crude trail.

CLOSE-UP—
Now the man's face reveals a grim look of determination, with tightly clenched teeth; we see a sheriff's badge on his vest.

LONG SHOT—
(Reestablishing)—Another long shot reveals that the sheriff has reached the city limits just as the sun sets.

If this basic script were given to five different directors, each would film it in a slightly different way. *Long, medium, close-up* are only approximate terms for these shots. Some long shots are longer than others, just as some close-ups are closer than others.

This basic order of shots makes psychological sense because this is the way we see things in reality. Imagine entering a classroom on the first day of school. First you look around the room to establish where you are—a long shot. Then you begin to look around at who is in the room and to scan faces— your medium shot. Third you see someone you know and narrow in on an empty desk nearby— a close-up. After you sit down you go back to examining the entire room again—the reestablishing shot.

This basic order of shots is widely used, and you should be able to spot it easily in almost any film. You will also be able to spot many exceptions to this basic order, just as there are exceptions in reality. If your main concern as you enter the classroom is the rumor that your favorite teacher is teaching the course, you might look first to see who is standing in front of the room. In a film in which the person entering is concerned about the teacher, the first shot would be an extreme close-up of the smiling (or scowling) teacher instead of a long shot of the room. A film director has to be part technician, part artist, and part psychologist to select the right shots.

In film there are as many general rules as there are exceptions to the rules. This basic shot order can even be completely reversed. Most often this is done for a shock effect. For example: An extreme close-up of a spider crawling; cut to a medium shot revealing that the spider is crawling on a person (shock number one); and finally a long shot showing a cobweb-covered dead body complete with dagger (shock number two). If this sequence were shot in normal order, the shock effect would be lost.

Editing

Every art form has some kind of "editing"—the process of selecting the best words, colors, lines, building materials, or sounds and rejecting those that are less good.

When a film is finally shot, all the bits and pieces must be put together skillfully so the viewing audience will follow the story and be entertained. Putting together the bits and selecting the best is called editing. Editing in film can be done with scissors and tape, but special editing machines make the job easier and faster.

The person editing the film works with a copy of all the footage shot, while the original is safely stored until the final steps of the editing process. (In making your own movies, you probably won't want to spend the extra money to have a copy of your film made.) The editor joins the shots into scenes, the scenes into sequences, and the sequences into a film. He or she rejects film that is incorrectly exposed, scenes that are poorly acted, or shots that contain too much or too little information. For professionally-made films, ten to twenty times as much footage as is needed will be shot. To edit a one-hour film, the editor may have ten to twenty hours of film from which to select.

Just as the sentences and paragraphs of a book must be linked together by transitional devices, so a film must fit together according to the logic of its story. A film must be put together so that the audience is involved rather than confused. For example, an editor putting together the scenes from our "Goal Line Stand" sequence could thoroughly confuse the viewers by changing the order of the shots. If the shots of the center snapping the ball were followed immediately by one of the pass receiver running after the ball, a confused audience would conclude that the center had somehow snapped the ball to the receiver.

Editing is the magic by which houses hundreds of miles apart can be made to appear on the same street. Take a piece of film of a person looking out a window, join to that a two-second shot of ocean surf, and the viewer will conclude the person is looking out the window at the ocean. In reality, the person is in a Hollywood studio where there is nothing outside but a parking lot. The shot of the ocean shows a beach in Hawaii and was made three weeks later. Through the magic of editing, an audience will be led to believe the person is on the ocean's shore.

There must be some logic to splicing one piece of film to another. If you were making a home movie of a baby and you first showed it crying into the camera, then followed with a shot of a huge black spider, the audience wouldn't know what connection there was between the spider and the baby. If, however, you first showed the baby sitting next to a small tree and smiling into the camera, then looking toward the righthand side of the picture frame (where the tree is) and starting to cry, and then you spliced on a shot of a spider crawling on a tree branch toward the left side of the frame (a shot you may have made years ago), the audience would assume the baby was being attacked by the spider. The act of looking toward the edge of the frame leads the audience to expect the next shot will be what that person sees.

Many years ago, a Russian director took a strip of silent film that showed an actor's face staring down. The director spliced this same shot in between a shot of a steaming bowl of soup, one

Shown here is an editing machine. Notice the digital counter to help find single frames, the small size of the screen, and the presence of two screens to aid in matching shots.

of a dead woman in a coffin, and another of a child at play. His finished film was (1) face, (2) soup, (3) face same as in shot 1, (4) coffin, (5) face same as in shot 1, (6) child, (7) face same as in shot 1. Pretending it was a screen test for the actor, he screened the film for a small audience. The audience praised the unknown actor, commenting on his subtle expressions of hunger at the sight of the soup, grief at seeing the coffin, and amusement as he watched the child play.

This experiment illustrates the power of editing as well as its ability to make film acting much easier than stage acting. Even the world's worst actor can turn in an acceptable performance in a film if the editing makes it so. If a scene requires an expression of fright, our nonactor is told to look to the right and register an expression such as a person would have if there were a 20-foot-tall rabbit outside the window about to eat the house. The director would have the actor (or nonactor) simply look to the right and express fright. If the actor cannot do even that, perhaps a well-timed and unexpected firecracker from a stagehand would accomplish the task. As edited, the actor's fright at the noise of the firecracker would be followed by a shot of the giant rabbit, and the audience would conclude that the actor is reacting to the sight of the rabbit.

When the editor works with the copy of the film, he or she cements together the bits and pieces of film that will eventually make a finished product. This glued-together film is then copied in a film lab into one complete piece of film. The magic of the movies has again been created out of skill, hard work, and patience.

MEDIALAB

The Grammar of Film

1. While filming, you (a) shot a few seconds of a friend standing against a wall; (b) stopped filming but left the camera absolutely still, mounted on a tripod; (c) told your friend to walk away while the camera was not running; (d) began filming again without moving the camera. Describe the resulting film.

2. Describe what would happen if, while filming, you did these steps. (a) You again pointed the camera at your friend standing against the wall. This time you ran the camera for as short a time as possible—ideally, advancing the film only one frame. (b) You stopped filming and left the camera absolutely still. (c) While the camera was not running, you told your friend to move four inches to the left. (d) You again ran the camera for one frame or as little as possible. (e) You stopped and had your friend move four inches to the left again. (f) Repeat this process until your friend is out of view of the camera. What would the resulting film show?

3. You are assigned to film a sequence in a railroad station. The script calls for the star to kiss the co-star, get on the train, and wave from the window as the train leaves. You arrive at the railroad station only to find that no engineer is available to move the train. No one else is able to drive the train and you cannot change the script. How would you solve this problem?

4. An editor can arrange the following three shots in ways that will give the audience an impression of either cool courage or cowardice. Do you see how?

Face Filled
with Fear

Gun
Pointed

Face with
Confident
Smile

5. Using either a short film or a TV program, find clear examples of:

an establishing shot

a scene

a sequence

a shot

a scene or portion of a scene in which a long shot is followed by a medium shot, followed by a close-up

6. Study carefully one scene or sequence in a film and see how it was made and put together.

7. What would happen if a director arranged the following events? An actor located at A shoots an arrow as indicated in the sketch. The camera begins to film as the actor shoots the arrow and then quickly pans around and stops so actor B is in view. Actor B already has an arrow lodged in balsa wood underneath his shirt back. As the camera stops on him, he staggers forward and falls to the ground. How would this appear on the screen?

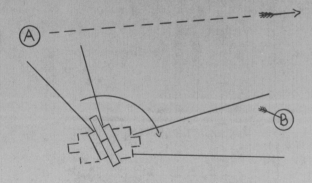

8. Write a shooting script (no longer than one page) for the following action: A person approaches your house at night while you are asleep, leans a ladder against the house, and begins to climb it. Halfway up his foot breaks through a rung on the ladder and awakens you suddenly from a deep sleep. Make your shooting script clear enough so that a director and actors could actually make the scene from your directions. Number each shot and indicate about how long each should

last. The entire scene should last no longer than 45 seconds.

9. What effect on the meaning of the film would the elimination of shot 114 have in the example that began this section? (Shot 114 was a long shot of the bank building on a busy street.)

10. In the editing process, one of the critical decisions to be made about each shot is how long it should be left on the screen. How would a shot that lasts too long affect an audience? A shot that is not shown long enough? Be aware that a shot left on the screen too long will have a different audience reaction than a shot left on the screen for too short a time.

11. Watch at least a few minutes of any kind of sport televised within the next week. While you watch, note to yourself the beginning of each new shot. Look for cut-ins and cut-aways. Be aware of the use of close-ups, medium shots, and long shots.

12. Prepare a rough draft of a shooting script (no longer than one-half page) that condenses time. Take any action that would normally take several minutes and condense it down to a few seconds. Your script should be clear enough for a director to use in making a film and should leave no doubt about what has happened.

13. Do you think the experiment of the Russian director involving the actor's face and the soup/coffin/child shots would work today? Remember that the people who viewed his experiment were very unfamiliar with film.

HOW THE CAMERA GIVES MEANING

Movies move. Give a beginning filmmaker a camera, and he or she will move the camera back and forth, up and down, and play with the zoom lens like a new toy. An experienced photographer moves the camera only when necessary and only after careful thought about how the movement will affect the viewer.

You should be able to recognize the most commonly used camera movements.

PAN

The tripod remains in place, but the camera swivels from left to right or right to left. The resulting shot duplicates a person surveying a situation by standing in one place and turning his or her head. A pan (short for "panorama") is used in film, as in reality, to survey a scene or to follow a moving object.

Tilt

A tilt shot is a vertical (up and down) pan. The tripod remains in place while the camera pivots up or down. This seldom-used movement gives viewers a trip up or down a building, a person, or other tall object.

DOLLY

The camera rolls smoothly toward or away from the subject. In professional films the heavy camera is mounted on a special cart called a dolly. In amateur filmmaking the same effect can be obtained by moving the camera on a wagon, skateboard, or any wheeled platform. The ground must be smooth for this shot to work.

 Tracking Shot

Also called a traveling shot or a follow shot. This is a variation of the dolly. If you want to move the camera parallel to a fast-moving car, the camera can be mounted on a second car and moved alongside the car that is being filmed. If the camera is to move smoothly along rough or sandy ground (to follow two people walking on a beach, for example), a special wooden track is laid down and the dolly "tracks" along it for a smooth shot. (Note that in television film production the universally used term for tracking shot is trunk left or trunk right.)

BOOM

This shot involves mounting the camera on a special crane on the end of a hydraulic arm. The camera mounted on this "boom" can be moved very fluidly in almost any direction.

zooM

This shot is used for a dramatic or shocking effect. A zoom lens is manipulated while the camera remains stationary. The effect created is similar to looking through a telescope or binoculars and moving from the least to the greatest magnification (zoom-in) or the reverse (zoom-out). A zoom can be very fast or gradual. A zoom lens is available for home movie cameras and is much overused by amateurs. It is seldom used in professional films because there is no comparison to this kind of "seeing" in reality. Our eyes are not equipped with zoom eyeballs.

Hand-Held

All the previous techniques of camera movement depend on the fact that cameras are usually mounted on a tripod. But newer cameras are light enough to be carried by hand so that a film can be made by picking up a camera and walking around with it. This is most often done in documentary films and in filming for news.

Camera Angle

A basic problem in any filming is where to place the camera. Part of that problem is solved by deciding what you want to appear on the screen. But the question remains, from what angle will you film?

Let's say you need a shot of a fighter standing alone in a boxing ring in an empty auditorium where tomorrow he will face the champ. Do you place the camera in one corner of the ring and look the boxer in the eye? Do you place the camera below the ring and look up at him, or perhaps even go into the rafters and look down on him? Each of these choices will produce a different emotional effect on the viewer. Your final choice will depend on the story line and on what you know about camera angle. There are three basic vertical camera angles:

Eye level

1. You can place a camera rather normally so that you are looking at people or things from eye level.

2. You can place the camera below the person, looking up. This "low angle" shot is used when you want the viewer to "look up" to someone. A low angle shot will make a person appear strong and superior, even superhuman.

Low angle

3. A "high angle" shot involves placing the camera so that it looks down on the subject being filmed. When we are above somone, looking down, we tend to feel superior to that person. So a high angle shot is used to make a person appear small, inferior, lonely, or looked down on.

High angle

If, in filming the boxer, we want to emphasize the fact that the boxer is small and alone in the face of the champ, the best angle would be in the rafters looking down. If the script calls for showing the boxer as superior and confident, then it would be best to place the camera below the ring, looking up at him.

An awareness of how different camera angles make pictures look different is necessary to solve one of the basic problems of movies. Reality is three-dimensional, but the movie screen has only length and width. The problem is to give an appearance of depth to flat pictures. A movie camera is like a one-eyed person unable to see depth. If you close one eye and try to touch various objects a few feet from you, you will have difficulty because you can no longer see in three dimensions.

Front

3/4 Profile

Camera operators rely on angles to give the illusion of depth. Consider these two pictures of the same face.

The picture on the right has more "depth" to it, because we see two sides of the face. The picture on the left is "flat" and dull because it shows no depth. If you look at the faces in the ads in magazines, you will notice that rarely is a face shown straight on. A slight angle off to the side reveals more of the head and adds depth to the picture.

There is a simple law governing the filming of novels: if it is worth doing it can't be done, if it can be done, it isn't worth it.

—JOHN SIMON, film critic

A movie screen, a TV picture tube, and a photograph all have only two dimensions and yet are called on to represent three-dimensional reality. Let's say your assignment is to take a picture of an automobile so that a person looking at it will have a good idea of what the car looks like from the outside. Where would you place the camera to take such a picture?

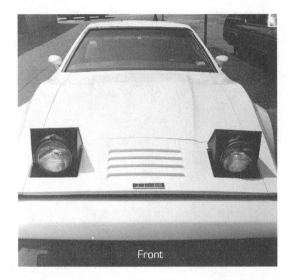

Front

Low Front

3/4 Profile

To give three-dimensional reality to static objects, you would use an angle-on-angle camera position. To use angle-on-angle positions, you take the film or picture from both an angle other than straight on *and* an angle other than eye level. If you look at pictures of products in ads, you will see that angle-on-angle shots are common indeed.

MEDIALAB

Camera Movement and Angles

1. If there is at least one movie camera available for class use, make a film in the classroom with as many people participating as possible. The purpose of the film is to illustrate the various camera movements and angles discussed in this section. The film should contain examples of the following:

Pan from right to left

Pan from left to right

Tilt from bottom to top

Tilt from top to bottom

Dolly shot toward an object

Dolly shot away from an object

Tracking shot

Hand-held following a person or moving object

High angle shot

Low angle shot

Zoom—slow zoom *in* on an object

Zoom—slow zoom *out* from an object

Zoom—fast zoom *in* on an object

Zoom—fast zoom *out* from an object

These last four shots are possible only if the camera is equipped with a zoom lens.

Make no attempt to have the film tell a story. Simply illustrate the above shots without making any attempt to connect one shot with the next. Use a film that needs no special lights.

2. When the illustration film is developed, watch it as a class. Discuss the different effects of each shot. For example, does the pan from right to left feel any different from the pan from left to right? Does the "dolly in" toward a subject feel any different from a "dolly away" from a subject? What feeling does a zoom shot give? Judging from your own film, why do you think professional filmmakers seldom use a zoom shot?

MEANING THROUGH COMPOSITION, COLOR AND SOUND

COMPOSITION

A painter, a photographer, and a filmmaker all share a concern for the composition of a picture. Composition is how the parts of the picture are arranged, or "composed," within the frame. A poorly composed picture will look somehow "wrong" and will be distracting to the viewer. Seeing good composition in pictures takes a trained and knowledgeable eye. But even a beginner can quickly learn a few basic ideas of composition.

The kinds of lines used in a picture are important. If the film calls for a shot of the office of a strict male army sergeant, the director will know that straight, angular lines should be part of the picture. Straight lines are considered masculine, curved lines feminine. The army sergeant would not have a round desk or rug or a chair with a curved back. If the film calls for a shot of the bedroom of a female character presented as traditionally "feminine," the lines will be curved—oval rugs, paintings with curves, a vase. The choice of the kinds of lines in each room communicates to the viewer something about the person who lives or works there.

If the director wants a quiet, peaceful sequence, he or she will compose using long horizontal lines. The horizontal line is restful, perhaps because it suggests the line of the body asleep or at rest.

Vertical lines inspire awe. The sight of a skyscraper as seen looking up from its base, the majestic vertical height of a distant mountain, or even the imposing appearance of a six-foot-tall adult as seen by a three-year-old are all awesome. If a group of people are to be filmed sitting around a table and one of the people is supposed to be strong and determined, the director might have that person stand up, thus creating a vertical line.

Diagonal lines suggest action and dynamism. If the script calls for a long shot of a racing car, the director will often place the camera so that the car moves across the screen diagonally.

People go to the movies for the various ways they express the experiences of our lives, and as a means of avoiding and postponing the pressures we feel. This latter function of art—generally referred to disparagingly as escapism—may also be considered as refreshment, and in terms of modern big city life and small town boredom, it may be a major factor in keeping us sane.

—PAULINE KAEL,
America film critic

In this still from the film *Up the Down Staircase*, the boy's leather jacket forms a massive dark shape filling nearly half the screen. His right arm extends directly across the other half of the frame suggesting a barrier. If the camera were placed where the three spectators are, the idea of the huge dark shape blocking the way of the actress would be missing. The boy with the jacket is not actually blocking the sidewalk, but the careful use of shapes suggests that idea. The boy's head is also carefully placed in relation to the background. If the white wall with the graffiti were not placed where it is, the picture would be much less effective.

The boy in this film still from *400 Blows* is trapped. The picture is composed in such a way that his head has little room to move within the frame. The fence also acts as a visual barrier adding to the feeling of imprisonment.

Low angle gives this character an added dignity and impressiveness. The contrast between the white face and the darkness of the rest of the picture also adds interest (*Legend*, Pyramid Films).

The angle of the raft makes this picture more exciting than if it were positioned parallel to the base of the photo *(Rapids of the Colorado,* Pyramid Films).

A picture of a girl skipping rope sounds like quite an ordinary shot. But to make the picture more intriguing in this frame from the visual poem documentary *Jumprope*, the cameraperson used an extremely low angle *(Jumprope,* Pyramid Films).

COLOR

Most of the film *Fiddler on the Roof* was shot through a camera lens covered by a piece of brown nylon stocking bought at a local department store. Director Norman Jewison wanted the film to be filled with a warm and earthy feeling, befitting the peasant people and rural location of the story. He found that a very sharp focus and bright colors gave a slick, too-contemporary look. He also realized that "modern life is perceived sharply, but the moment you move into a period [of the past] it becomes, somehow, faded and a bit hazy. Your references to it are through old photographs and books and things. You don't see it quite as clearly as you see life today." To give the film the earthy look and to establish the mood of its taking place in the remembered past, the best solution was to shoot it through some kind of filter. The best results were obtained with a stocking that gave the film a subtle tint and softened the focus very slightly.

In addition to the unusual filter, nearly all primary colors were taken out of the sets used in the film. There are few pure reds, blues, or yellows in *Fiddler on the Roof*. The film gives the "feeling" of black and white, although it was filmed in color.

Does the average viewer notice that certain colors are missing or call out to the projectionist to get that stocking off the projector? Of course not, but the techniques give the film a subtle reality it would not have had under more conventional shooting conditions. The careful use of color, composition, angles, camera movement, and other film techniques should not be so obvious that they are noticed by the viewer, but they should *influence* the viewer. Film techniques work best when the audience is not aware they are working.

Chiaroscuro: use of light and dark tones

The *Godfather* was carefully colored, and many shots were composed to resemble Italian chiaroscuro painting. This served to link this story of the Mafia with its origins and to give the picture a properly historical look.

Film directors do not take whatever color comes along. They realize that color, like composition and movement, influences the feeling the film creates in the audience. Often the color of a costume, an automobile, a room, or even an entire stage set is changed for a scene of a few seconds.

A film about a joyless future world that is run by a dictator and allows no personal freedom would not look right shot in "living" color complete with bright, gaudy splashes of color. Such a film would very likely be shot in a very subdued, almost colorless, style, perhaps tending toward an overall bluish cast.

In the 1939 version of *Jesse James*, the James gang holds up a railroad train near sunset. Jesse leaps atop the train and runs along the top while it is still moving. The camera is alongside the train and shows James silhouetted against the darkening sky; below him the train windows glow with an orangish lamplight. Such care in filming was not done to make a "pretty" picture, but to point out through color the difference between the dangerous, cold world of the criminal and the comfortable, warm world of the law-abiding citizens.

A film director must be sensitive to colors and their effects on the mood of the audience.

SOUND

When film was new, people marveled at pictures that moved. They called this new medium a "movie." When sound was added in the late 1920s people were astonished at pictures that talked. They called this innovation a "talkie."

We still use the quaint term "movie" (which is a bit like calling a car a "horseless carriage"), or even a "flick" (although a flickering image is no longer a problem). But we don't call films "talkies" or "soundies." Our choice of words reveals we have lost sight of (there's that visual bias again) the importance of sound in film. All films today are multi-media—sight and sound. The study of film must include careful analysis of sounds as well as sights.

In Movies, Hearing Is Believing*

By Frank Spotnitz

Humanity's bigotry against the ears has a long and ignoble history. "Men trust their ears less than their eyes," Herodotus noticed some 25 centuries ago, and the eyes have been steadily outdistancing the ears ever since.

Herodotus could not have predicted the advent of a visual art where hearing—not seeing—is believing. In the darkness of a movie theater, we are only too aware that the images before us are illusions. It's the film's sound track that surreptitiously seduces us, mysteriously altering our perceptions of reality. The intangible nature of sound, combined with our bias toward the visual, has led to a shocking neglect of the subtle and yet powerful role sound plays in the movies.

"People are generally not aware of the direct effect the sound track is having on them," says Ben Burtt, sound editor for the *Star Wars* and *Indiana Jones* trilogies. "They tend to accept what's there on the speakers as being natural. Audiences have become educated to look for matte shots, animation, or whatever, but sound is still a magical area. It comes into the mind in a different way."

In a film like *Raiders of the Lost Ark*, eye-popping visual effects are all part of the filmmaker's cache. We are wowed by the sight of a mammoth boulder careening down the cave on the heels of Indiana. The ominous rumble makes it real, but only Ben Burtt knows that the roar of that rock is actually an amplified recording of his Honda Civic rolling down the driveway at Lucasfilm Ltd. in San Anselmo, California. Such trickery is the trade of an elite corps of sound-effects wizards who have virtually reinvented the craft since the early '70s—the biggest technological and qualitative leap forward in sound since the advent of the talkies themselves. These sound specialists, who, in addition to Burtt, include Alan Splet (*Eraserhead, The Black Stallion, Blue Velvet*), Walter Murch (*The Godfather, The Conversation, Apocalypse Now*) and the now-retired Frank Warner (*Raging Bull, Close Encounters of the Third Kind*), stand out for their originality—both in their use of sound and their scrupulousness in creating new effects—as well as their technical precision. They have redefined their craft so thoroughly that Murch even dreamed up a new credit to describe what they do: sound designer.

The term occurred to Murch while he was mixing the quadraphonic sound for *Apocalypse Now* a decade ago. "It seemed like a sort of interior design to me," he says. "You were hanging sound on the walls of the room, and it had to be done just right. I expected [the credit] to disappear, but it seemed to be a word whose time had come."

The art of designing sound effects is what Walter Murch calls making "little lies that add up to a truth." Aural reality is shaped to fit the dynamics of a microphone. Bending a sheet of metal sounds like thunder. Walking through cornstarch sounds like trudging through packed snow. In a thousand ways, the sound editor tricks us into thinking we are hearing the real thing. In fact, he does more than that—he creates a noise that is more exciting than reality (realistic sound work is the province of Foley artists).

"The early Hollywood filmmakers discovered that a punch requires an exaggerated thwack to emphasize that it might really hurt," three-time Oscar-winner Burtt says. "Literal reality couldn't be as exciting."

If you doubt the impact that sound makes in a film, sound-effects editor

*Originally entitled "Stick It in your Ear"

A sound editor at work

Richard Anderson (*Beetlejuice, Poltergeist*) suggests taking home a videocasette and trying to watch it with the sound off. The silence is deafening. Even if you're able to follow the story, the film's emotional impact is blunted. "Most modern movies are based on sound tracks," Anderson says. "It's very important. I'm not going to say it's 50 percent of the experience—that depends on the sequence in the film—but it's certainly a big part of it."

Just as the quality of special effects has been revolutionized in the past two decades, enormous changes have occurred in motion-picture sound—and only the fanatics have noticed.

Indeed, the explosion of big-budget pictures and science-fiction extravaganzas in the late 1970s and early '80s exerted a tremendous pressure on sound-effects men to come up with new and dazzling noises. Stock sound effects in studio libraries sounded flat and tired in the Dolby stereo that was coming into vogue. In addition, digitized sound, synthesizers, and computers opened a whole new range of sound manipulation that no one had dreamed of before. The technology had the effect of concentrating creative power in sound-effects editors, who no longer needed huge crews to go out and record sounds or a band of technicians to mix them in the studio.

"The sound designer has all kinds of new processing gear," Burtt says. "There's been a revolution in reverb with devices like the Lexicon, in which you can put sound effects and make them sound as if they're inside a cathedral or a cave or a bathroom. You can take a gunshot and make it sound like it's in a parking garage. You can manipulate a sound much more efficiently than you ever could in the past."

Producers trying to squeeze out ounces of value rediscovered an age-old Hollywood truism: Sound is the cheapest special effect there is. In the opening scenes of *The Elephant Man*, when Frederick Treves (Anthony Hopkins) discovers the deformed John Merrick, sound designer Splet's calliope music and the shrieks and murmur of the crowd do more to suggest the atmosphere of a large circus than the much costlier standing set and dozens of milling extras.

Until the '70s, audiences had been listening to the same gunshots, wind noises, and face slaps for decades. The Paramount face slap, for instance, has been standard in the industry since it was recorded for, but apparently not used in, the Marx Brothers film *Monkey Business* (1931). Creepy, whistling "yellow wind" has been used countless times since it first was heard in *Frankenstein* (1931). Incredibly, both sound effects are still a staple in television sound editing, but the fussiness of the new feature sound editors, as well as the higher fidelity of latter-day theater sound systems, demanded change.

The new generation of sound editors prides itself on recording as many fresh sound effects as time allows. "To quote Julia Child, The best cooking comes when you use the freshest ingredients,' " says Murch. "So if you simply return to the library, the way a bored cook returns to canned food, the food you produce is going to have a harder time being interesting." Those stock sound effects that are used either end up being distorted in a new way or combined with other sounds so as to be unrecognizable. Frank Warner was said to be such a purist about using fresh sounds that he recorded all new gunshots for Martin Scorsese's *Taxi Driver* and all new punches and face slaps for *Raging Bull*—destroying the tapes of them all after the films were finished, to prevent others from reusing them.

Although no one is sure how the first face punches were created, typical methods used today include smacking animal carcasses such as turkeys and roasts, breaking lumber, and snapping crisp vegetables like celery and carrots. Violence in the cinema, in fact, sounds nothing like violence in real life—we just think it does. Ask any police officer about the pathetic popping sound a real gunshot makes in an open boulevard—far from the deafening pow of Dirty Harry's .44 Magnum on the streets of San Francisco. Ditto for just about any other weapon. On playgrounds across America, kids employ an arsenal of sounds to make their weapons sound "right." Violence just isn't as much fun outside of a theater.

Of course, the images of swashbuckling swordplay and heroic gun battles have something to do with that, too. But sound editors subtly abet the movie world's use of violence as entertainment. Says Burtt, "A punch in real life is nothing like a movie punch. You'd hear the grunt of the victim much louder than the impact of the fist." A victim's cry of pain, Hollywood sound editors know, might be more disturbing than exciting. So to maximize excitement and avoid upsetting the audience, the punch is turned up and filled out, the cry of pain is turned down.

When sound designers aren't called upon to create new worlds in sound, they keep busy reshaping the old one. Murch, who has become a director since his ground-breaking sound work with Francis Coppola on *The Godfather* and *The Godfather, Part II* (1972, 1974), *The Conversation* (1974), and *Apocalypse Now* (1979), is a master of what he calls "hypersensitivity."

"Your brain can tune sounds in and out," he says, so that you can, for example, filter out extra sounds in a restaurant to concentrate on the conversation at your table or perhaps the conversation of someone attractive standing next to you.

With his mixing board, Murch performs the same function for an audience. One of his most celebrated examples comes from *Apocalypse Now*, when Frederic Forrest and another soldier are patrolling the jungle, looking for the source of a noise. Gradually, as the men get closer and closer to the source, the sound of the crickets fades out, then the monkeys, then—silence. Suddenly, we see a tiger jump out, hear his roar, the sound of a rifle firing, another roar, and the jungle screams with sound as Forrest flees in panic.

"The audience doesn't notice 'instruments' dropping away—that it's getting quieter and quieter—because the sound is close to the way they're feeling, leading them slightly, but never ahead," Murch says. "They've been turning up the volume in their minds."

The feat is pulled off with stunning success, although it's an effect that's been around almost as long as sound in the movies. The same effect has been achieved countless times when the leading man spots a beautiful woman across the platform of a crowded train station. The music comes up, the sound of the crowd is drowned out momentarily, and presto! We actually "hear" the love between the two actors.

"Sound can say, 'This is how I want you to take what you're going to experience' and do it quicker than anything else. Like a picture frame which enhances a painting by echoing the colors inside, sound sets you in a mood to allow you to take certain things," Murch explains.

MEDIALAB

Aural Reality vs Sound Effects

1. Imagine you are a sound technician or editor for a major motion picture. You decide to pioneer a new approach to sound based on reality. For footsteps, you simply record footsteps for your sound track. For a fight, you record people hitting each other—without amplification. How do you think the audience at opening night would react to your revolution in sound?

2. Watch at least part of a film with a superior sound track such as a *Star Trek* movie (which sound editor Mangini worked on). Ignore the visuals, plot, or voice track. Pay attention only to sounds other than the spoken word. Note how they differ from reality. Note how they influence feelings.

3. Find a specific example in a film that illustrates how sound can be the voice of the director saying, "This is how I want you to feel."

4. Countless films and television shows used "canned" instead of fresh sounds. Can you tell the difference?

5. Gunshots on film sound more explosive than in real life. Punches on film sound louder and more violent than in real life. Do you believe this unreality in film causes unreal (and perhaps dangerous) expectations about guns and fistfights?

6. Do you remember better what you see or what you hear? Are your earliest memories of sights or sounds? Can you remember advertising sounds (jingles, for example) from many years ago? How well do you remember the visuals that accompanied those commercials? Why do we usually say "seeing is believing," instead of "hearing is believing"?

Preserving Great Films

Great books and plays from the past are preserved through reprinting. There is little danger the works of William Shakespeare or the books of the Bible will be lost forever. A modern printing of *Hamlet* has as much power as one created hundreds of years ago—only the cost will be different. The best creations of film artists, however, are far more fragile.

Early film stock contained the chemical silver nitrate, which slowly turns to powder. Librarian of Congress James Billington estimates that half of all movies made before 1950 and 80 percent of those before 1930 have been lost forever. Billington observes that "We have a better record of the early days of our Founding Fathers than we do our early days of American film." Many early films were also lost through poor storage, carelessness, and the simple failure to recognize their lasting value.

In 1988 Congress passed the Film Preservation Act, which called for naming twenty-five outstanding movies annually beginning in 1989. These outstanding films will be archived and preserved in the Library of Congress. The films chosen are not intended to be a list of best American films. Rather, the choices suggest the breadth of great American filmmaking. Once selected for the National Film Registry, the film cannot be colorized or cut unless it bears a label stating it was altered "without the participation of the principal director, screenwriter, and other creators of the original film." No film less than ten years old was eligible.

The list below shows the first twenty-five chosen for the National Film Registry. Find out which films were added in 1990 and 1991. Most films are available in videocassette. Watching as many as possible would provide a fine background for a study of American film.

National Film Registry

Films selected by the Librarian of Congress for inclusion in the National Film Registry; available on video tape unless otherwise noted.

The Best Years of Our Lives: 1946; William Wyler, director; received Academy Award for Best Picture

Casasblanca: 1942; Michael Curtiz, director; received Academy Award for Best Picture

Citizen Kane: 1942; Orson Welles, director

The Crowd: 1928; King Vidor, director

Dr. Strangelove (or, How I Learned to Stop Worrying and Love the Bomb): 1964; Stanley Kubrick, director

The General: 1927, Buster Keaton, director

Gone With the Wind: 1939; Victor Fleming, director; received Academy Award for Best Picture

The Grapes of Wrath: 1940; John Ford, director

High Noon: 1952; Fred Zinnemann, director

Intolerance: 1916; D.W. Griffith, director

The Learning Tree: 1969; Gordon Parks, director

The Maltese Falcon: 1941; John Huston, director

Mr. Smith Goes to Washington: 1939; Frank Capra, director

Modern Times: 1936; Charlie Chaplin, director

Nanook of the North: 1922; Robert Flaherty, director

On the Waterfront: 1954; Elia Kazan, director; received Academy Award for Best Picture

The Searchers: 1956; John Ford, director

Singin' In the Rain: 1952; Gene Kelly, Stanley Donen, directors

Snow White and the Seven Dwarfs: 1937; Walt Disney, director; not available on video tape

Some Like It Hot: 1959; Billy Wilder, director

Star Wars: 1977; George Lucas, director

Sunrise: 1927; F. W. Murnau, director; received Academy Award for Best Picture; not available on video tape

Sunset Boulevard: 1950; Billy Wilder, director

Vertigo: 1958; Alfred Hitchcock, director

The Wizard of Oz: 1939; Victor Fleming, director

Source: Video Adventure, World Almanac

WRAP-UP

From its beginnings in the 1800s to today's technical miracles, the mass medium of film has been examined. You have learned what it means to be a film critic and the difference between a subjective and an objective film review. You have discovered why the 1930s and 1940s are called film's "golden age" and been challenged to explain why movie theater attendance is not what it used to be. Now you know how movies move and how directors and camera crews, along with sound technicians and editors, work together to create a motion picture that "works," using the principles of film composition, color, and sound. Have you seen any good movies lately? Now that you understand more about this fascinating medium, you can answer that question as a film critic might.

CHAPTER 5

Comics and Cartoons

Cross Media Study:

Like film, comic strips and cartoons are popular mass media. In this chapter, you will learn about comics, editorial cartoons, gag cartoons, and more.

Comics and Film

Learning about the techniques of any one mass medium often helps to understand other media. This is particularly true for films and comics. In a sense, comics were the first movies. Like films, they use a series of still pictures to tell a story. In film the movement is supplied by the camera and projector, while in comics the movement is supplied by the tricks of the artist.

The following article was written by Steve Gerber, who writes comics for the Marvel Comics Group and also makes his own amateur films. He is well aware of the similarities between film and comics. Since the previous chapter of this book was about film language, you should have little trouble applying film techniques to the world of the comic artist.

What Comics Can Teach You About Movies

by **Steve Gerber**

"A comic book is essentially a film . . . in shorthand." Here's a look at the techniques of comics writers and artists as they create their stories.

On the most basic level, the creators of comics and of cinema are faced with an identical task: *telling a story in a series of still pictures designed to give the illusion of motion.* Visual narrative and movement are at the heart of both. And the similarity doesn't end there. Even the mechanics of the creative processes are remarkably alike for the two media. Much of the terminology is the same. Indeed, the only major differences between comics and film— with regard to storytelling, at least—are technological ones.

Otherwise, a comic book is essentially a film . . . in shorthand. And what comics teach about movies is something all filmmakers, whether their interest is documentaries, sports

reportage, or biblical epics, need to know: how to construct a dramatic event in pictures; how to make the pictures move.

Comics Writer as Screenwriter

A comic book begins as a typed synopsis in which the writer describes the action of the story page-by-page, often even panel-by-panel, for the artist. Every relevant detail is noted: what each character is thinking and feeling, the expression on his or her face, what they're doing with their hands, their physical appearances, and the settings, costumes, and props. Diagrams and sketches of these items may be attached to the synopsis. And snatches of dialogue are often included, along with ideas and suggestions for unusual artistic approaches and spe-

cial effects. Fight scenes are choreographed. The need for an establishing shot here, a close-up there, is specified. And perhaps most importantly, the writer includes his estimation of how much space (one panel, one page, more?) each scene should require.

Thus, in form, style, and content, the writer's synopsis for a comic book bears a distinct resemblance to a story treatment for a film. In the case of a silent Super-8 short, it could even suffice as a shooting script. Chances are a film will require *more* separate shots than a comic book, but consider the advantages of planning your shooting on paper as tightly as I plotted the following sequence (shown in Illustration One) for a comics story called "The Return of

Illustration One: Comic book as shooting script for opening sequence of mystery thriller; four panels outline storytelling techniques

your camera.) You might dolly in slowly, silently, until the crate dominates the scene. Then you halt, holding the same shot for several seconds. Next, the crate itself rocks every so slightly, creating the first sound of the film. Suddenly, one arm smashes out, splintering the wood; then you cut to the other arm, as it comes through the opposite side of the crate; then a foot, a knee—each shown separately in a series of quick cuts. Then you take a long shot as the entire crate flies to pieces, revealing the full, fearsome figure of the Living Mummy.

The point here is that the storytelling techniques of comics are directly translatable into cinema *if* you, the screenwriter, remember that the comic book is presented in visual "shorthand." That "if" cannot be overemphasized because the image on the movie screen is constantly changing. The viewer isn't able to flip back a page or reread a panel to see if he's missed something. This means that the "information gap" between panels in comics can be much wider than the gap between shots in film; every action need not be detailed in comics. Nevertheless, the technique of getting from "point A" to "point B" in the plot is virtually identical.

Comics Artist as Filmmaker

Working from the writer's synopsis, the comics artist draws the story in pencil, breaking down each page into an arrangement of panels, composing each individual drawing, deciding which panel, if any, should dominate the page. In so doing, the artist also contributes to the overall rhythm and continuity of the story, and performs functions similar to those of the filmmaker.

The *size* of a panel drawn by the artist, for example, is roughly analogous to the *duration* of a shot—but only roughly. In this respect, comics are somewhat more flexible than film. The artist is not bound to a rectangular frame of predetermined size

the Living Mummy."

Scene One: Four-panel opening page with sequence as follows: (1) A wooden crate resting on the floor of the Egyptology Room of a New York museum; the room is dark except for moonlight streaming in from a skylight in the ceiling. (2) Same shot, but a bandaged arm is smashing out from inside the crate. (3) Entire crate flies apart as Mummy breaks out. (4) Large panel; long shot of Mummy looking around him, seeing the various Egyptian art objects, etc.

Now let's look at the techniques involved in creating these panels. A picture of a wooden crate in a dark room (panel 1) is not particularly exciting in itself, but it poses a mystery immediately. And the lighting, a single shaft of cold silver from above, casting stark, shifting shadows, at once establishes a mood. Without a word of dialogue or sound effects, we've made it clear that whatever is inside the crate poses a threat.

To create the same mood in a film, you might open with a long shot of the Egyptology Room, with the crate standing upright in the center of the shot. (Actually, the panel shows you where to position the crate and

for his panel; the filmmaker, obviously, is. Then too, the effect on the audience of certain approaches to a scene are different in comics. For example, a page consisting of, say, nine small panels may either elongate a scene, if the content of those panels is calm, or produce a staccato effect, if the content is rapid-fire action. A series of short, quick shots in a film is almost always likely to produce the staccato effect, regardless of content.

Aside from these differences, though, the function of the artist is like that of the filmmaker who does all the shooting, as well as directing and editing. The artist, in effect, sets up the shots, blocks the actors' movements, and generally provides the print equivalent of shooting and cutting. Dialogue and captions are added later by the comics writer, much the same way background music and voice-overs might be added to a silent film. As a rule, the tighter the writer's synopsis, the more likely it is that the artist will draw what the writer had in mind.

This principle can be applied to cameramen and screenwriters, too. Take, for example, the 3-panel sequence shown in Illustration Two. Matt Mudrock— the blind attorney who is secretly Daredevil— hears a voice from "off-screen." We cut immediately to the source of that voice as Matt perceives it with his radar sense, the unique power that compensates for his lack of sight. For the comics artist, Sal Buscema, each of these panels required written description down to the last detail. The direction from which the voice is heard, the "radar sense" special effect, the matched action from the "real" shot to the "radar" shot, and, of course, the urgent emotions and movements of both characters all had to be carefully written out for the artist to render the sequence correctly. For the cameraman/filmmaker the same tightly written directions are useful. If you construct your shooting

Illustration Two: Comic-book version of off-screen voice, special effects, and matched cuts

scripts meticulously, the chances of making the film you set out to make are greatly enhanced.

At the same time a certain flexibility is desirable. Just as the comic artist may visualize a shot differently than the comics writer, you-as-cameraperson may discover possibilities that you-as-screenwriter never anticipated. For example, look at Illustration Three, which shows the final comic-book sense of a drama about a clown who commits suicide in a swamp. The monster you see is Man-Thing, here returning to his home. The scene is composed of three panels (note the vertical dividing lines that do not completely separate the panels), and is the comicbook equivalent of a "tracking shot." The idea for this scene was entirely the creation of artist Mike Ploog. My

own unimaginative little ending for the story had Man-Thing wander off into the marshy swamp in a typical "wide angle" type panel. Mike, on the other hand, created a more powerful image by depicting the monster in two stages of movement: standing fairly straight and then slouching deeper into his swamp.

The monster seems to lumber towards the reader. If you were filming him, he'd be moving closer to the camera even as you move it, tracking him from left to right. Meanwhile, the characters who are delivering their final lines about the clown's suicide, seem to recede in the background. Of course, this type of scene should be carefully planned *before* it is shot on location, but you should also give yourself room to maneuver once you get there. Lots of good ideas come at

Illustration Three: Comic-book equivalent of a tracking shot; the monster is shown in two stages of movement across the two panels

the last minute from unexpected sources.

Besides sharing responsibility with the writer for visualizing the overall flow of the story, the comics artist shares a concern for using a variety of panels. Nothing is duller in comics than a page made up entirely of close-ups (or long shots, or medium shots). In breaking down a page, the artist again plays the role the film-maker and film editor play in shooting and cutting a scene— all the same rules apply. The shots must be varied, but they must come together to form an integrated whole. And just as the overuse of "trick shots" is to be avoided in film, overly fragmented layouts are shunned in comics. If the cinematic technique is to be effective, it must be "invisible." It must not distract the viewer or it defeats its own purpose.

We turn to Matt Murdock again—this time in his Daredevil out-fit (see Illustration Four)— for a lesson on placing diverse shots together.

Gene Colan drew this fight sequence using several separate panels arranged to present a coherent picture of the action. First, you see the scene from street level (low-angle shot); then, from the points of view of the villain, the hero, and the spectators. The result is a fast-paced action sequence (it *had* to be fast paced, we ran out of pages) in which the reader alternately sees the fight as if he were a partici-pant and an observer. Comic books are filled with sequences like this one; for the filmmaker, they are the perfect guide to new framing techniques and the provocative use of various camera angles.

Summing up, then, it seems clear that the problems to be solved by the comics artist and the filmmaker are very nearly the same. How best to tell the story? Convey the mood? Follow the action? To find answers to these questions, you can study the work of the best comics artists: Jack Kirby, John Buscema, Rich Buckler, Jim Starlin, Will Eisner, as well as those

whose work is displayed here. Their names are usually listed in the credits which appear at the beginning of each comic-book story.

How Comics and Movies Differ
Despite all the parallels, comics are not movies, and understanding their dissimilarities is equally vital to learn-ing about one from the other. First, and perhaps most crucial, even though the goals and the creative mechanics of the two media are anal-ogous, the technologies involved are vastly different.

Given a little imagination and a sharp pencil, the comics writer-and-artist team can tackle anything from a sock hop to an intergalactic war. Most Super-8 filmmakers, it's safe to assert, will probably have to content them-selves with the more mundane end of that spectrum. So it's wise not to let yourself be influenced by the subject matter of the comics, enticing though it may be. Don't attempt the sequel to "E.T." as your first film—or even

Given a little imagination and a sharp pencil, the comics writer-and-artist team can tackle anything from a sock hop to an intergalactic war.

Illustration Four: Comic-book version of a fight sequence; the series of panels shows how to place together different camera angles and points of view.

your second.

But realize, too, that it would be far more difficult to portray the sock hop scene in comics than it would be in movies! The finite areas of space on the comic-book page, the limited number of pages in each book, and the relative unsophistication of the four-color printing process, make subtleties extremely difficult to achieve, both in dialogue and illustration. Generally speaking, the artist gets only one chance at each panel. The printer has a range of only thirty-two shades. If the writer writes too much copy, he covers up the picture.

The filmmaker has a far greater range of moods, textures, and colors to work with. He need not rely on archetypes and stereotypes as substitutes for real characterization. (True, the comics are maturing, coming out of that phase, but it's still possible to tell the hero from the villain by the color of their respective longjohns.) The themes that film can explore are much richer, much more complex. And they can be dealt with, even by the novice, with a pretty fair degree of success.

MEDIALAB

Comparing Comics and Film

1. As a class, list ways in which comics and films are alike and ways in which they differ.

2. Could an intelligent person who has never seen a comic strip understand a comic like *Batman* or *Wonder Woman* right away, or would it take some learning first? Support your answer.

3. Which do you think would be most difficult to become—an expert creator of comic books or a film director?

4. Find examples in comics that would match the following devices in films. Make a chart of examples, labeling each one and explaining why each particular technique is used.

Films	Comics
frame	
scene	
low angle	
high angle	
camera movement	
subjective camera	
color to influence feeling	
lighting to influence feeling	

THE COMICS CODE

COMICS MAGAZINE ASSOCIATION OF AMERICA

PRINCIPLES OF THE COMICS CODE AUTHORITY

PREAMBLE

The Comics Magazine Association of America was formed in 1954 by a group of publishers committed to the principle that the public deserved decent and wholesome comic books as entertainment for children. To that end, those publishers set content guidelines, created a reviewing authority and established the Comics Code Seal. This seal was to appear on covers of CMAA member comics as a way of communicating to the public their shared commitment to uphold these standards.

While the comic book industry has changed over the intervening three decades, as has almost every other facet of American life, the publisher members of the CMAA remain committed to providing decent and wholesome comic books for children. This new updated version of the Comics Code is a reaffirmation of that commitment.

The member publishers of the Comics Magazine Association of America hereby reaffirm our joint commitment to our shared principle: that comics carrying the Comics Code Seal be ones that a parent can purchase with confidence that the contents uphold basic American moral and cultural values.

Reprinted with permission.

APPROVED BY THE COMICS CODE CA AUTHORITY

THIS SEAL OF APPROVAL appears only on comic magazines which have been carefully reviewed, *prior to publication*, by the Comics Code Authority, an agency operating apart from any individual publisher, exercising independent judgment — and found to have met the high standards of morality required by the code of the Comics Magazine Association of America, Inc.

Look for the comic book with this seal

Comics Magazine Association of America, Inc.
355 Lexington Avenue, 17th Floor, New York, N.Y. 10017

APPROVED BY THE COMICS CODE CA AUTHORITY

CODE OF THE COMICS MAGAZINE ASSOCIATION OF AMERICA

CMAA

INSTITUTIONS

In general, recognizable national, social, political, cultural, ethnic and racial groups, religious institutions, and law enforcement authorities will be portrayed in a positive light. These include the government on the national, state, and municipal levels, including all of its numerous departments, agencies, and services; law enforcement agencies such as the state and municipal police, and other actual law enforcement agencies such as the FBI, the Secret Service, the CIA, etc.; the military, both United States and foreign; known religious organizations; ethnic advancement agencies; foreign leaders and representatives of other governments and national groups; and social groups identifiable by lifestyle, such as homosexuals, the economically disadvantaged, the economically privileged, the homeless, senior citizens, minors, etc.

Socially responsible attitudes will be favorably depicted and reinforced. Socially inappropriate, irresponsible, or illegal behavior will be shown to be specific actions of a specific individual or group of individuals, and not meant to reflect the routine activity of any general group of real persons.

If, for dramatic purposes, it is necessary to portray such a group of individuals in a negative manner, the name of the group and its individual members will be fictitious, and its activities will not be clearly identifiable with the routine activities of any real group.

Stereotyped images and activities will not be used to degrade specific national, ethnic, cultural, or socioeconomic groups.

LANGUAGE

The language in a comic book will be appropriate for a mass audience that includes children. Good grammar and spelling will be encouraged. Publishers will exercise good taste and a responsible attitude as to the use of language in their comics. Obscene and profane words, symbols, and gestures are prohibited.

References to physical handicaps, illnesses, ethnic backgrounds, sexual preferences, religious beliefs, and race, when presented in a derogatory manner for dramatic purposes, will be shown to be unacceptable.

VIOLENCE

Violent actions or scenes are acceptable within the context of a comic book story when dramatically appropriate. Violent behavior will not be shown as acceptable. If it is presented in a realistic manner, care should be taken to present the natural repercussions of such actions. Publishers should avoid excessive levels of violence, excessively graphic depictions of violence, and excessive bloodshed or gore. Publishers will not present detailed information instructing readers how to engage in imitable violent actions.

CHARACTERIZATIONS

Character portrayals will be carefully crafted and show sensitivity to national, ethnic, religious, sexual, political, and socioeconomic orientations. If it is dramatically appropriate for one character to demean another because of his or her sex, ethnicity, religion, sexual preference, political orientation, socioeconomic status, or disabilities, the demeaning words or actions will be clearly shown to be wrong or ignorant in the course of the story. Stories depicting characters subject to physical, mental, or emotional problems or with economic disadvantages should never assign ultimate responsibility for these conditions to the character themselves. Heroes should be role models and should reflect the prevailing social attitudes.

SUBSTANCE ABUSE

Healthy, wholesome lifestyles will be presented as desirable. However, the use and abuse of controlled substances, legal and illicit, are facts of modern existence, and may be portrayed when dramatically appropriate.

The consumption of alcohol, narcotics, pharmaceuticals, and tobacco will not be depicted in a glamourous way. When the line between the normal, responsible consumption of legal substances and the abuse of these substances is crossed, the distinction will be made clear and the adverse consequences of such abuse will be noted.

Substance abuse is defined as the use of illicit drugs and the self-destructive use of such products as tobacco (including chewing tobacco), alcohol, prescription drugs, over-the-counter drugs, etc.

Use of dangerous substances both legal and illegal should be shown with restraint as necessary to the context of the story. However, storylines should not be detailed to the point of serving as instruction manuals for substance abuse. In each story, the abuser will be shown to pay the physical, mental, and/or social penalty for his or her abuse.

CRIME

While crimes and criminals may be portrayed for dramatic purposes, crimes will never be presented in such a way as to inspire readers with a desire to imitate them nor will criminals be portrayed in such a manner as to inspire readers to emulate them. Stories will not present unique imitable techniques or methods of committing crimes.

ATTIRE AND SEXUALITY

Costumes in a comic book will be considered to be acceptable if they fall within the scope of contemporary styles and fashions.

Scenes and dialogue involving adult relationships will be presented with good taste, sensitivity, and in a manner which will be considered acceptable by a mass audience. Primary human sexual characteristics will never be shown. Graphic sexual activity will never be depicted.

ADMINISTRATIVE PROCEDURE

I

All comics which member publishers wish to bear the Comics Code Seal will be submitted to the Code administrator for review prior to publication. The administrator will review them according to the guidance he has received from the permanent committee and will either approve them to bear the seal, or return them to the publisher with his comments. The responsible editor from the publisher will either revise the comic in accordance with those comments, or discuss with the administrator the concerns raised with him and reach agreement on how the comic can properly bear the Code Seal either without being revised or with a mutually-agreeable set of alternative revisions. In the event no agreement can be reached between the editor and the administrator, the matter will be referred to the permanent committee, which will act promptly to determine if, or under what conditions, the comic in question can bear the Code Seal. Decisions of the permanent committee will be binding on the publishers, who agree not to place the Code Seal on any comic on which it is not authorized.

II

The members of the Comics Magazine Association of America include publishers who elect to publish comics that are not intended to bear the Code Seal, and that therefore need not go through the approval process described above. Among the comics in this category may be titles intended for adult readers. Member publishers hereby affirm that we will distribute these publications only through those distribution channels in which it is possible to notify retailers and distributors of their content, and thus help the publications reach their intended audiences. The member publishers agree to refrain from distributing these publications through those distribution channels that, like the traditional newsstand, are serviced by individuals who are unaware of the content of specific publications before placing them on display.

III

Recognizing that no document can address all the complex issues and concerns that face our changing society, the member publishers have established a permanent committee composed of the senior editor of each member's staff. This committee will meet regularly to review those issues and concerns as they affect our publications, and to meet with and guide the administrator of the Comics Code, and will replace the previous written guidelines of the Comics Code.

SOME CARTOONS BITE

Every year Americans spend about 300 million dollars on comic books, according to the *Comics Buyers' Guide*. Comic strips are most people's first contact with a newspaper, and every survey about newspaper readership comes to the same conclusion— the comics are the most widely read part of the daily paper. For many adults comic strips are a daily ritual, and for many youngsters comic books are their main contact with reading.

Almost all newspaper comic strips are "syndicated." That is, a cartoonist draws one cartoon or strip a day (or one a week) and sends his or her work to a newspaper syndicate, such as Tribune Media Services. The syndicate distributes the strip to those newspapers that subscribe, and the cartoonist receives payment through the syndicate from each subscribing newspaper. Gag cartoons (one box rather than a strip) that appear in magazines are done by free-lance cartoonists who work in much the same way as free-lance magazine writers. The free-lancer works at home and sends cartoons to various magazines; payment ranges from $25 to over $600, depending on usage, if the cartoon is published.

Some comic strips or gag cartoons are purely entertainment, while other cartoons give serious advice, preach, or make political or social comments. Many newspapers feature such editorial (opinion) cartoons, usually as a single frame placed in the editorial section of the newspaper. These cartoons are designed to send a message; they may be "biting" or satirical.

This colonial cartoon was one of the earliest published in what is today the United States of America.

MEDIALAB

Newspaper Cartoons

1. Make a list of comics—comic books, comic strips, editorial, or gag cartoons—that are read by class members.

2. Find out the names of syndicates who supply the cartoons carried in your local papers.

3. Select the comic strip or comic book that you read most often. Write a brief article about the strip or book explaining why it is fun to read, what some of the cartoonist's favorite subjects are, what the comic says about life, and what kind of person probably would not enjoy that particular comic.

4. Study the editorial cartoons on the previous page and below. Determine what each one says.

5. Find political or editorial cartoons in your local newspapers, or elsewhere, and bring them to class. Collect them on a bulletin board; when there are enough gathered, discuss those that seem most effective.

6. Create your own editorial cartoon and add it to those on the bulletin board.

THE LANGUAGE OF COMICS

Each mass medium has its particular language, one that most of its users understand but if asked, probably could not describe. Film viewers know that a fade or a dissolve means a long passage of time, book readers expect a new chapter to mark a new time frame and location for the action, TV viewers know a station break does not mean the end of a program, and newspaper readers do not confuse the news with the ads. Why? Because users are familiar with each medium's language. They have learned these languages by experience with the media rather than through schooling or formal training. An adult who for some reason first saw a film at the age of 25 might find it confusing and meaningless. The language of a medium is made up of the conventions, the rules, and the traditions that media creators use.

An adult who read a comic strip for the first time at the age of 25 would wonder what all those strange blobs are over the characters heads. Of course, most comic readers learn the language when they are children. They learn that those strange blobs are dialogue balloons. Dialogue balloons show many examples of the conventional language of comics. The tail pointing to the speaker is one such example. If the balloon line is perforated, the character is whispering—the cartoonist need not print out "this person is whispering." Tiny letters in a huge balloon show the speaker is frightened or ashamed. A cry has a jagged outline, while a telephone voice has a zig-zag shape with an arrow going into the telephone.

If a balloon has little icicles underneath it, the words or thoughts are taken to be cold and cruel or filled with hatred. If the balloon has a series of small smoke-puff circles instead of a tail pointing to the character, the contents of the balloon are thoughts or dreams rather than spoken words. If the balloon has an arrow pointing outside the cartoon frame, the speaker is off screen.

Swearing is expressed by "$#*@" or "!!!!." A lightbulb above a character's head means a bright idea, dark clouds signify depression, and musical notes symbolize music or singing. The boldness of the letters indicates the volume of the speaker's voice.

Speed lines indicate movement and are sometimes used to hide violence. A split panel can be used to indicate the passage of time without having to write "and several hours later. . . . "

These bits are only a few examples of the hundreds of details that make up the grammar of comics. They are rules, but they are not strict and can be changed and modified in many ways.

MEDIALAB

Looking at Language and Visual Techniques

1. Go through a single comic book or a variety of newspaper comic strips and find examples of at least a dozen comic-strip language techniques. Include at least three that are not mentioned in this chapter.

2. Look at several comic strips and comment on the size of the characters' head, hands, and feet. Explain what you find.

3. Comment on the different drawing styles used in various strips. In writing, attempt to describe the style of a particular cartoonist or strip.

4. Why do you think comics are so popular? What needs do they fulfill for the millions who read them so faithfully? Do different comic strips satisfy different needs?

5. Find characters who appear both in comic books or comic strips and in other media—television, film, recordings, radio. Compare how the same character is portrayed in different media.

6. Bring a comic book to class. Go through the comic and note visual techniques that are also used in film.

7. Prepare a research report on the history of comic books in the United States.

THE GAG CARTOON

A gag cartoon is a single picture, a comic strip is a row of pictures, and a comic book is a collection of stories told through comic-style drawings. All these comic forms share the same language or drawing devices discussed earlier in this chapter. But the gag cartoonist has to use the most finely developed bag of techniques to evoke laughter. Because the whole point of the cartoon must be carried by a single printed line beneath the cartoon, nothing in the drawing must distract from the point. Sometimes the gag is done in pantomime, without any words. The restrictions of the form make gag cartoons the ultimate in cartoon art. The following article explains some of the subtle and finely developed techniques of the gag cartoonist.

READING

The Techniques of the Gag Cartoonist

by **John L. Hulteng and Roy Paul Nelson**

How are those wonderful gag cartoon jabs at our shams and illusions carried out? Here are some of the techniques.

To the real cartoon connoisseur, gag cartoons represent the ultimate in the cartoon art. A gag cartoon is to be savored, not just looked at and read. The subtleties of the art are considerable. Note that the whole point revolves around a single line printed underneath the cartoon, and everything within the drawing must substantiate that point. The gag cartoonist keeps his cast of characters down, his setting simple. He must make it clear at once, without benefit of balloon, just who within the drawing is doing the talking.

Sometimes he can put his gag over without a single word below. He does his gag in pantomime.

Unique among the cartoonists, he has no particular axe to grind. His objects of ridicule, when they are there, are hard to pin down, because he deals less in personalities and issues, more in general statements about mankind. He's never happier than when, in the words of Steven Becker, he is "jabbing away constantly at our shams and illusions."

Gag cartoonists come onto their gags in a number of ways. Sometimes they dream up a scene and then try to imagine a scene that will make it funny.

Most gag cartoonists buy ideas from outside sources. They pay the writer 25 percent of what the cartoon earns and keep 75 percent for themselves. Only the cartoonist signs the cartoon.

It has been said that the novelist has only a few basic plots to work with. Similarly, the gag cartoonist has only a few basic ideas. The setting, the props, the characters change; the words in the gag lines vary; but the ideas stay the same. Perhaps you will recognize them:

1. *The cliché.* Most journalists avoid the cliché. Not the cartoonist. He can take a cliche and let a character act it out literally and get a laugh. Virgil Partch (Vip) is a master of this kind of gag. Vip shows a man lying dead on the sidewalk while a companion, unaware of the tragedy, turns to

watch a cranky woman walk by. He says: "Boy! If looks could kill, eh, Steve?" Dana Fradon makes a slight change in a cliché in a *New Yorker* cartoon dealing with deteriorating telephone service. An executive leads a caller to the door and says: "Don't try to call me. I'll try to call you."

If you'd like to be a gag writer or cartoonist, see what you can do with these cliché lines:

"Mind if I smoke?"

"You'll only encourage him."

"You're putting me on!"

"Been waiting long?"

"Am I getting warm?"

2. *That's life.* This includes any gag that depicts life as it is, so that the reader will identify with it, and say, in effect: "Ain't it the truth!" Tom Henderson in *The Saturday Evening Post* shows a lazy, unshaven man reading the paper, the phone on a table at his side. His wife has just picked up the receiver after rushing in from in front of the house where she's parked the car. She's dropped groceries all the way in and knocked over a chair in her rush to answer the phone. She's saying: "Yes, he's here."

3. *Ridiculous situation.* The opposite of "That's Life." It just couldn't be that way! Jerry Marcus in *True* shows a worried woman driver with her husband sitting beside her. In back of her is a line-up of cars: a tow truck, a police car, and an ambulance. The husband says: "Relax, it's probably just a coincidence."

4. *Out of character.* Sweet little old ladies act like gangsters. Kids talk with grownups. Ministers sit in bars with worldly ladies. Mulligan in *The New Yorker* shows a perplexed man and wife looking at

a painting of a haggard, hungry woman holding a baby with a frightened child at her side. The scene is dark, desolate. The painting is signed "Norman Rockwell." The man says: "Well, there must be more than one Norman Rockwell in the world."

5. *In character.* People act out their roles to the point of absurdity. B. Tobey in *The New Yorker* shows a young man smooching with a girl on a park bench. With his free hand, and without looking, he's reaching into a bag of popcorn and feeding a flock of pigeons and squirrels. An older couple is walking by, and the man says to the woman: "Now, there's a warm human being for you."

6. *Understatement.* This is a favorite theme for the cartoonist; and British cartoonists have no corner on it. Jim Stevenson in *The New Yorker* shows an art expert examining a fine painting while the owner looks on. The expert has rubbed his finger across the painting; his finger is wet with paint. He says: "Well, this initial test suggests that the authenticity of your Rembrandt may be questionable."

7. *Exaggeration.* The opposite of understatement. Chon Day in *The Saturday Evening Post* shows a tired, middle-aged man asleep on a couch. His wife, a little portly, and a lady visitor are talking. The wife says: "He's had a bad back ever since he carried me over the threshold."

8. *Ingenuity.* When man solves some problem in an unusual way, readers—even readers of gag cartoons—appreciate it. Rodrigues

in the *Saturday Review* sets up a situation in which a father tries to tell his side of the story to the rebel generation. He's fat, balding, middle-aged, well dressed; he stands on stage at a run-down coffee house, strumming a guitar. Hippie types sit watching him, frowning. He's singing: ". . . Oh, my kid's twenty-three and he don't like to work/Oh, he don't like to work/When I was twenty-three I worked very hard/Oh, I worked very hard . . ." You could classify it as "out of character," too.

9. *Stupidity.* This kind of a gag especially satisfies the reader, because the cartoonist always lets the reader know something a chief character in the cartoon doesn't know. The reader feels superior. Jerry Marcus, again, this time in *The Saturday Evening Post*, shows a middle-aged couple already in bed, looking bored. Another couple, obviously visitors, stand nearby. The man, hat in hand, says, "Well, we really must be going."

10. *The letdown.* Some definitions of humor suggest this is the real core of humor. The reader is led to believe one thing, then finally disappointed. Jim Stevenson again, in *The New Yorker*. A guru sits in front of his high mountain cave. Around him are signs scrawled on the rock: "Smile and the world smiles with you, cry and you cry alone"; "Early to bed and early to rise makes a man healthy, wealthy and wise"; "A penny saved is a penny earned"; and so on. A disappointed, slightly hippie-ish couple has just arrived. The girl says to her male companion: "Something tells me we've come to the wrong guru." Again, classification can never be exact. This gag could serve as an example of "Understatement."

MEDIALAB

Having Fun with Gag Cartoons

1. What is a gag cartoon?

2. Make your own gag cartoon. If you do not want to draw, use existing drawings or magazine cut-outs, or use an existing cartoon but change the punch line.

3. Make a class collection of gag cartoons.

4. The article suggests ten types of gags commonly used in cartoons. Find examples of at least five of these techniques.

5. Are these same techniques used in other forms of humor? Find examples.

6. Provide titles or captions for the illustrations on this page. Your captions can be satire or "gag humor." Show an understanding language of comics.

b.

a.

c.

d.

Comics and cartoons appeal to most everyone. Many people turn to the "funnies" even before they read the front page of a newspaper. In this chapter you have learned about the similarities between comics and film. Many of the same visual techniques, such as close-ups and strategic use of color, are used in both. You have read about the special language cartoonists use and looked at the more serious side—the editorial cartoon. Having been introduced to the cartoonist's techniques and having tried your hand at creating cartoons, you can now fully understand what makes comics and cartoons such popular mass media.

CHAPTER 6

News Media

WHAT IS NEWS?

Before you read this chapter, spend a few minutes thinking about your own definition of news. In one or two sentences write your definition. Do this now before reading any further.

If you were to ask a dozen professional news people for their definition of news, you would collect a dozen different opinions.

The dictionary definitions are most unsatisfactory. For example, one dictionary's first meaning for "news" is "recent events and happenings, especially those that are unusual or notable." The fact that you cleaned up your room yesterday for the first time in two years would fit this definition, but it would hardly make the morning paper or the evening newscast. The dictionary next describes news as "new information about anything previously unknown." When you walk into math class and learn for the first time how to factor a quadratic equation, that is new and previously unknown information to you. But again your math class would not make the news. So what is news? Can it be defined?

For you and me, the consumers of news, news might be defined as what newspapers and newscasters decide is newsworthy. The people who run the papers, write the stories, and edit the news have to decide what is news and what is not. They do this by following tradition and by making educated guesses about what the reading, viewing, or listening public wants to know.

If a person eats a fish, that is not news; but if a fish eats a person, that is news. If a fish eats someone in your town, it will certainly be news in your town. But if a fish eats a celebrity or world leader, it will be news worldwide. News favors events that are unusual. The fact that thousands of airplanes land and take off safely every day is an amazing feat of technical competence and human expertise, but it is not news. However, if one airplane crashes, or even blows a tire while landing, that is news precisely because it is so uncommon.

The desire of journalists to report the unusual (a desire encouraged by their readers' attraction to the out-of-the-ordinary and the bizarre) explains why so much news is "bad news." People often ask why newspapers and TV newscasts dwell on tragedies, accidents, crimes, and generally negative human events. Given that planes are safe, people are usually honest, buildings rarely burn, and criminals are only a small part of the population, such negative events are precisely what is *unusual*. It is normal for things to work fairly well and for people to lead their lives with a certain degree of contentment. A society in which the good news would be out-of-the-ordinary would be a sorry place to live.

But all that is unusual is not news (cleaning your room, for example), nor is all news unusual. There are other qualities that make items newsworthy.

Timeliness

News should be new. There is no such thing as old news—only history. Instant news has become the standard.

Significance of the Event

This news value demands the most personal judgment on the part of the news editor. News events must be events that are important in some way to the audience.

Closeness to the Audience

A fire in the house next door would certainly be news in a neighborhood paper, or even a city paper. But the fire would not be news on national television since it would not be close enough to most viewers. A national election in Austria might not even be mentioned in American papers, but the national election in America will fill several editions of most American papers.

Importance of the People Involved

If your next-door neighbor is famous, the fact that his or her house burned down might make national news. A speeding ticket is rarely a newsworthy event unless the person speeding is well known.

Drama of Human Interest

The news has to be interesting (some say entertaining) or the audience will not read or watch it. Some stories are included with the news because they are particularly dramatic or have human interest value; this news value can make an otherwise minor event into real news. If the fire in your neighbor's house happened on Thanksgiving Day, for instance, the human value in the story might make it national news.

> Why is news so often *bad* news? Because the journalist, like the doctor, deals in illness. You don't go to the doctor to find out what is right.

MEDIALAB

Thinking About What Makes News

1. Examine each story in the first three pages of your local newspaper and decide which news values they embody. In doing this, you will be answering the question "Why is this news?" Apply the five news qualities mentioned earlier, in order to make your judgment. Do the same for the first three stories carried on a local TV newscast.

2. Decide if each of the stories on the first three pages of the newspaper fits the definition of news you wrote at the beginning of this chapter. After doing this, you might want to change your definition of news.

3. Discuss the various definitions of news proposed by class members and try to find one that most of the class agrees is valid.

4. Debate or discuss the idea that news reports should place more emphasis on good news than on tragedy and violence.

HOW ARE THE VARIOUS NEWS MEDIA ALIKE ?

The news media are united by their concern for reporting news and the need for an audience. They all depend on advertising to make a profit. They all rely on the Associated Press and United Press International as main sources of news, and all have a "gate-keeper" who controls the flow of news to the public.

News, in the United States, is a product that is sold to consumers. In some countries, news is whatever the government wants the people to believe. The fact that the United States government does not run the news media gives journalists a certain independence and a willingness to point out flaws and to criticize the government. This ability of the press (both print and electronic) to criticize government and industry is essential to freedom of the press. It is common for governments to at least bend the truth they give out. It is the mission of the press to dig for the whole truth. For this reason many politicians, from mayors to presidents, are antagonistic toward the press. If the press were subject to the government, it would do little but print whatever the government told it to. The Watergate scandal would never have been uncovered (*Washington Post* newspaper reporters were the first to report it); mistakes made in Vietnam would still remain hidden (it was the *New York Times* that first published the "Pentagon Papers"); and scores of dishonest politicians and businesses would still be in power preying on the ignorant and uninformed.

> News in the United States is a product that is sold to consumers.

But the press must pay a price for this freedom. Since no news medium is supported by taxpayers' money, the high cost of gathering and spreading the news is assumed by advertisers and the news-buying public.

The second similarity among the news media is their reliance on wire services, such as Associated Press (AP) and United Press International (UPI). If you were to walk into the nerve center of news-gathering activity in any TV or radio station, newspaper, television network, or even newsmagazine, you would see teletype equipment transmitting news from all over the world.

If you look at the beginning of each newspaper story, you will see how many are supplied by wire services. A wire service collects stories and sends them via teletype machines to subscribing newspapers.

> All the news media rely on wire services for a large proportion of their news.

Newspapers and news departments of broadcast stations subscribe to or join the wire service. Each subscriber pays a fee to the wire service and also agrees to supply it with coverage of local events that might have national interest. The reports from the wire services arrive 24 hours a day. AP and UPI reporters all over the world phone or send stories to the New York headquarters. From there the stories are sent to subscribers who can print them as news, rewrite them, use them as a research source, or ignore them.

An average newspaper contains more news from the wire services than from its own reporters. The smaller the paper, the truer this is. Many small-town papers are little more than a collection of wire service reports and syndicated material. The average radio news broadcast is at least 90 percent wire service material. Edward Jay Epstein, in his five-year study of network (not local) TV news, concluded that the source for 70 percent of NBC-TV's "Nightly News" was wire service reports. There is no way for the news consumer to know the source of a TV or radio news story.

The third similarity all news media share is the use of a "gatekeeper." A news medium could be pictured as a funnel. Into the wide and always open mouth of the funnel flows a steady stream of news. Since there are over 5 billion humans on earth, billions of potential news events happen every day. Someone has to make the decision as to what is worth presenting to the public and what belongs in the wastebasket or on the floor of the film-editing room. The person who performs this function has different titles in each news organization. In many places he or she is called the managing editor or simply the news editor or news director. Social scientists use the term *gatekeeper* to describe this person, since he or she acts as a kind of control for the news, deciding which items make the paper or the broadcast and which do not gain entry.

Newspapers brought the Civil War home to Americans. The Second World War was heard by Americans on the radio. Vietnam was the first television war.

Although gatekeepers are extremely important to the news process, they are usually unknown to the general public. They do not get by-lines in newspaper stories, nor do they read the news on television. The gatekeeper is a powerful ongoing influence, but when decisions are made on important stories, the publisher of the newspaper or the director of the TV or radio station may step in. However, the sheer volume of news that flows into news media headquarters and the limited amount that comes out means that the gatekeeper is the one person most influential in deciding what is and what is not news.

All the news media have a "gatekeeper" who controls the flow of news to the public.

In newspapers the gatekeeper uses only about one in five stories that come in; in television and radio the number is probably closer to one in ten or twenty. On large city newspapers, news pours in so fast that only one in ten items scanned by the gatekeeper makes the paper. The gatekeeper is given a certain amount of air time or magazine space or newspaper pages to fill. This number is determined by the amount of advertising available. A large amount of advertising means less news; less advertising gives the consumer more news. Because ad space has already been committed, it is figured first, and the news must fit in the space that is left over.

MEDIALAB

Analyzing Similarities

1. This section suggests only a few similarities among the news media. List several other qualities they all share.

2. How do you think news in the United States would be different if it were government controlled and paid for from tax money?

3. Find some current examples showing the news media and the government in conflict.

4. Do you think it is dishonest for a government agency, a corporation, or an individual to release news about itself that presents it in the best possible light? Support your answer.

5. How much advertising does each news medium generally contain? Use a single issue or broadcast as an example. Express all answers in terms of percentage. For example,

time a 30-minute TV newscast; use a stop-watch to count the exact number of minutes and seconds of news. Count the number of minutes and seconds of ads during that half hour. If there are 20 minutes of news and 2 minutes of advertising, then you can say that 10 percent of the news time is devoted to advertising. For newspapers, measure in terms of column inches.

6. Draw two conclusions from the statistics on the amount of advertising in each news medium.

7. Do you think the need to show a profit and to sell advertising influences the kind of news the various media report? Explain your answer.

8. Determine what percentage of all the news in your local papers is provided by AP, UPI, or other wire services.

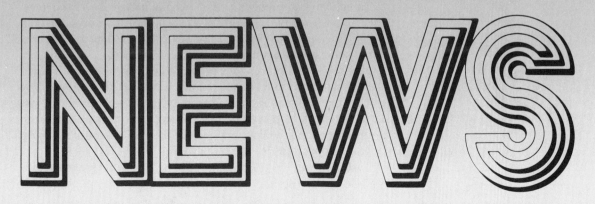

How Do the News Media Differ?

Each news medium may report the same news, but the words, the images, and their effect on the news consumer differ. Let us consider how the four major news media (TV, radio, newspapers, newsmagazines) differ in their presentation of the news.

TELEVISION

Television, and to some extent radio, use one or two individuals to present the news. The television viewer sees a person who is regarded as trustworthy or hears a radio announcer with a voice that rings with authority. Newspapers and newsmagazines lack this element of personality and instead must depend on the printed word. Television news commentators are often highly paid public celebrities. Some TV newscasters are not reporters at all; they are announcers with a favorable public image. Newspaper editors are seldom recognized on the street and rarely become celebrities.

Television can present a strong visual image. A written news story about poverty will probably make less of an impression on a reader than a powerfully filmed story of a starving family. A live telecast of some important happening is far more memorable and emotionally powerful than a series of printed words in the newspaper. Television news is at its best when it can show what is happening as it happens—cameras in outerspace, congressional hearings, wars, disasters, and sports. But the national networks require events of great national interest before they will preempt regularly scheduled programs for a live telecast.

Another form of network news that is almost as powerful as a live telecast is the documentary. These network specials have included in-depth programs on topics such as poverty, AIDS, terrorism, racial conflict, pollution, drug abuse, and other topics of vital concern. Such documentaries are usually produced by one of the three networks for nationwide broadcast, but some are done by individual stations on topics of local concern. Documentaries are expensive to produce and invariably lose money for the networks. Although they do rather poorly in the ratings, they are still seen by millions of people and sometimes have a noticeable effect on governmental agencies and future legislation. It is in these documentaries that television is at its best in providing in-depth news coverage. A one- or two-hour documentary can give the depth lacking in the evening news as well as present powerful visual images to influence opinions.

The viewer has less control over which items she or he sees. It's a very brutal way to get the news.

Abraham Lincoln or Franklin Delano Roosevelt would have trouble getting accepted as a legitimate presidential candidate today.

For the majority of viewers, TV news *is* the evening network news or cable's CNN. A television newscast permits less viewer selectivity than a newspaper gives its readers. A newspaper reader scans the headlines first and reads complete stories only if the headline promises a story of particular interest. Television news is usually watched in its entirety. The TV viewer is not as free to select which items he or she will watch. Older Americans find TV news difficult because they had not been subjected to serious news until the mid–fifties, when networks began to develop serious news programs. Before that, people read daily newspapers. They read the sports page, the comics page; they glanced at the front page. If people didn't want to read about an ax murder, they didn't have to read about it. If they didn't want to read about the race problem, they didn't have to read about the race problem. Then came television, and in order to see any news you pretty much have to see it all. It's a very brutal way to get the news. You can either accept the news that comes from the tube or turn it off completely. You can't pick and choose.

Another unique quality of television is that the presence of film or TV cameras at an event can change what happens there. In the presence of a camera, we all become actors; and the TV news becomes a stage on which we can act out our viewpoint. Some members of Congress objected to the idea of television for congressional hearings on the grounds that the presence of TV cameras would create a "circus" atmosphere. Such fears turned out to be groundless, but the TV camera does have far more effect than a newspaper reporter with a notepad or even a radio reporter with a small tape recorder and microphone. Many states still forbid cameras in courtrooms.

Still another aspect of television news, not shared by the other media, is that a person who looks and sounds believable can influence viewers' opinions. The same person's statement in print might be far less convincing. However, the opposite can also be true. This importance of the "image" a person can project over television has become an important factor in political campaigns.

Radio

For the most up-to-the-minute, quickest, and most frequent news, no medium currently does better than radio. Many stations carry news every 30 minutes; most, every hour, and large cities are served by one or more "all news" stations. Radio is available anywhere in the country, thanks to transistors and radios that have become standard equipment in automobiles. Using a telephone, a radio station can present news almost as it happens. A newspaper has to wait at least until the next edition, and television has to wait (with the exception of special bulletins) until the next evening news broadcast. Radio serves the nation more as a headline service. Many radio news broadcasts are what is called "rip and read." The disc jockey (the same one who announces songs and reads commercials) is given news reports ripped off the wire service teletype machines to read for five minutes.

Better radio stations, usually in large cities, have news departments and reporters out looking for stories. But radio news today functions best as a headline service, as a first alert for important news, and as the best source for current weather and traffic information.

Radio functions as a headline service

Newspapers and Newsmagazines

The ability of television to provide up-to-date evening newscasts has caused a decline in the number of evening edition newspapers. The decline began in 1977, and, during 1988 alone, 27 cities lost their daily evening newspaper. The physical problems associated with publishing a newspaper make the news at least a few hours old by the time the paper hits the street. But of all the news media, newspapers offer the reader the greatest variety and the greatest personal choice. Each newspaper reader is his or her own editor, selecting the news that he or she thinks is important and ignoring what is not. Newspapers have been in the news business far longer than any of the electronic media and have the most people working on gathering and writing the news.

News is the same thing happening everyday to different people.

Newspapers and newsmagazines provide the most in-depth reporting, while radio and television (with the exception of documentaries) go into comparatively little detail. The newsmagazines often provide the most detail about national stories but are a few days or a week behind the newspaper in getting the news to the readers.

There are currently three national news weeklies with a large circulation—*Time* with over 4 $1/2$ million readers; *Newsweek* with over 3 million; and *U.S. News and World Report* with over 2 million.

The newsmagazines report the news with a more entertaining and lively writing style than do newspapers. They have more time to prepare in-depth stories since they are not under the pressure of putting out a daily publication. However, both *Time* and *Newsweek,* which are printed on a Sunday, can publish a story about an important event that happened on Saturday in time for the newsstand copies available Monday morning. *Time* is printed in a number of printing plants around the world and begins selling each edition on Sunday night and Monday morning in more than 150 countries.

The newsmagazines provide the most retrievable form of news. Radio and TV news is gone once the show has ended. A listener or viewer cannot easily go back and check what was said or find the text of the news broadcast at a public library. A newspaper is more retrievable, but its size and inexpensive paper make it hard to store without the inconvenience and expense of microfilm. Newsmagazines are available in any library or in the basement piles of back issues in thousands of homes. A newsmagazine also is on sale for at least a week, while a newspaper disappears from newsstands within twelve hours. Due to this longer sales period and the relative permanence of the newsmagazine, magazines have developed a policy of stressing facts and checking their accuracy.

> Newsmagazines present their opinions as part of the news. Newspapers keep their opinions as separate pieces.

Newsmagazines (as well as other magazines that use factual articles) have full-time "checkers" whose only job is to verify the facts reporters mention in their stories. The checkers are also charged with filling in facts that reporters leave out. A story might come to a checker with a line such as "The 00-person Sudanese army. . . . " It will be up to the checker to fill in the "00". Other news media are careful about reporting facts accurately, but none treat even the least important facts with the passion of newsmagazines. The presence of insignificant but often colorful facts is one of the aspects of newsmagazine writing that distinguishes it from newspapers. A newsmagazine story might begin: "Flowers were in bloom on the crumbling towers of St. Hilaron, and hawks turned soundlessly high above Kyrenia." A newspaper story, on the other hand, would begin simply by noting: "Strife-torn Cyprus was reported quiet today with only sporadic outbreaks of shooting."

Newsmagazines present the news in the form of dramatic stories. Unlike newspapers, they have no tradition of reporting unbiased news and restricting opinions to columns and editorials. They often present opinionated news and interpretations of events, sometimes in articles signed by the writer. Newsmagazines present their opinions as part of the news; newspapers keep opinion pieces separate; television editorials are clearly labeled on the local level, while interpretive documentaries are presented on the national level. The presentation of news in a TV documentary is somewhat similar to that in a newsmagazine.

MEDIALAB

Analyzing Differences

1. Construct a news media comparison chart using the general form given here. Before filling in the chart, discuss exactly how the questions should be answered, the amount of detail desired, the time spans to be used for comparison, and any other points of possible confusion. Either individuals or small groups can fill in the charts.

2. Compare charts with others in the class (or other groups) and discuss reasons for your answers. Draw the chart on the blackboard or a transparency for an overhead projector and fill in the boxes with answers that reflect general agreement (where possible) among the class members.

3. Draw two general conclusions from the charts.

	NEWSMAGAZINES	RADIO	TELEVISION	NEWSPAPER
1. How much time or space does each medium devote to actual news?				
2. How much detail does each medium provide?				
3. How fast does each provide the news? Which is fastest and which slowest?				
4. Which media depend on advertising to make a profit and thus stay in business?				
5. Is the news part of the medium economically profitable?				
6. Which are the best-known nationwide suppliers of news in each medium?				
7. Which are the local news suppliers in each medium?				
8. Which do you think has the strongest emotional effect on the audience?				
9. Which do you think most influences people's opinions?				
10. What is the strongest point of each?				
11. What is the weakest point of each?				
12. Which covers each of the following best:				

sports   events at your school
local politics   tragedy
human interest   weather
in-depth news stories financial news
world events

MAKING NEWS

Most of what appears on televised news is not really the "news"; it is people reacting to the news. How can you gain television time on the news other than by committing a crime or hitting a home run to win the World Series? Easy. Represent a special interest group (political party, police, union, corporation, entertainer) and stage an event (pseudo-event) to which the press is invited.

Once television time is gained, you either prepare a favorable statement or stage an event with visual interest that makes your point. If you are interviewed by a local reporter, you try to control the interview to create the impression of yourself as the good guy.

Joe Saltzman is a former journalist and now a journalism professor and media consultant. Here are his reflections on media control by major corporations and special interest groups and the fine art of controlling interviews.

R E A D I N G

HOW TO MANAGE TV NEWS

All the world's a stage, at least if you know how to manipulate local television reports.

by **Joe Saltzman**

It is a blunt fact of life that the local television news we see every night—the only news source for more than 60 percent of the American people—has been staged for television by outside special interests.

Consider the following cases and use them as a guide when watching tonight's local news programs:

A politician wants to get publicity for legislation he is sponsoring. He calls a news conference. Reporters from every television station show up. Viewers will see the news conference on the evening news but probably little else. What they won't hear about is any political wheeling and dealing out of the glare of the television lights. . . .

A major company holds a news conference to issue its year-end report. The figures are glowing, the cameras are rolling, everyone is smiling. If the reporter works harder than most do, the viewers might hear figures questioned and policies doubted when the story gets on the air, but that kind of information can't be dug up in the course of a press conference. No one will call in cameras and reporters to reveal economic reverses, mishandling of funds, or worse. And if reporters find out something suspicious on their own, they probably won't even get to talk to the company president, much less record an interview with that person.

A picket line goes up around a market to protest higher prices. A spokesperson is there when the television reporters arrive. For the next hour or so, the cameras cover the staged event. The reporters thank the spokesperson and leave. Five minutes later, the picket line disappears.

The list is endless. Politicians, police, the military, entertainers, government agencies, corporations, businesspersons, individuals, and groups all stage news "events" for their own benefit. And those with money to hire a savvy public relations firm can get their news—and usually their version of the news—broadcast into living rooms with sports and the daily weather.

"Any sharp public relations person can get the story covered by television," says Robert Irvine, a former news director of the Eyewitness News team at KABC—TV in Los Angeles. "He knows how to schedule a story for maximum exposure, how to alert the news media and make sure they show up, how to get the inexperienced reporter to put his PR release on film, how to make sure it will get on the evening news. Most of what you see on television news is stuff handed to . . . assignment desks who then feed it to reporters who are usually guided in their coverage by the public relations person involved. . . ."

A local television news reporter who has worked for 25 years for several stations shares Irvine's opinions. He says news executives like well-organized stories that don't leave unanswered questions. "Investigative reports or stories that take a lot of time and effort never look as smooth or polished as the simple PR story," he explains. "Nobody is very happy about partially finished, dull, or nonvisual stories. So eventually you either give up or keep fighting until you get fired or change jobs."

Thousands of stories from special interests make the air only slightly altered from their staged creation. It takes money to cover stories well and most local television stations don't have the funds. Assignment desks, faced with limited budgets and a handful of inexperienced personnel, look for stories they can film fast—and most of the time those are staged for the media by outside sources. ABC producer and former NBC reporter Mike Gavin explains: "Every demonstration, every scheduled interview, every news conference, every notification of a planned story, every time a person wants to get his or her point across—it's 'staged.'" . . .

Most editors and reporters insist that the bulk of these staged events is not inherently bad. They often provide information the public should have. The danger is that this is the *only* news the public usually gets while enterprising, investigative television reporting is becoming a thing of the past.

Couple that with television management that is entertainment-oriented and wants short, snappy stories with no loose ends, all packaged neatly into less than two minutes, and it is easy to see why most local news shows are filled with stories that are the easiest to get. . . .

In the past, reporters were more expert than special-interest group representatives in creating and fleshing out stories for the media. No longer. Major corporations and other special-interest groups are training their people in how to deal with the media in specific and formalized ways.

A prototype for this new sophistication is the Standard Oil Company television training seminar, a two-day, intensive education program for top company executives on how to handle the broadcast media. Executives are brought to a rented television studio, interviewed by a hired reporter, then "critiqued.". . . By the time executives "graduate," they are ready to handle any radio or television reporter in any local news market in the country. More and more companies have copied the Standard Oil television seminar, which itself was modeled after the very successful program pioneered by J. Walter Thompson Company in the early 1970s.

As one of the university specialists brought in on several occasions by Standard Oil for its "Television Training Seminar," I came to understand that we were preparing Standard Oil executives to cope easily with reporters who have never received such comprehensive briefings. . . .

We would teach these managers and administrators, these top representatives of Standard Oil how to overcome nervousness (before being introduced "take a deep breath, hold it for about three seconds, and then let out slowly . . . "); how to stand and relax ("Stand naturally with your feet about shoulder-width apart; let your hands hang naturally. Relax your fingers. Then start vibrating your fingers and wrists as fast as you can. Then let that vibration flow through your body to free your muscles of tension").

We would teach them how to get rid of butterflies in the stomach and how to wet a "dry mouth": "A dry mouth can make speaking uncomfortable. Just before you go on, work up a quantity of saliva in your mouth and swallow. It will moisten your mouth and throat and speaking will be easier."

What to do if, under stress, the voice becomes shrill: "Don't talk from the throat, talk from the diaphragm. Use your lungs and entire chest as a sound-source resonator. That way you won't have to shout. It improves the sound of authority in your voice."

We emphasized that the executives must speak clearly, not mumble; they must be aggressive, not passive. After various other voice-training procedures, we showed them how to project a good image through the eyes and we emphasized the importance of good grooming: Dress comfortably; wear solid colors; avoid sharp, flashy clothes; avoid large cuff links or gaudy jewelry. . . . Shave before an appearance, TV accentuates the beard. . . . Wear knee-length hose; avoid short socks, garters, argyles; if they don't have high socks, wear boots. . . .

Those were just the preliminaries. The main event was how to deal with reporters on television. The first part of the lesson was how to prepare for the interview. By Sunday afternoon, after an intensive weekend, the executives would go home feeling confident, knowing a good deal more about interview techniques than the majority of broadcast reporters they would run into.

We put the executives through a rigorous interview schedule. Thrown cold into a television studio, they were interviewed by a seasoned reporter specially paid to make the guest feel uncomfortable. Every ploy was used, from argumentative and personal questions to cheap shots and dropping film cans off-camera. The tape was later played back while two media experts—in a carefully rehearsed piece of criticism—ripped it apart. After that, the executive was interviewed again, and those tapes were evaluated.

Avoiding "question traps" and learning how to control an interview were the most important parts of the lesson. We insisted that the executives be prepared, that they have specific objectives in mind when being interviewed and be ready to talk about them whenever possible by taking charge of the interview. The most important single technique is called "bridging." Months later, I happened to see one of our executives use it. He responded to a question by saying, "That is not my area of expertise, –(reporter's first name). I came here to talk about oil and that reminds me of . . ." Before the reporter knew what was happening, the executive was into a two-minute summary of what he wanted people to know about Standard Oil. The answer had nothing to do with the question, but the confused reporter thanked him and that was that.

Besides bridging, we demonstrated to the executives how to handle all types of questions. One was "the loaded preface question" that "stacks the deck and colors any answer." It implies charges and guilt and "puts you in a corner before you even get a chance to open your mouth." An example goes something like this: "You're a representative of a company that polluted the Bay of San Francisco with its tanker collision, ruined the shrimp and oyster business in the gulf with an oil well blowout, and foisted a phony gasoline hike on the public. In light of that track record, what is the new management of your company doing to mend the error of its ways?" How should they handle this? First, as the interviewer

sets out this laundry list of charges, we taught the executive not to try to remember all the charges and not to try to answer them all. We instructed him to zero in on one he was sure he could respond to and by implication discredit the rest. The executive was taught to say, "Hey, wait a minute. That's quite a laundry list of accusations,–(reporter's first name), and I doubt that we have enough time on this program to answer them all. I can assure you that you're way off base on all those charges. For example, let me deal with just one of those. That well blowout in the gulf had no effect whatsoever on the shrimps and oysters. A study by the University of Texas biology department proved this, and the courts dismissed all suits that were brought against us alleging harm to marine life."

Executives were also made to understand that they could not have personal opinions. "Everything you say on radio or television or to a reporter will come across as a statement of a representative of the Standard Oil Company. It will be interpreted as an official statement. Even if you say, "Well, I can't speak for my company, but I think personally that . . .' it will come out as a representative of Standard Oil says this and that.'" The executive was warned: "You cannot have a personal opinion. Only an official opinion. Do not give your private feelings."

We warned executives against falling for questions that pose "either/or" choices. They were also cautioned against "A–B–C ranking" questions: "Sir, list the four most important problems the industry faces today and tell us how to deal with them." They were taught not to make a list but to pick out one point, deal with it, then bridge to their own point. A sample answer: "Well,—(reporter's first name), with the kind of problems facing our whole economy today, I don't think we could cover any indus-

try's total problems in 30 seconds. But I'd like to say this . . ." then bridge; it's just like dancing: one, two, three, bridge.

On occasion, the executive was told, there would be reporters who cut off answers, interrupt the most carefully plotted bridges, make snide comments, and be downright rude. "If this happens, ride it out and try to capture audience sympathy with facial expressions and body language. If you engage in verbal battle with the interviewer, you will lose. He's on his home turf and is familiar with the techniques of broadcasting. He will win the battle. There is no way you, an amateur, can win over a professional . . ."

We told the executives always to keep their cool, always to be friendly and gentlemanly. No personal battles, "If you get hostile, you'll probably lose audience sympathy and end up in a bad situation." Other tips offered were to always listen carefully to the questions, never let accusations stand, only answer questions with which they were familiar and not concerning any controversial subjects, and bridge often to what they wanted to say, not what the reporter wanted said. . . .

There may be occasions when the executive would not want to answer a question, but he was urged to avoid saying, "No comment," at all costs. That sounds evasive, as if he has something to hide. If the executive can't or won't answer a question, he was urged to say so and explain why.

Executives soon learned one way to avoid answering the question was to ask another question they liked better. Example: "Why haven't the oil companies reduced their gasoline prices and their earnings a little instead of making such obscene profits?" Answer: "You know,–(reporter's first name), what we should be asking ourselves is why you and other people seem to think the idea of profits is in any way obscene. We ought to be

asking ourselves if we're providing enough incentive for the economy to generate the level of profits we need to expand energy supplies." And the executive kept going, bridging to another little speech.

We warned the executives never to lie—never to make up anything, shade or distort facts. "It is a good probability that sooner or later you'll be found out if you do not tell the truth. It will blow your credibility. There is no chance to recover. No more believability. Never play games with the truth."

They were taught how important it was to keep their answers brief. "Twenty to 30 seconds is a target time; make it lucid and brief." A nice 20 to 30-second speech would make the editor's work easy and improve the chances that the executive's statement would be used. They were told to avoid the use of jargon, to give support to generalizations, to use an authority —an expert who holds the same view—to use statistics to illustrate a point, to use analogies to support answers: "Raising taxes on our industry would be like buckling a lead belt on a long-distance swimmer." . . .

It is small wonder that much of what we see on local television news is created by special interests who only want their version of a story told. In many stories, two special-interest groups collide, and sometimes the public gets enough facts to make an educated decision. . . .

The danger that special-interest groups' staged news is becoming TV's primary news has already been realized. Individual reporting enterprise is becoming less and less the norm as special-interest groups become more and more sophisticated. Only when newspapers and magazines do the leg work, does television discover that there are stories not being regularly supplied to it. . . .

MEDIALAB

Looking at Local TV News

1. Why are so many of the stories on local news provided by special-interest groups or individuals with a product or viewpoint to sell?

2. Watch the local news on television tonight. If you have more than one local television station, be sure someone is watching each newscast. Note each local story carried and determine which are examples of some person or group using television to present a favorable impression. Discuss your findings in class the next day.

3. Station managers defend the use of "staged" or "managed" news items on the grounds that they still provide the public with useful information. The danger is that because such news is so easy to report, it might become the only news. How much investigative reporting is done by local television and radio stations?

4. Interviews on local TV newscasts usually fall into one of two categories: an interview with an ordinary person who has just become a victim/hero/witness, or an interview with professional person (corporate spokesperson, politician, public official) who is defending a viewpoint. In the first category, the reporter is not looking for information as much as for emotion. People being emotional on camera will attract attention. You will see interviews with victims of tragedy as well as heroes and lottery winners. Such interviews are televised to add emotional content to the news broadcast; sometimes this is called human interest.

What is your opinion of this first kind of interview? How valuable is it in terms of news? How would you react if your house just burned down and a reporter asked you, "How did it happen?" or "What are you going to do now?"

5. The article deals with training for the second kind of interview. What techniques were taught to help the executives control an interview?

6. Watch news interviews of corporate executives, government official, or politicians. Study how and if the person being interviewed controlled the interview. Look for examples of the techniques discussed in the previous reading.

7. Work in groups and demonstrate one or more of the interview techniques illustrated in the article. Volunteers should play the roles of reporters and of interviewees. Illustrate how to:
- avoid question traps
- take charge of a possible hostile interviewer
- control an interview by bridging
- survive a loaded or biased question
- avoid the "either/or" trap
- avoid answering a question

HOW HAVE MASS MEDIA CHANGED POLITICS ?

Television has changed the concept of news more than any invention since the printing press. Television invented the idea of national news. Radio had the potential to unite the nation and create national news, but its impact was limited. Radio required the listener to use imagination. It did not show angry mobs, extremes of poverty or wealth, or the grittiness of war.

The first to use radio to strengthen the image of the presidency was Franklin D. Roosevelt. In the 1930s and 1940s, Roosevelt's fireside chats were a perfect match of the man to the medium. He might not have been able to survive the television news camera. Voters would have been constantly reminded that he was crippled and spent most of his time in a wheelchair.

Before televised national news, a presidential candidate could hope to get away with making a special promise in one part of the country that would go unnoticed elsewhere. But today, a promise made to factory workers in Ohio is seen on the evening news by farmers in Mississippi. So candidates avoid local issues in favor of national or even global concerns.

Presidents use television to communicate with the entire country, taking time on all three major networks for policy statements and even press conferences. Compare that to pre-television days in which a president had to travel around the country on arduous speaking tours. Woodrow Wilson defended his idea to establish a League of Nations with a cross-country speaking tour. Some historians believe the strain of the trip led to the stroke that ended his presidency.

Presidents once delivered the annual "State of the Union" address to Congress at noon. Today it is done at nine at night on the East Coast. True, this time is less convenient for the people in attendance, but the time is best for a national TV audience. Nine o'clock is prime time in the East and Midwest and still late enough to garner a large audience on the West Coast. Every trip a president (or a presidential candidate) makes is carefully planned to give the maximum television coverage. A president can now afford to address a small gathering— even a high-school assembly or a local meeting of autoworkers. The real crowd for such speeches is the millions who will see a few seconds of the speech on the evening news. Meetings are timed and planned for maximum television coverage. The live audience is more a stage prop provided to cheer and applaud. The audience communicates a sense of support and excitement to the millions watching at home.

Television gives a president a powerful tool to earn the nation's support and to unite the country in times of crisis.

The real audience for a televised political speech are the millions of TV viewers who will be watching it on the nightly news.

MEDIALAB

News and Politics

1. Imagine that television ceased to exist. How would that fact change a presidential campaign and election? In particular, what kind of impact would debates have?

2. How does the current president use television to gain public support of his policies and influence public opinion?

3. Make a note of any politician who appears on a newscast. Why is the politician gaining television time? Is the "live" audience important or merely a prop for this occasion?

4. When a president makes a policy statement or conducts a news conference, it is often carried in prime time on all three television networks. Do you think this is (a) important for the good of the nation, (b) government domination of media, (c) a shame since you sometimes miss a favorite program, or (d) not needed since it could be covered by newspapers and one network instead of all three? Support your answer.

THE NEWS BUSINESS

Reporting the news is a high-speed business involving many layers of information and people. Just exactly how is it done? Here is the story of a story: a look behind the scenes of news gathering. An early-morning school bus accident in a Midwestern town is reported on the network news from New York the same day. How do the information and the pictures get to the producer in New York? How does the producer decide which stories will be shown on television? Step-by-step, the process is explained in the following article.

R E A D I N G

THE ACCIDENT
A CROSS MEDIA STUDY

by John Chancellor and Walter Mears

How does a school bus crash in the Midwest turn into a news story on national television and in newspapers around the country the next morning?

The break in the wooden guard rail is hard to see in the gray morning, as the rain slants across the ravine. Several cars pass over the bridge before a farmer in a pickup truck notices the broken rail and stops to look down.

The school bus is on its side, bright yellow against the green slope, its headlights on, its warning lights blinking. The farmer can hear the sound of children crying.

He passes the message to the state police on his citizens' band radio. It goes from there, by telephone, to hospitals. In a few minutes, the red lights of ambulances and police cars flash across the stubble of the harvested cornfields.

And so begins a news story. The school bus accident will join thousands of other events and occurrences on that day, part of a great river of information, carried by satellite links, high-speed teletypes, and computerized word processors. The high-speed machines of the Associated Press transmit about 400,000 words a day, 1,000 stories every 24 hours.

Thirty miles from the scene of the school bus crash, a reporter at the city desk of a small Midwestern paper learns of the event while making his routine morning check with the state police. At the radio station across town, a broadcast reporter hears the news on the police radio frequency. Their reflexes are the same: find out what happened. At this point, they don't know much, only that a school bus has crashed and that children have died.

The radio station interrupts its disc jockey with a bulletin saying just that. Essential but cruel—no one knows yet who has survived and who has not. The newspaper reporter tells his editor. Reporters and photographers head for the scene and the hospital.

It is wrenching catastrophe for the town—and a story across the country. For those initial reporters relay word of the crash to the organizations that will tell the world of it. The newspaperman telephones the Associated Press bureau in Kansas City. The radio man calls United Press International. They are stringers, paid space rates to cover local stories for the wire services.

The story is developing. AP and UPI send their first, sketchy stories across the nation. Then come advisory notes:

"Editors: A reporter and photographer are en route to the scene of the school bus crash. There is as yet no word on the number of casualties."

At NBC News in New York, a copy clerk tears the copy from the printer and takes it to the editors. The producer in charge of national stories for "Nightly News" has just had his first sip of office coffee. The program is nine hours away, but there is work to be done right now. This is a story that will be prominent on the evening news; and he knows it.

He pulls out a map, looks for the closest NBC television affiliate, picks up the phone, and calls the news director there. Crews are on the way, he's told, and some of the videotape they will shoot will be available in time for "Nightly News." Next step: Call NBC

Chicago; and order a network reporter and camera crew to the site of the crash. They'll charter a plane and be there in a couple of hours.

By now, the wire services have their own reporters and photographers on the road. They will be the first out-of-town reporters to get there; their bureaus are widely deployed, and there's one close to almost any place a story breaks. There are more than 120 Associated Press bureaus in the United States.

They'll check with the local stringers, get to the scene, talk to the police, get the casualty list, telephone the details to the bureau in Kansas City. The story is put together by editors there, relayed to New York, then transmitted to newspapers and broadcast stations that take the service.

When journalists talk about this, it is in a language as old as the first telegraph lines. A story "moves" on the "wire." It may be transmitted by way of a satellite, but the language of the business is rooted in the days when telegraphers wearing green eyeshades tapped out stories in Morse code, on wires that ran along the railroad tracks.

Today the wire services, the great engines of news gathering and distribution, are at the center of the news business. The wires provide both the text and the context of the news. In the editor's office, on the telephone, or in the conference room, every daily news organization sorts and sifts the day's events to decide what will be

published or broadcast, how much space or time it will get, and whether it belongs on the front page or back with the classified ads.

AP and UPI are central to the process of decision. They are the basic wire services. They deliver news, photos, and radio reports at the local, state, national, and international levels. They cover the state governments and distribute stock market tables and weather reports. The objective is to deliver everything an editor needs to put out a daily newspaper.

The Associated Press is the oldest and biggest, a cooperative that serves about 1,350 daily newspapers and more than 5,700 radio and television stations in the United States. It is a nonprofit organization, owned by the newspapers it serves. They aren't customers; they are members. . . .

United Press International is a privately owned company, with a news and photo staff of about 1,000. UPI says it has more than 1,000 newspaper clients. After losing money for years and changing ownership in 1982, it faces an uncertain future.

Each television news department —at NBC, ABC, and CBS—employs over 1,000 news people, including technicians, and can call on help from several hundred radio affiliates and more than 200 television affiliates.

Although Reuters, the British news agency, has expanded its operations in the United States, and

competes with the American wire services, it is strongest abroad and in international financial reporting.

New York wire supervisors control the wire. On the story of a school bus crash in the Midwest, they would be in frequent telephone contact with Kansas City as the story developed. It would belong on the daily news digest, the menu of major stories each wire service transmits to advise newspapers what is coming. There's a late-morning digest for newspapers that will be published the following morning, a midnight digest for afternoon newspapers.

In the trade, those are the "cycles," AMs and PMs. The evening news on television is, in effect, an AM operation, with access to the same stories that will be in the morning papers. The PMs' news cycle is comparable to that of breakfast-time television programs.

The process of deciding what stories will be shown on television on any evening and published in AM newspapers the next day is one that begins at midmorning, Eastern time.

At 10:30 A.M., about a dozen people sit down in a fourth-floor conference room at the Associated Press Building, overlooking Rockefeller Plaza in New York, to talk about the day's news.

Across Manhattan at UPI headquarters, the process is more informal; no set meeting, but a series of discussions and telephone calls.

In Rockefeller Center, the staff of "NBC Nightly News," about ten people, meets at 11:45 A.M.

There, and at like meetings in newsrooms across the country, editors have been assessing the day's events, the wire copy, the staff reporting, the stories assigned but yet to come. Now they begin planning the product, deciding what's important, what to do about

it, and where to play it.

Editors must decide long before deadline which national and international stories belong on the front page, and at what length. The decision is subject to change, because the news doesn't stop, and what seems most important at noon may be forced further back in the paper by what happens at night.

The story of a school bus crash in the Midwest would be a subject of those conferences. It is a cold, impersonal process—the mathematics of the news business. If that crash killed two children, it would be a small story nationally. If it were twenty-two, it would be a major one.

Were that the case, the story would be at or near the top of AMs news digests moved by the wire services. It happened early in the day, on PMs time. But few afternoon papers in the East would be able to print more than the first sparse reports, scant on detail that would come later, after their deadlines.

News digests are agendas, and they are a factor in the decisions made in all newsrooms. The digests are brief summaries of the most important stories of the day—twelve, sometimes fourteen of them. They deliver the lead paragraph, and an editor can write a headline from them before the story arrives.

These digests are put together by editors who have been writing, editing, and judging stories for years, and much of what they do is instinctive. Former Supreme Court Justice Potter Stewart once said that he could not define pornography, but knew it when he saw it. That's sometimes the way it is with news. The pros know it when they see it.

The story lineups assembled by the two wire services, and the story decisions at the networks and the newspapers, usually are similar and

sometimes are almost identical.

That is the case simply because good, seasoned editors looking at the same set of events will come to many of the same conclusions. Some of those decisions are automatic. If the President is going to make an announcement on foreign policy at 3 p.m., that belongs on the digest, and the story about it belongs in the paper and on the air. If there is a major flood in the South, a government shake-up in the Middle East, those stories do too.

The more difficult calls come on another kind of story: the piece that is not of compelling importance today, but may be next month; or the investigative story; or the complex but potentially significant science story; or the politician who announces he wants to be President but nobody knows his name. . . .

At a morning newspaper and in network television, the pace accelerates as the day goes on. By 2 P.M. in New York, Europe is beginning to shut down, and Asia has been fast asleep for hours. Washington is generating its stories, at the midday briefings by White House and State Department spokesmen, in the debates and votes of a Congress that does much of its work late in the day or at night. The dynamics of public relations are at work too. Across the country, press agents have timed their releases, their client's speeches, their staged happenings, to take place in time for the evening TV news and the morning papers. In the age of television, presidential campaigns are shaped by the deadlines of the networks. Candidates want to be on the air.

That can work in reverse. Public relations people in a government agency or a corporation that has to acknowledge bad news know that an announcement made at 5:30 on a Friday afternoon produces little coverage on television, and fewer newspapers are sold on Saturday than on other days. Federal government announcements that will affect financial markets are issued after Wall Street has shut down at 4 P.M. White House press agents choose the time of announcements according to the way they hope to see the story played. If it makes the President look good, it comes early, in time to be seen on television. If it makes him look bad, it comes late. . . .

By 3 P.M., it is decision time at "Nightly News." There's another conference, but this time it is limited to the executive producer, his three deputies and the anchorman. It is a time for blunt talk about the importance and quality of the stories available for the evening's program. There are going to be some stories that will be broadcast without pictures, written by the anchorman. Anchormen usually argue for those stories, and producers press to get their videotape on the air. . . .

At 3:30 P.M. there's a final meeting at "Nightly News." The lineup is set, and the executive producer announces it to his staff. It includes the stories that are going to be covered, the order in which they will be presented, and the exact amount of air time the anchormen

and the correspondents will get to tell them. They'll have to edit their own copy to fit the assigned time.

The school bus crash is going to be high in the program. Eleven children are dead; the driver and seven others are gravely injured. It will be covered in exactly one minute and forty-five seconds.

Not long after that last formal meeting at "Nightly News," the editors of the *New York Times* hold their first formal meeting of the day. They've been at work on tomorrow's paper since mid-morning. The foreign desk, the metropolitan desk, the national desk and the other departments have been preparing and updating "skeds," short for "schedule," meaning the stories they see coming. They make their cases for space for those stories. They get a hearing, no decisions yet.

There, as everywhere, the process involves some internal competition. At any newspaper, the city editor wants a piece by one of his reporters at the top of the front page. The editor who handles foreign copy argues that there is a better piece coming from Moscow, and it ought to be the lead. The editor who handles features wants front-page space for a story about the zoo.

By 5:15, when the newsroom at

NBC is hectic, and getting more so, the senior editors of the *Times* are meeting to plan their front page.

The executive editor, the managing editor, and their departmental editors discuss the stories ready or coming for tomorrow's *Times*. The *Times* man in Washington listens on a telephone hookup. When he has something to say, his words issue from a speaker in the ceiling in New York. *Times* voices often seem that way.

After about fifteen minutes, the discussion is done. The department editors go back to their desks, and the top editors decide what the front page is going to look like and what will be relegated to pages of lesser prominence. They do it by themselves because they want no further debate. They decide what will be out front in the *Times*, and they make a sketch of Page 1. In journalism, a page sketch like that is a "dummy."

So the decisions that shape the news most people read the next morning or see that evening are made within a few hours in the afternoon and early evening. The process is repeated, time zone to time zone, Boston *Globe* to Los Angeles *Times*. . .

MEDIALAB

Thinking About News Gathering

1. In the school bus accident example, which medium reported the story first? Is this medium usually the first with the news?

2. Sometimes a citizen will report a story (usually a crime or accident) to a newspaper or radio or TV station. What other means are used by news organizations to learn of the news? (The answer to this question is not "reporters." Reporters are sent to cover the event once the news organization learns of its existence.)

3. How did NBC News learn of the bus accident? What action did the producer in charge of national stories for "Nightly News" take when he learned of the bus accident? How would this differ from the action taken by a producer of a local newscast in some other part of the country? How would it differ from the action of a producer in the city where the accident took place?

4. What role do stringers play in news gathering?

5. AP, UPI, and the British Reuters are commonly called wire services. Where do you think the name came from? What would be a more accurate name?

6. What is the main source of news for local newspapers, radio newscasts, and local televised news programs?

7. Research how television networks now use communication satellites to relay communications during news programs.

8. From what you have learned about news gathering so far in this chapter, how would you go about setting up a one-person newspaper without hiring reporters?

9. What are the AMs and PMs? If the school bus accident happened after school instead of before, how would its coverage on television and in newspapers differ?

10. Timing is important in controlling news. Imagine you are public relations director for a corporation that is very important to the local economy. When and how would you alert the local press about the fact that your company just received a multi-million-dollar government contract? When and how would you inform the press that your company is about the fire 10 percent of its workers?

11. Editors face tough decisions in selecting the news. The article points out "it is a cold, impersonal business. . . . If that crash killed two children, it would be a small story nationally. If it were twenty-two, it would be a major one." Why does the "mathematics of tragedy" play such an important role in selecting the news?

12. What role does timing play in staged news, such as press conferences, press releases, and announcements of economic indicators?

13. The decisions about what you will read in the morning paper and what you will see on the national evening news are made (barring major last-second emergencies) around what time of day?

14. The availability of pictures (photos, film, or videotape) can influence news decisions. Explain how the presence or absence of pictures might influence a TV news producer and a newspaper editor.

15. From which medium—television or the newspaper—would you learn most about the bus accident? Which medium might present the most emotional coverage?

16. Research how television coverage of the war in Vietnam on the nightly news influenced the American people's reactions to U.S. involvement (1965–1973). In addition to library research, you may wish to interview parents or older brothers and sisters who remember watching actual combat scenes that had been filmed in Vietnam the day of the broadcast.

17. How might the American Civil War have been influenced by the presence of nightly televised newscasts?

WRAP-UP

Now that you've been introduced to the news media, you can answer the often-asked question: Why do we see, hear, and read about so much *bad* news? You've learned how important wire services are to the news media and how the news director or managing editor serves the important function of "gatekeeper." You've discovered who makes the news and who manages it and learned about the function of a reporter and the interview process. From the days of Roosevelt's fireside chats on the radio to today's televised campaigns and presidential addresses, you've seen how mass media have changed politics. Finally, you've learned how local news becomes national—or even international—news.

CHAPTER 7
Newspapers

Take a look at another mass medium, the newspaper, and discover how this medium developed and how news is published today.

THE GROWTH OF NEWSPAPERS

Publishing a newspaper requires a machine that will print large quantities of words at a relatively low cost. Such a machine could not exist until the fifteenth century when Johannes Gutenberg invented a system of setting type that used movable, reusable type. Yet, one hundred years after the invention, newspapers were still almost unknown. Why the long delay between the invention and its application?

Two major obstacles existed for the would-be newspaper publisher before the Industrial Revolution in the late 1800s: first, most people could not read, and second, the technology did not exist to make mass production of newspapers possible. Literacy was needed so there would be enough people willing to buy and read newspapers; literacy has been common only in the past five or six generations. Technological advances in the late 1800s, such as the invention of the linotype (a machine that produces each line of type in the form of a solid metal slug) and high-volume presses, enabled newspapers to become a truly mass medium.

Democracy and wide-spread literacy often go hand-in-hand, so it was only natural that the first popular democracy—the United States—would be the birthplace of a popular free press. Today, one out of every five newspapers printed is published in the United States, and, even though the United States has less than 5 percent of the world's population, it has about 20 percent of the world's news readers.

American newspapers began as bulletins hung on tavern walls or printed sheets from the local postmaster or printer. Anyone could start a newspaper, and this fact was important in the development of a free press. Most schools have small newspapers that cover only events in school, but there is no legal reason why these papers could not be expanded to become neighborhood newspapers. On the other hand, a school radio or TV station cannot broadcast to the public without a government license. New, inexpensive offset printing systems make it possible for anyone with a few hundred dollars to produce a small newspaper with a circulation in the thousands.

> It was only natural that the first popular democracy would be the birthplace of the popular free press.

In spite of increasing competition from TV networks and cable news networks, a great number of newspapers are financially successful and socially responsible. The closest to an official daily newspaper is the *New York Times*, a paper found in most libraries and often considered the official record of the day's events. Other respected national papers are the *Wall Street Journal* and the *Christian Science Monitor*. A newer national newspaper is *USA Today*, which started in 1982 and boasts a circulation of well over one million daily. The paper is owned by the Gannett chain of papers and, like other nationally-circulated newspapers, is printed in various plants around the country using satellite transmission.

Today there are about 1,650 daily newspapers in the United States, about the same number as existed in 1920 and actually fewer than in the late nineteenth century. At the end of 1984 the number of TV stations caught up with the number of daily newspapers. In spite of the popularity of television, 63 million people still read a daily newspaper.

Newspaper ownership has recently become increasingly concentrated, with a smaller and smaller group of people owning the nation's newspapers. The owners of all the newspapers in the country could assemble in an average-sized high school gymnasium or auditorium. This increasing concentration of owners means there is less competition among papers. Competition helps ensure the news consumer that the papers will try to do the best possible job of finding and reporting the news.

Without local competition, a single paper can establish a news monopoly in a city and can succumb to the temptation to turn out a paper that is a collection of wire service items, press releases, and syndicated material. Such a paper will give a certain amount of news and information to the people. But it will not ask the news-makers hard questions, send reporters to dig around for the truth behind the press releases, attempt to expose corruption in local government or business, or spend large sums of money for investigative reporting. Very likely it will not attract the best possible talent in reporters and editors.

A paper with a local monopoly can make a substantial profit from advertising without making any effort to actively pursue local news. The people in that city have then lost freedom of the press for all practical purposes, even without censorship or government restrictions. A local monopoly does not always lead to this situation, but it is all too common, especially in small American cities.

Journalism Quarterly studied a city in which a news monopoly was established and then looked at how the situation changed when a strong competitor started business. The study found that the original monopoly paper gave 41 percent of its nonadvertising space to local news (local news is the most expensive to obtain since it requires reporters, travel, and time). When the competing paper began operation, the percentage increased to 51 percent—the people in the town got more news, thanks to the competitor. When the competitor failed and went out of business, however, the amount of local news slipped back to 43 percent.

> A good newspaper, I suppose, is a nation talking to itself.
> —ARTHUR MILLER, dramatist

How common are newspaper monopolies? In 1880, 61 percent of all newspaper towns had competing dailies. By 1930 that figure had dropped to only 21 percent; in 1940 it was only 13 percent; and today about 2 percent of newspaper towns have competing dailies. There are only 15 cities left with competing papers published at the same time of the day (for example, competing morning or evening papers). Some cities have two papers but one is sold to those who prefer a paper in the late afternoon and the other to those who prefer a paper in the morning. Many cities have lost their evening edition newspapers because of the competition from TV nightly newscasts. A few cities have two papers owned by the same person or company, but the papers do not really compete.

About half of the nation's daily papers are owned by chains, companies that own more than one paper. The largest chains include the Chicago Tribune, Scripps-Howard, Hearst, Newhouse, Knight-Ridder, and Gannett papers.

The decreasing amount of competition and the increase of concentrated ownership is not necessarily a bad influence on news, but the tendency in such situations is for both the quality of news and variety of opinions available to decrease.

MEDIALAB

Newspapers in Our Society

1. What two factors enabled newspapers to become a mass medium? Why do you think the United States is a dominant force in newspaper publishing?

2. Find some foreign newspapers and compare them with American papers. Even if the paper is not written in English, it can be compared in terms of appearance and advertising. Some libraries and large newsstands carry foreign papers.

3. Find out which local paper most of the class members' families subscribe to.

4. Take a survey of class newspaper reading that will show how many people in the class read a paper daily, which sections they read most, and how much time each day they spend reading a newspaper. Expand the survey to include the families of everyone in the class.

5. Find copies of national papers such as *The Wall Street Journal, Christian Science Monitor, USA Today,* and *National Observer.* Have a class member report on them, or make the papers available for class reading.

6. Find out if your area has competing papers or a newspaper monopoly. Who owns the local paper or papers? Find out what other communications businesses the owners run. (For example, do they own any other papers as part of a chain, or do they own radio or TV stations?)

7. Make a careful study of your local papers and discuss various opinions about them. Do they do a good job of providing news?

HOW NEWS IS PUBLISHED (THE PROCESS)

The basic function of a newspaper is to report the news. How is this fundamental purpose carried out? Local news stories must be covered by reporters who follow leads, conduct interviews, make innumerable phone calls, and write their stories—all under deadlines. The reporter and the city desk (the managing editor) work together to bring a story into being. The reporter may be working at top speed to assemble facts and possibly locate an angle to the story. Supporting the reporter and making sure that stories are accurate and presented clearly is the copy editor. The copy editor smooths out the writing, checks the spelling of names, reminds the reporter if a crucial fact is missing, and in many ways helps get the story into print. The following article follows a story (a large theft of uncut diamonds) from the first police report to the printed page.

R E A D I N G

FROM

MORE LANGUAGE THAT NEEDS WATCHING

by **Theodore M. Bernstein**

The following story, told by a former copy editor of the *New York Times*, shows how one local news story moves from the event to the printed page.

It is mid-afternoon and the office of the morning newspaper is quiet except for the typewriters or computer keyboards of a few rewrite men tapping out short stories of routine events. The man covering police headquar-ters phones the city desk to report a rather large theft of uncut diamonds from a dealer's office—"Looks like a pretty fair story." Should he cover it or does the city desk want to assign another reporter to the story? He is instructed to remain on his beat.

Arnold Dittenhouse draws the assignment. He is told the nature of the story and goes to work.

From the headquarters man, Arnold picks up the basic facts by phone. A diamond merchant, Gregory Lee, has reported the loss of

$100,000 worth of uncut stones from the safe in his office at 1661 Sixth Avenue. Lee says the stones were there the previous afternoon but were gone this morning. The police have questioned everyone in the office except a clerk ("Haven't got his name, but the precinct cops can give it to you"). The clerk has not been questioned because he left on a two-week vacation last night and no one seems to know where he is.

Arnold next travels to the precinct station house and buttonholes a detective on the case. He learns that the clerk is Julius Feinguy, 22 years old, who rooms with a family named Fickett in Queens Village. He also discovers that the F.B.I. is investigating because of a suspicion that the diamonds may have been transported across state lines. Do the police suspect anything phony about the case— a staged theft to collect insurance or anything like that? No, they do not. Was the safe jimmied open or blown open? No, there were no signs that it

had been tampered with in any way. Then it looks like an inside job, doesn't it? The police are offering no theory about it just yet.

A visit to Lee's office seems to be in order so that Arnold can at least get some idea of the physical layout. At the Sixth Avenue address the reporter is fortunate enough to find Lee in his office. He thus is able, in addition, to gather a few details about the personal appearance of the distraught, bespectacled, round little man who has suddenly found himself a figure in the news. Arnold is curious about how the safe was opened. Lee suggests the possibility that he may have left it open and unwatched very briefly the previous afternoon when he stepped into another room to answer a phone call. He has nothing else to add to what Arnold already knows.

At this point the reporter phones the city desk to report how the story shapes up and to see whether the office has any further information that would require outside checking

before he returns. Time is getting shorter now, and he is told to come in.

Back at his desk, Arnold knows there are still one or two angles to be explored. There is also one piece of routine that he senses he must still perform, but for the life of him he can't recall what it is. He phones the F.B.I. press officer, but, as he expected, learns nothing except that the investigators would like to question Feinguy. No, they cannot say where they are looking for him.

Next he searches through the phone book for the Ficketts. (What is that piece of routine he has overlooked?) Mrs. Fickett tells him what she knows about her roomer, Feinguy, which is not much. No, she doesn't know his home town or where he went on vacation.

Ah, yes, that piece of routine. Send to the newspaper morgue to see if there are any clippings on Feinguy. Not very hopeful, but you never can tell. While he is waiting, he organizes his notes. At last the copyboy hands him the slim folder from the morgue. It contains a single small clipping: A five-year-old dispatch from St. Louis relates that Julius Feinguy, 17, won a citywide essay contest. St. Louis? An angle, perhaps.

It is getting late, but Arnold now has a couple more phone calls to make. First he checks back to headquarters. Are the police looking for Feinguy in St. Louis? The police won't say. Arnold drags out a St. Louis phone book. There's a chance. Feinguy is an unusual name. He finds a number and puts through a call. Yes, this is Julius Feinguy's mother. No, Julius hasn't been there. No one else has phoned, but a detective did visit her to ask the same question. What is it all about? Thanks, Mrs. Feinguy.

Arnold decides to let his paper's resident correspondent approach the St. Louis police and puts in a call for him. Meanwhile, he has a story and probably an exclusive angle. It is time to begin writing. He checks with the city desk to inform the editors about the story and to get instructions about how much to write. He returns to his desk, feeds some paper into his typewriter (or accesses his computer terminal) and begins. He must hurry, he knows. The deadline is an hour and a half away. But it will take him perhaps an hour to write the story. And it has been drummed into him that every story that is to appear in the paper cannot go to the composition room at the deadline, because if that happened the paper would never be printed. So he writes as rapidly as he can, sending the story to the desk in short sections, or "takes." He pauses only to consult his notes and to take a call from the St. Louis correspondent. Out rolls the story, take after take.

What has happened up to this point is the exercise of the creative faculty of newspapering. The city desk and the reporter combine to bring the story into being. The reporter, now working at top speed, is almost completely preoccupied with his subject matter. Many fine points of writing, of presentation, even of accuracy may escape him. But he is backstopped. The critical faculty is now brought into play on the copy desk. His story is passed to a copy editor. Except for the news editor and his assistants, who oversee in a general way everything that goes into the newspaper but obviously cannot read closely all the thousands and thousands of words, the copy editor exercises final responsibility.

Let's call him Harold Aufseher. The diamond story is now in his hands. He has been told by the city desk how long the story is to be. As a practiced editor, Hal knows that Arnold probably will exceed his limit (most reporters understandably do that) and so he is on the alert to trim out the soft spots as he proceeds. In addition he will try to tighten the wording wherever he can to save precious space. When the reporter writes, "one of the employees," Hal will condense it to "an employee"; when the reporter writes that the police "rushed to the scene," Hal will strike out the phrase as an unnecessary and self-evident detail. In the second paragraph he discovers an involved fifty-word sentence; he breaks it into two short, clear sentences. When he reads that "the tray with its little bags and boxes of stones were missing from the safe," he almost automatically corrects the grammatical error. He sends the lead to the composing room and picks up the next take.

Here he finds that Arnold has inadvertently begun to refer to Gregory Lee as "Mr. Gregory." Rather than interrupt the reporter he checks in the phone book to make sure of the man's name. However, when he notes that there has been no elaboration of the statement in the lead about $100,000 worth of uncut diamonds, ranging up to nine carats in weight," he decides he will have to interrupt the reporter. "Who made the evaluation—the dealer, the police, the insurance company?" He returns to his desk and inserts the necessary information.

Next he deletes a quotation from Mr. Lee: "I always thought there was something a little shady about Feinguy." Libelous. He also deletes a quotation from Mrs. Fickett: "He was careless personally—fingernails always dirty and that sort of thing." Poor taste and irrelevant.

Smoothly and swiftly, his critical faculties always on the alert, Hal makes his way through the story. As he goes, he writes subheads in the copy—those little headings of boldface type that are inserted to break up long stretches of gray type. And as he goes, he is trying to resolve in his mind what the headline should say. When the story is finished, he tackles the head. His job here is to condense the main news of Arnold's 600-word story into half a dozen words.

Arnold has been writing under pressure; Hal has been editing under pressure. Each has a multitude of things to keep in mind. The story, as it presently appears in the paper, is as accurate as they can make it; it is a smooth, lucid job of narrative and exposition, and it may even have some literary quality. Both have worked hard, if hastily, to make it a finished piece of newswriting. For Hal, incidentally, it is only one of a dozen or more stories he has processed before deadline. He has had to switch his attention rapidly from robbery to rocketry, from budgets to bullets, from grand slams to great slums, from racket busters to filibusters. Is it extraordinary, then, that something has eluded him, that he has allowed a mistake to slip into print? It is perhaps not excusable, but it is at least understandable.

Newspaper Chain of Command

Owner
Sometimes the owner and publisher is one person.

Publisher
Publisher usually stays out of day-to-day production of the paper, but is responsible for all aspects of the paper.

Editor-In-Chief
Sometimes called executive editor or simply "The Editor." Responsible for only nonadvertising content.

Business Manager
Has a staff who takes care of:

Advertising	Classified
Circulation	Section
Delivery	Production
Pay Bills and	(Printing,
Collect Money	Typesetting)

Editor of Editorial Page
Takes care of editorials, letters to editor, political cartoons, and syndicated columns.

Managing Editor
Coordinates the news gathering of various department editors

Copy Editor
Checks language style, writing, headlines.

News Editor
Selects and edits national and world news.

Editors of Various Sections — Sports, Home, Food, etc.

City Editor
Responsible for local news. Some papers will have a state editor also.

Layout Editor
Makes it all fit.

Wire Service Editor

Stringers
Part-time reporters usually paid on the basis of stories published.

Local Reporters and Photographers
A reporter's story has to pass through the critical eyes of City Editor, News Editor, Copy Editor. Editors determine what is news, reporters are assigned to stories of the Editor's choosing. Some reporters regularly cover certain "beats"—city hall, the police, etc.

As you can tell from the chart, a newspaper has many editors. The people most associated in the public mind with a newspaper are the reporters, yet their job is at the bottom of the totem pole of the news process.

Each person along the line of the news process makes decisions about the news, and each decision is subject to possible veto by the boss. The owner of a paper is the most removed from the paper's daily operation, perhaps visiting the paper only occasionally. Yet the owner can influence the kind of news the paper prints by making the basic policies it follows.

MEDIALAB

The News-Publishing Process

1. In Bernstein's story, what is the main force that prevents the reporter from doing a thorough report on the crime?

2. Would your local newspaper rely on the police report of the gem theft or would it assign a reporter to dig up the facts? Support your answer.

3. What is the newspaper morgue?

4. What does *libelous* mean?

5. In the chapter on the news media and in the glossary, the word *gatekeeper* is explained. Who, in the newspaper chain of command, acts in any way as a gatekeeper?

6. Check the front of your local newspaper and find out who the publisher, the editor, and the managing editor are.

7. Looking at the newspaper chain of command, what could be some of the bad effects on the news if the business manager were the boss of the news editor?

WHAT NEWS IS PUBLISHED
[The Contents]

Unless you live in an area with a number of competing papers and have compared them carefully, you may not know whether your local paper does a good or a mediocre job of reporting the news. To make such a judgment, you must be able to compare it with other papers in cities the same size as yours, and you must be able to tell where the news comes from and have some idea of the bias of the paper and the values on which it makes news judgments. In order to make a news judgment on your local paper, or on any paper, it helps to know what is inside the paper and where it comes from. Let's take a close look at the contents of a newspaper.

Masthead

Edition

Lead Story

Deck

The "masthead" gives the name of the paper and other details, such as the date and number of pages. Often the name of the paper will be printed in an old-style type simply because that style used to be the darkest kind available; often it has become a kind of trademark for the paper. Many papers have redesigned their front pages to look more modern.

The edition of the paper is usually listed in the upper right-hand corner. Editions are called three star final, suburban, market final, and so forth. Large papers publish a number of editions during the day, each basically the same but with more recent news and details than the preceding edition. Smaller papers publish only one edition a day.

The edition's most important story, or lead story, is the one with the largest headline. It usually starts in the upper right-hand part of the front page.

Newspaper headlines are traditionally written in the present tense, even if the story happened in the past.

Since newspapers are folded in half for sale on newsstands and in boxes on the street, the top half of the front page is often designed with the most attractive, dramatic, or saleable parts on it.

Headlines in newspapers are written to fill a certain amount of space. (In magazines a headline or title is written first, and then editors decide how much space to give it.) Newspapers are partly responsible for nicknames being applied to public figures such as the president. Since space is so limited, a newspaper headline will often use shortened forms like Ike (for former President Eisenhower), JFK, or LBJ. Any president with a long last name will be renamed to fit the headlines.

A second and smaller headline (usually one column wide) below the story's main headline is called a deck.

1439 Year — No. 314 © Chicago Tribune   7 Sections   ★

East Germans open Berlin Wall

Citizens on both sides dance atop barrier

The Berlin Wall: 1961-89

1961: An East German border guard, seeking to join his family in the West, leaps to freedom not long after the Berlin Wall went up with the blessing of then-Soviet leader Nikita Khrushchev.

1971: On the wall's 10th anniversary, tourists in West Berlin photograph crosses erected to remember those killed trying to escape; officials estimate 191 people have died trying to get out.

'Long-awaited day has arrived'

By Ray Moseley
Chicago Tribune

BERLIN—East Germany on Thursday night opened both the Berlin Wall, the most dramatic and bitter symbol of the Cold War, and its border with West Germany to all of its citizens for the first time in 28 years. Thousands began streaming across to a delirious welcome in the West.

West Berliners, drinking champagne and cheering wildly, greeted the first East Germans to cross at Checkpoint Charlie and other crossing points through the 103-mile-long wall that was built across and around the city in 1961.

They hosted East Germans, including smiling communist border guards, to their shoulders and cheered them repeatedly. They hugged and kissed. They danced on the wall and used hammers and chisels to break chunks of concrete from it as souvenirs.

At Checkpoint Charlie, a crossing normally reserved for foreigners, East German police made no attempt to keep their own people from using it. The West Germans sent special shuttle buses to the other side to collect jubilant East Germans for a trip to Kurfürstendamm, the glittering street of shops in the heart of West Berlin.

"Can you believe this is happening?" exclaimed Angela Ebertus, an East Berlin clerk, as she and her husband strolled through Checkpoint Charlie early Friday morning. "No," he replied. "No, this must be a dream."

The emotional scenes at the checkpoint, where more than 2,000 West Berliners gathered, were repeated at all 12 crossing points in Berlin. Early Friday huge traffic jams developed in the center of West Berlin as the curious flocked to the wall.

Some East Berliners were reported to have climbed over the wall, unhindered by border guards, at the Brandenburg Gate, the heart of Berlin as it existed before 1945. There were similar reports of a human flood through checkpoints all along the East-West German border.

"The long-awaited day has arrived," West Berlin Mayor Walter Momper exulted. "The Berlin Wall no longer divides Berliners."

In Washington, despite almost universal surprise, the Bush administration didn't want to give anyone the impression it was gloating.

"We are handling it in a way where we're not trying to give anybody a hard time," President Bush said as he leaned back in his chair, twirling a pencil in his hand.

Bush soberly described the liberalized emigration policy as "a great victory" for democracy but also said he doubted "any single

See Germans, pg. 14

Young East Germans climb atop the once-feared Berlin Wall near the Brandenburg Gate early Friday as they celebrate the government's announcement opening the borders to the West.
Reuters photo

Wire, concrete symbolized era

By Charles M. Madigan

There is no modern piece of symbolism, no barbed-wire border, no prison cell that carries more powerful meaning than the 103-mile wall that surrounds West Berlin, separating a small island of democracy from the stormy sea of communism around it.

It is 13 to 15 feet high, made of concrete and topped in some places by razor wire. It has self-firing guns and booby traps, guard towers and spotlights powerful enough to illuminate every inch of the no man's land it circumscribes.

At the height of the Cold War, it was the place that produced powerful images of what communism was actually like, from dramatic photos of border guards hurdling barbed wire to cold, black-and-white news pictures of victims sacrificed in a desperate run toward freedom.

Since its construction in 1961, the wall has served as the final barricade for as many as 191 people who died trying to escape, according to estimates from West German human rights groups.

Its existence was proof that, given the chance to leave, few people would opt for life in a communist world. Getting out was worth risking everything, even life itself

West German Chancellor Helmut Kohl says Berlin situation may cut short his visit to Poland. Page 16.

- Fears dampen hopes of a reunited Germany Page 14.

That free passage would be offered through the wall was inconceivable—until Thursday.

For the people on the inside in West Berlin, the wall serves as a concrete canvas for colorful graffiti acclaiming democracy and freedom, and a constant sign that their city is a Western anachronism trapped deep in communist East Germany.

For the East Germans on the outside, it is an ever-present reminder that when a war ends, the spoils collected by the victors often include the souls of the defeated. More than anything else, geography and timing that placed them behind Soviet lines determined the course of their lives.

Although updated and reinforced many times, the Berlin Wall is the product of another era, when the superpowers were testing their strengths on a playing field still raw from the carnage of World War II.

President John F. Kennedy and Soviet Premier Nikita Khrushchev were in a bitter contest of wills in the summer of 1961.

Kennedy was frustrated by the failure of the Bay of Pigs invasion in Cuba and felt Khrushchev had upstaged him during meetings in Vienna in June. He left those sessions full of apprehension about the Russians, who were insisting on their right to back "wars of liberation."

Khrushchev was deeply concerned about West Germany's growing military and economic power and its alliances with Western Europe. The ailing East German

See Wall, pg. 14

Indiana to toughen waste rules

By Casey Bukro

Fearing that Indiana is becoming a national dumping ground for solid waste, Gov. Evan Bayh on Thursday ordered a crackdown on rail and truck shipments carrying garbage from out of state.

Bayh issued an executive order that overhauls Indiana's waste management program by April, 1991—focusing on the growing tide of waste exported by Northeastern states to the Midwest.

"In recent months, the national solid waste crisis has brought new and more serious threats to the well-being of the people of Indiana," Bayh said. "I have directed that our enforcement agencies make sure that every train car and tractor-trailer loaded with trash in Indiana

Indiana Gov. Evan Bayh discusses solid waste Thursday.
AP Laserphoto

by the Indiana Department of Environmental Management, the state police and the state board of health to curb public health and safety risks from garbage shipments.

Indiana officials have been jolted in recent weeks by reminders that their state is a target for out-of-state trash. Trucks carrying food to the East Coast return west carrying garbage, po-

New York to pay for Wall St. woes

By Pat Widder
Chicago Tribune

NEW YORK—When all the bloodletting is done on Wall Street this year, almost 50,000 fewer people will be gainfully employed in the securities industry than there were at the peak of the roaring '80s bull market.

The layoffs these days, two years after the Oct. 19, 1987, crash, are taking on the attributes of Chinese water torture.

They just keep coming, a little here, a little there, prompted by the Street's continuing efforts to cut costs in an industry that has never recovered from the crash.

This week, Shearson Lehman Hutton Inc. and Drexel Burnham Lambert Inc. confirmed they were letting more people go. Observers predict there will be other cuts in the coming weeks and months.

On Thursday, Chemical Banking Corp. signed an option

to move at least 3,000 employees to New Jersey. The bank, citing the high cost of New York real estate, said it will keep only a small "flagship" headquarters in Manhattan.

New York is expected to bear the brunt of the cuts, though the extensive networks of branch offices maintained by big firms have not been exempt. (Illinois, for example, is the headquarters of only about 30 securities firms,

See Wall Street, pg. 2

Slate more women, Democrats told

By Thomas Hardy
Political writer

Democratic women turned up the heat on state party leaders Thursday, as comptroller candidate Dawn Clark Netsch and treasurer candidate Peg McDonnell Breslin appeared with 50 members of a Breslin campaign committee to demand endorse-

up more than 55 percent of the [Democratic] vote and that Democrats cannot expect to win next November without having more than just one woman on the ticket," Breslin said at a joint news conference.

Neither Breslin nor Netsch has the same assurances of virtually uncontested nomination that any secured by several male

Central Committee will formally endorse a slate when it meets Nov. 27, raising the possibility of both women having to slug it out with other candidates in open primary contests.

Unrequited loyalty by the party to such a major constituency, the Democratic women predicted, would have the same impact as if blacks were not represented.

Photographs are often referred to in the newspaper business as "cuts," from the days when illustrations were make from woodcuts. The description or explanation given with a newspaper photo is called a cutline. In the magazine or book business it is called a caption.

Newspaper Advertising

There are only two kinds of space in a newspaper—advertising and the news hole.

Few people would answer the question, "Why do you watch television or listen to the radio?" with the reply, "For the advertising." But many people do buy and read newspapers because of the advertising. In newspaper advertising the potential consumer is told exact prices and places to shop. Newspapers carry ads for neighborhood stores and tell what is on sale tomorrow. Magazine and television commercials are more concerned with motivation and persuasion; newspaper advertising gives information. The classified section contains almost pure information, with little of the psychological techniques of the kinds of ads discussed in the advertising chapter. Newspaper advertising is most often cited by people as being useful and reliable.

Not only is advertising a service to the public, but it is also the way the paper makes a profit. The subscription or delivery price of a newspaper helps to pay expenses but is not sufficient to make an attractive profit. A full page of advertising space costs from a few hundred to many thousands of dollars, depending on the circulation. Space is sold by pages, half pages, column inches or, as in the classified section, by the column line. Sixty percent of the average paper is advertising; this helps account for the fact that newspapers as a business enterprise are among the most profitable in the nation.

In this chapter we will consider over a dozen different kinds of news items that are printed in a paper. From the viewpoint of the publisher and editor, however, there are only two kinds of space—advertising space and the "news hole." The news hole is the amount of space left to fill once all the advertising is accounted for. Still, not everything that goes into the news hole is news.

Why do you buy the newspaper?

Associated Press sportswriter at work in his New York office. He simultaneously receives information from a teletype machine (on his left), types the story on his computer terminal, and verifies last-minute facts by telephone.

Wire Service Material

The news hole in the average paper is 40 percent of its total number of pages. About 37 percent of that space is filled by wire service material. Such material is clearly marked as a press release.

Sometimes the wire service report is rewritten, sometimes it is published as it is received.

Storms renew fury on West Coast
Associated Press

Pacific storms, which have been pounding the West Coast with wind, rain and snow for nearly a week, struck with renewed fury Tuesday, touching off more floods, mudslides and power failures. A tornado caused heavy damage to an air terminal in central California.

The tornado raked the Fresno, Calif., Air Terminal, shattering plateglass windows and ruining sections of a roof on a hotel-restaurant. Cars were overturned and utility poles snapped in half, but authorities reported no injuries.

THE TWISTER. spawned by a string of valley thunderstorms, left a layer of hail three to five inches deep on fields around the air terminal. After spinning away from the facility, it touched down two more times near the neighboring community of Clovis.

Thunderstorm after thunderstorm hit California after midnight. Winds hit 50 knots. Commuter traffic was snarled with freeways and streets covered with water up to five feet in depth. Mudslides closed many arteries. Power was knocked out at the San Jose, Calif., Police Dept., causing communications problems for headquarters.

Traffic officers said many cars became stalled in water during the morning rush hour, putting a heavy strain on tow trucks.

More rain pounds California

Los Angeles (UPI)—Heavy rains pounded the Southern California coast Wednesday with a winddriven intensity which guaranteed new flooding and destruction in a region saturated by week-long storms, which have killed 22 people and have wrecked scores of homes.

The new storm, powered by 40 mph winds, was the latest in a series of savage Pacific onslaughts blamed for millions of dollars in property losses—mostly from uncontrollable mudslides.

Compostion of a Typical Daily Newspaper

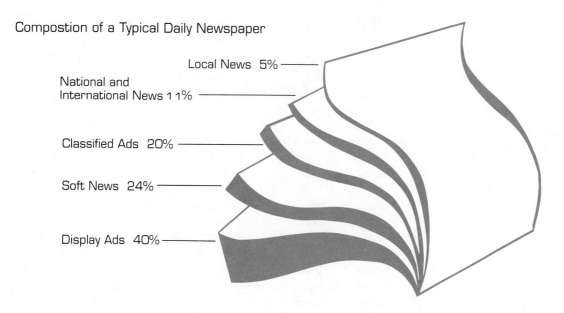

Local News 5%

National and
International News 11%

Classified Ads 20%

Soft News 24%

Display Ads 40%

Syndicated Material

Syndicates are another source of material for newspapers. Feature syndicates supply comic strips, cartoons, columns on topics from cooking to politics, and longer feature stories. Syndicates do not supply "hard" news. The material arrives by mail at the newspaper ready for printing or typesetting. Papers pay for what they use on the basis of circulation—the larger the paper's readership (circulation), the higher the fee for using the item. Some of the larger syndicates include King Features, Universal Press Syndicate, Religious News Service, and United Feature Syndicate. Some syndicated material is marked with the name of the syndicate for copyright purposes. About 10 percent of the entire average paper (about one-fourth of the news hole) is taken up with syndicated material.

Most newspapers feature one or more syndicated columnists. A good paper will serve its readers a varied diet of columnists with different viewpoints. Since columnists can write about whatever they please, they are usually very opinionated and biased. It is their purpose to argue strongly for their viewpoint rather than to present straight news reporting. Many columns are political, but others are about religion, bird watching, gossip, or almost any conceivable subject.

A newspaper editor can select only very conservative or very liberal columnists or only those he or she personally agrees with. But such a limited selection does not serve the needs of the readers. One way to evaluate the slant or bias of any paper is to study the viewpoints of its regular columnists and other syndicated material.

The *New York Times* throws away 168 bushels of wastepaper everyday. Much of it is press releases.

Sections and Departments

Almost every daily paper has a sports section and many have either pages or separate sections for society news, food, family features, arts and entertainment (movies, theater, music), books, business and finance, real estate, and travel.

On larger papers each of these sections might have a full-time editor and staff. Such sections can provide readers with news, valuable how-to information, consumer advice, and features. In cities with competitive papers, these sections have a great influence on which paper people will buy.

Unfortunately, there is a tendency to allow these sections to become little more than disguised advertising. A real estate section, instead of giving news about real estate trends in the city, will be filled with articles written by realtors advising people to buy a house now or by developers extolling the beauties of their latest suburban housing tract. A good section or department can provide, for instance, economical and creative recipes, shopping advice, articles on how to select quality meat, advice on which foods are good buys and which are not. A good section could report on sanitation conditions at local food stores and restaurants and even give comparative prices. On the other hand, a food section can print recipes supplied by advertisers (using brands advertised a few pages later) or ads disguised as articles from product promotion groups.

The temptation for the paper is to keep the advertisers contented. An article in a real estate section about the shoddy building at a local housing project is hardly likely to make that builder spend money to advertise in the paper. An article warning consumers that a certain supermarket has a confusing labeling system for meats might be uncomfortable for the supermarket—which spends thousands of dollars a year for newspaper advertising.

Filling special sections and departments with press releases is tempting because they are free and already written, and they pour into the newspaper office by the thousands. The *New York Times* throws away 168 bushels of wastepaper every day, according to one of its associate editors. Much of the wastepaper is press releases.

People everywhere confuse what they read in newspapers with news.

—A. J. LIEBLING,
media critic and writer

The Editorial Page

One section of the newspaper where editors can exercise some influence on the city is the editorial page. It is on this page that the paper (that is its editors or owners) can speak its mind. On page one the newspaper has the obligation to present the facts, but on the editorial page it can indulge in argument and opinion. On this page it also often prints letters from readers. The editorial page should offer a variety of opinions and a fair sampling of the letters sent to the editor.

Press Releases

Every large corporation as well as government agencies, large institutions (such as universities), and other groups have a public relations (PR) department, whose aim is to tell the community—or the world at large—about the good things the organization does and to create a favorable public image.

One of the jobs of the PR or media relations department is to send press releases to newspapers, radio, and TV stations. The press release is usually written so that it can be reprinted almost word for word in a newspaper or magazine. Such press releases, or slightly rewritten versions of them, form the basis for many items in newspapers. The news item on the right is an example of a story based on a press release.

The problem with press releases is that they are a form of managed news. They are usually truthful, but most often the truths are carefully selected to give a favorable impression of the company, government agency, or other organization responsible for the release.

An average large-city newspaper receives about one hundred press releases daily. They are either thrown out, rewritten and used, used as is, or used as a lead for a reporter to investigate and supply more objective details.

Below is an example of a press release and the resulting article:

New Shopping Center to be Constructed on Northwest Side

J. D. Bosch, Inc., today announced plans for a new three-million dollar shopping center to be constructed on the city's northwest side near Newburg Park. It is scheduled to open for business next April with nearly 85 stores.

The new complex will be designed by R. G. O'Brian and Company and built by the Atlas Construction Company of Rochelle. Mr. Gerald Bosch, chairman of the board of J. D. Bosch, Inc., proclaimed the new shopping center a welcome addition to the northwest side community. He said the new center will enable area residents to shop without the long trip downtown and will provide about 900 parking spaces.

Bosch promised that the new center will be the most modern shopping facility in the entire area.

Release Date: Immediate

Contact: Les Bears

Grover Mitchell

MOBILE HOMES TO BE ANCHORED

AUSTIN, (TX), July 6—Texas Mobile Home Owners will soon have the responsibility and expense of properly blocking and anchoring their homes as a result of an act recently signed into law by Texas Governor Dolph Briscoe, according to E. L. Murray of Corpus Christi who is Chairman of the Board of Directors for the Texas Mobile Home Association.

The law becomes effective 180 days following the effective date of the minimum standards which are to be established by the Texas Performance Certification Board, the policy-making body for the Mobile Homes Division of the Texas Department of Labor and Standards. Only mobile homes purchased after this effective date will be required to be blocked and anchored in accordance with this law. Exempted are mobile homes located more than 300 feet from any other occupied or inhabited building or structure.

Actually, two sets of standards will be in effect: Mobile home dwellers within the first two tiers of coastal counties in Texas will be required to block and anchor their homes to withstand hurricane force winds.

(more)

AUSTIN, Texas—Mobile home owners will soon have the responsibility and expense of properly blocking and anchoring their homes as a result of an act recently signed into law by Texas Governor Dolph Briscoe, according to E. L. Murray of Corpus Christi, chairman of the board of directors for the Texas Mobile Home Association.

The law becomes effective 180 days following the effective date of the minimum standards which are to be established by the Texas Performance Certification Board, the policy-making body for the Mobile Homes Division of the Texas Department of Labor and Standards. Only mobile homes purchased after this effective date will be required to be blocked and anchored in accordance with this law. Exempted are mobile homes located more than 300 feet from any other occupied or inhabited building.

THE HOUSTON POST
Columbia Journalism Review

MEDIALAB

Looking at Your Local Newspaper

1. Find out how much your local newspaper or papers charge for advertising space. This information can be obtained from the newspaper or the library.

2. What percentage of your local paper(s) is advertising? The national average is 60 percent—compare your paper(s) to this average.

3. Which local advertisers pay the newspaper the most money for advertising? Your answer will probably have to be an educated guess based on an examination of as many editions as possible. In some cities, a few large stores contribute half or more of a newspaper's advertising revenue.

4. What percentage of your local paper's average edition is the news hole? To measure it, subtract the answer to Item 2 above from 100 percent. (The average paper comes in with 40 percent news.)

5. Which wire service does your local paper(s) use the most? What percentage of its news hole is filled by wire service material? How does this compare with the national average?

6. Find examples in your paper of syndicated material other than comics or cartoons.

7. Which syndicated columns are available in your local newspapers? What is the subject matter and viewpoint of each?

8. Does each local newspaper offer a variety of syndicated columnists or do they favor those with a particular political viewpoint? Support your answer with specific examples.

9. Work alone or in small groups to evaluate various sections and departments of local papers—sports, finance, real estate. Report the findings to the class. Be sure to determine whether much of the material in the sections is puffery—press release material praising certain products or companies.

10. Does your local paper have an editorial page? If so, does it express a consistent viewpoint? Does the editor tackle important local and national issues?

11. Does your local paper print letters to the editor? If so, do they represent a fair cross section of opinion or are they limited to those who agree with the editor?

12. Find one or two examples in your paper of what seems to be a press release. Discuss the pros and cons of printing press releases. Does your school send out press releases?

13. Using the sample newspaper page found on page 218, identify the following parts:

a) lead story   d) edition title
b) headlines   e) decks
c) masthead   f) cutlines

WHAT FILLS THE NEWS HOLE?

Local News

Each newspaper needs its own reporters, especially to handle local events that the national news services will not cover. Reporters are either part of a general reporters, pool assigned to stories as they break, or are given regular beats, such as city hall, the police, or the state legislature. A small paper, of course, will have only a few reporters to cover everything.

Reporters write their own stories, which are then subject to rewrite by various editors. For a last-minute important story, a reporter may phone the information directly to the paper, where a rewrite editor takes it down and hurries it into an acceptable form for the paper.

A reporter covering a story never knows whether the event will be considered newsworthy enough to make the paper or how much space it will be given. For this reason, news reporters often write in what is called the "inverted pyramid style." They arrange the news item so that the essential details are all in the opening paragraph. Each paragraph thereafter is more general and less important. A good reporter writing in the pyramid style will answer the questions *who, what, where, when, how,* and *why* in the first paragraph. With this done, the news editor can fit the story into any available amount of space. A reporter might write 1,000 words on a story and have only 100 used in the paper. You can see the difference between the pyramid style and other writing styles by reading a front-page newspaper story and stopping after any paragraph—the story still seems complete. If you try this with a magazine article, the item will not seem complete and will very likely lack some essential information.

A by-lined story carries the reporter's name. Most reporters are unknown to the general public and receive few by-lines. The reporter's job is sometimes exciting but involves many long hours of boring meetings, writing and rewriting, and simply waiting.

Newsmakers

One common reporting assignment is to cover a speech, airport arrival, dedication, or whatever by a famous person—a newsmaker. This is more common in large cities than in small towns where few newsmakers appear.

Newsmakers are people who make news when they talk, marry, divorce, date, write, or do almost anything. They are celebrities—media heroes, people in the public eye. What they do may not be terribly important or newsworthy, yet it somehow ranks as news. Some newsmakers, such as the President, do things that are really news. They can also make news by doing ordinary things, such as walking the dog, talking to people on a street corner, or playing golf. As discussed in Chapter 1, pseudo events can be staged to generate news coverage of celebrities or aspiring newsmakers.

Crime and Disaster

In 1976, 76 percent of adults polled said they read a daily newspaper the day before. In 1988, that figure dropped to about 60 percent.

Another common kind of local reporting covers the disaster or crime story. The story of a deadly accident, a fire, or a crime is the staple of the newspaper. Why these tragedies are so important as news is hard to understand, but they remain important to newspapers because people like to read them. The same subjects—crimes, fires, disasters—are important in novels, movies, and television programs as well as in news reporting.

Some sociologists claim that people like to read about the tragedies of other people to gain assurance that their own lives aren't so bad after all—things could be worse. Others guess that people like to read about crime and tragedy because they are exciting, something to break the ordinary and sometimes dull routine of daily life.

Investigative Reporting

There are many newspapers whose pages rarely see an investigative news report. Even the best papers can manage only a few a year. An investigative report is one that looks deeply into some situation and reveals facts not previously known. Often investigative reports reveal corruption in government or business. A newspaper might investigate the local ambulance services, for example, to look for corrupt practices, kickbacks, hidden charges, and the like. Or it can check on city workers to see if the taxpayers are receiving a full day's work for a day's pay from those employees paid by tax money. A paper can investigate short-weighting and other dishonest practices in grocery stores; unsanitary conditions at restaurants and fast-food chains; housing conditions among the poor of the city; or political influences in the city school system. Such reporting takes time, money, and courage.

Muckraking—an ugly word for investigative reporting.

Investigative reporting in the early 1900s eventually resulted in the passage of the Pure Food and Drug Act when reformers and writers like Upton Sinclair described unsanitary packing houses and meats filled with waste and dirt. Ida Tarbell's investigative reporting on the Standard Oil Company led to its breakup into a group of smaller companies. Such reporting was once called muckraking and is still called that by some newspeople today.

Investigative reporting takes a great deal of time to do well and, unfortunately, many papers consider it a luxury. It is true that investigative reporting sometimes leads to lawsuits, political pressure, threats, and loss of advertising revenues.

Human Interest Stories

A newspaper that reported only the facts, only the world's most important events, only the actions and ploys of world leaders and criminals, might soon find itself without the large number of readers it needs to stay in business.

Most newspapers include what are called human interest stories. Sometimes these are local stories written by staff reporters; other times they are provided by the wire services. Human interest stories are about non-newsmakers, about the troubles or heroics of the ordinary person. Whether tragic or humorous, they are often moving and dramatic.

MEDIALAB

Analyzing What Makes News

1. Look at the front page of any newspaper and notice how often the inverted pyramid style of writing is used. Take one of the following events (make up your own details) and write a four-paragraph news report about it:

   A fire at the school

   Your teacher has won one million dollars in a state lottery

   A student at school has broken the world record for sleeping without waking

The first (lead) paragraph should contain the who, what, where, when, how, and why of the event. Each following paragraph should be more general and contain less-important information. The story must be complete whether the editor decides to use one, two, three, or all four paragraphs in the newspaper.

2. Check to see how often your local paper uses reporters' by-lines—never, sometimes, or usually. What kinds of stories are usually by-lined?

3. Find a story in the paper either on the local or national level that involves a newsmaker or celebrity other than a politician. Find an example of pseudo events. Discuss the value of such news in the paper.

4. A fairly large percentage of news that makes up the main section of a newspaper is crime: murders, robberies, arson, riots. What do you think is the effect on readers of the news decision that crime is front page news? Do you think crime should be so important? What kinds of crimes are rarely reported?

5. Why do you think people read stories like the following about a murder victim? Do they enjoy it? How do they feel after reading it? One way of looking at this kind of news story is that it is included as a sort of violent form of entertainment. Certainly no paper would be justified in keeping such a story secret. Do you approve or disapprove of the way the details of the murder and the finding of the body are presented? Are they necessary? What purpose do they serve? How else could the story have been written?

Murder Victim Found in Garbage Can

The body of an unidentified 28-year-old woman was found last night, stuffed in an alley garbage can on the 1300 block of West Front Street on the city's east side.

The partially clad body was discovered by James Hanson, a resident of the block, after he had parked his car in a nearby garage. "I saw a leg sticking out of the garbage can," Hanson told police, "and looked in and saw the body. I rushed home and called the police."

The victim had been stabbed repeatedly and had a cord tied around her neck, according to police. The body has not yet been identified, and police have no suspects in custody.

6. Where does most of the information about crimes come from? How does the source influence the story?

7. If you live in a large metropolitan area, your newspaper probably does not report all crimes. Certainly it does not give the same amount of space to each crime. What do you think determines how much space is given to a local crime story?

8. A human interest story is featured on this page: "Steve's a stand-up type." Speculate why the story was interesting enough to warrant AP (Associated Press) attention and, subsequently, was picked up by many newspapers. Rewrite the story so that it is an editorial about the homeless. You do not have to use all the details in the story, but do use the item as a basis for some kind of expression of opinion.

9. Judging from other human interest stories you have read in your local newspaper, what qualities does an editor look for in such an item?

Steve's a stand-up type

Philadelphia (AP)—Stephen Tolvish has the only residence on the block with a folding door.

He lives in a telephone booth in northeast Philadelphia.

"It's nice and it's warm and I keep it clean," said the former mailer for a printing firm.

Tolvish, who is 54 and mostly unemployed and has never been married, said he has been living in the telephone booth "off and on for a year."

He stores his suitcase and clothes atop the booth. Tolvish does odd jobs for people in the neighborhood, and the "boys on the corner" take him home sometimes so he can get a bath.

He dines out, when he has the money. He sleeps standing up for obvious reasons, and getting a good night's sleep is often difficult.

"When people want to use the phone," Tolvish said, "they knock on the door. I wake up and get out."

10. Find out what kind of investigative reporting, if any, your local newspaper(s) have done recently.

Opinion vs. Objectivity
THE DILEMMA

To be objective means to eliminate personal opinion and prejudice from reporting. Some say that a completely objective story is not humanly possible; individuals can only express their viewpoints. They feel that if each reporter expresses personal opinion as well as possible and that if people read these various viewpoints, readers will then be able to reach their own decisions. Others say that this gives the reporter too much power; only the facts should be presented and opinions left up to the reader.

Newspeople themselves are undecided about the problem of objectivity. David Brinkley, well-known NBC-TV newscaster and commentator, said this: "A person presumably is expected to go on the air and to have no likes, no dislikes, no feelings, no views, no values, no standards—to be a machine. If I were objective, I would have to be put away somewhere in an institution, because I'd be some sort of vegetable. I make no pretense of being objective. Objectivity is impossible to a normal human being. Fairness, however, is attainable, and that's what we strive for."

A. M. Rosenthal, who was managing editor of the most powerful and well known newspaper in the United States, the *New York Times,* has said that objectivity is ". . . the determination to write and edit with the elimination of as much personal bias as humanly possible, to present facts and situations as close to reality as possible, to avoid our own pejorative phrases or comments, to give accused people or institutions the right of immediate reply, to present all shadings of opinion and counter argument, and most of all, to keep examining ourselves day by day and story by story to see if we are being as objective as we can."

HEADLINES

Headlines serve a number of purposes. They are a convenient way for a newspaper reader with only a few minutes to learn what has happened in the world. Sometimes the headlines are written to entice readers to purchase a newsstand copy. When this practice of using headlines to sell papers is carried to an extreme, it is called sensationalism. A paper might report a murder with a huge headline reading, "Mad Murderer Rampages Through City." Few

The Lower case

Fish & Game To Hold Annual Elections

Berkshire Courier
Great Barrington,
Massachusetts

Between 9:00 and 5:00, the noise was audible even over the daily street din, though apparently not enough to rankle the day people, who could only have heard it during brief forays from their insulated office buildings. Just we full-timers rang our hands in despair, for at night the roar was all ours.

New Times

The breaking down of most prejudices and discriminations has lifted women from mental work to important management and top professional positions.

The Scranton Tribune

A favorite piece by Tchaikovsky is highlighted as Andre Kostelanetz conducts the National Symphony Orchestra IN PERFORMANCE AT WOLF TRAP Monday, Dec. 23 at 8:00 p.m. on PTV. IN PERFORMANCE AT WOLF TRAP is made possible by a grant from Atlantic Richfield Company.

Aroostook Republican, Caribou, Maine

No Permit Needed For Accidents

The Times Argus
(Barre-Montpelier, Vt.)

Two innings later, Jefferson was beaned in the back of the head by a line drive off the red-hot bat of Mariner all-star Bruce Bochte. Jefferson was not injured on the play; the baseball, which ricocheted all the way to right field, was taken to hospital for X-rays.

Toronto Globe and Mail

CIA Reportedly Sought to Destroy Domestic Flies

San Francisco Chronicle

Only a third of state's voters went to polls on Nov. 5

One-third of the registered voters in Massachusetts stayed home Nov. 5, nearly a record for absence at polls.

The Boston Globe

Stolen Painting Found by Tree

The (Philadelphia) Evening Bulletin

The license fee for altered dogs with a certificate will be $3 and for pets owned by senior citizens who are altered the fee will be $1.50.

Santa Barbara News-Press

Bland Music Contest Set For Feb. 23

Page News and Courier, Luray, Virginia

Tuna Biting Off Washington Coast

Seattle Post-Intelligencer

462C UNIPRESSERS:

TO ALL OF YOU AND YOUR FAMILIES, MAY THIS BE A MOST PLEASANT HOLIDAY
AND MAY THE NEW YEAR BE BRIGHT AND PROSPEROUS.

   UPI 12-25 02:09 PPS

   EDITORS: PLEASE DISREGARD 462C UNIPRESSERS. IT WAS INADVERTENTLY
TRANSMITTED ON THIS CIRCUIT.

   UPI 12-25 02:21 PPS

---

papers practice such outright dishonest sensationalism any more, mainly because it is poor journalism and because most readers have the paper delivered to their homes rather than purchasing a copy from the newsstand. A more responsible headline for the same story might read, "Man Found Murdered in Hotel."

Headlines summarize the news. Some newspapers employ one or more people whose only job is to write headlines. They must be accurate, must contain the most important facts of even complex stories, and must fit into a certain number of spaces.

A headline can be written so that it summarizes a story accurately and clearly, or it can be written to express a slant or bias—an opinion about the story.

For example, a gathering of a large number of people in Washington, D.C., for the purpose of encouraging Congress to pass legislation favoring a ban on nuclear weapons could receive either of the following headlines: "7,000 Gather to Urge Ban on Nuclear Weapons" or "Mob Invades Washington to Push Weapons Ban." The use of a loaded word like *mob* in the second headline would tend to influence readers against the gathering. The use of the word *urge* in the first headline could be taken as a word loaded in favor of the action. A more neutral headline would be "7,000 Demonstrate for Ban on Nuclear Weapons."

The two headlines below appeared in two Chicago newspapers, both referring to the same event. Both headlines are true; the man was both a veteran and a gang member. But the second calls the dead person by a negative term while the first uses a more favorable label. Each headline has a different effect on the reader.

Veteran Shot in School

Gang Member Shot By Police

Newspapers can be quite objective and present a wide variety of viewpoints or they can consistently give readers slanted or biased news. Newspapers are often labeled conservative or liberal, or are known as probusiness or prolabor, or have certain viewpoints they stress constantly. For example, a newspaper editor who favored gun control might use every story possible in which innocent people were killed because of the careless use of guns. A newspaper can present opinions in many ways:

Editorials or items clearly labeled opinion

Slanted headlines

Loaded words in stories

Careful selection of what to print and what to omit

Selection within each news item of details

Placement of the stories (placing an item on the front page says it is more important than if it appears in the back pages of the paper).

MEDIALAB

Critically Reading Your Newspaper

1. Examine your local newspaper or papers to see if you can find any particular bias. Usually you will need to study more than one issue to make the bias clear. Ask adults who have been reading a certain newspaper for many years if they have found any viewpoint or bias. Do they object to it, or is it one reason they read that paper? Do you think newspapers should try to be objective or should they allow their own opinions to show in their news coverage?

2. Rewrite some headlines in your local paper so they are biased. Then rewrite the same headlines with a different bias.

3. If you find any examples of biased or slanted headlines, bring them to class—start a bulletin board of them if enough are found.

4. The following news item and speaker is fictional, but it is based on an actual event. Read it and then answer the questions.

This news story not only presents news, namely the fact that Richard Owen spoke to students at the community college, but it also reveals the opinions of the newspaper or, at least, of the writer of the story.

Tax Dollars Used To Pay For Anti-American Talk

Richard Owen, who apparently has switched from music to militancy, delivered a lashing lecture Tuesday against almost everything. He spoke at Lakeland Community College.

Over 1,000 listeners, most of them young college students, crowded the lecture hall to hear Owen attack America as a "sick, degenerate country run by a bunch of insane fool maniacs."

Owen was paid $1,500 for his ninety-minute scolding. The money was taken from the college's public affairs budget. He was invited to speak by the Culture Committee of the college.

Owen attacked the ". . . rich get richer system of the United States," and then flew back by private jet to his comfortable Palm Beach home.

Find specific words, phrases, and selection of details that reveal the writer's opinion about Owen and the talk.

Rewrite the news item (you can make up additional details) to show how it might have been written by (a) someone who wrote a fair and objective news story without revealing his or her personal opinion; and (b) someone who agreed very much with Owen's opinions and expressed that agreement in the news item. Your rewrite should also include a new headline.

5. If there are competing local newspapers in your area, obtain copies of each for the same day. Examine them carefully and decide which gives the most news, which is the most objective, and which the most interesting. Which one would you subscribe to and why?

6. Newspapers today are a mix of the tragic and the humorous, the historical and the insignificant. An ax murder is placed next to the weather map, and both are followed by an ad for bananas and grapefruit. In a talk to newspaper editors, Robert Hutchins, a renowned educator, told them that newspapers "should do as well as they can the things they can do best, and should leave to others the responsibility of entertaining the public." Do you agree with Hutchins or do you find other factors at work that make it necessary for a newspaper both to entertain and to inform? Support your answer.

WRAP-UP

As one of the first mass media, newspapers have a long history. In this chapter, you have learned that the U.S. was the birthplace of the popular free press. You have focused on American newspapers and learned how common newspaper monopolies are today. Reading a first-hand report of how a local news story gets published, you have walked along with a reporter and moved through a newspaper's chain of command. Now that you've taken a look at the contents of newspapers—hard news, soft news, advertising—and learned how important syndicated material and press releases are to a newspaper, you can now fully understand how much goes into making your own local paper. Recognizing the inverted pyramid style of journalism, the purposes of headlines, and how a newspaper story can be biased will make you a more perceptive reader of this important mass medium.

VOGUE

Ms

WORKING
MOTHER

New Woman

ents
Job

Woman

HOW AND WHEN
TO TELL SOMEBODY
TO SHUT UP

AFTERPLAY:

STAYING TOGETHER
AFTER ONE OF
YOU HAS STRAYED

Personal
Computer
World

COMPUTE!
SpeedScript 3.0
Our Enhanced Word Processor

Computer
BUYER'S GUIDE AND HANDBOOK

POPULAR
COMPUTING

AT&T'S UNIX PC

ASTRONOMY
The First Colors on Mars

EMERGING MARKETS: THE SMART HOUSE

high Technology

SPECIAL REPORT
AUTOMATION U.S.A.

DISCOVER

SCIENCE
digest

YALE'S ROBERT STERNBERG
INTELLIGENCE
WHAT, WHY
AND HOW CAN YOU

F

THE

5

INDUS

I

POPULAR
COMMUNIC

Rodding

Radio
Electronics

MATT DI

16

SUPER

VID

Rio

FRANKIE GOES
TO HOLLYWOOD

ROC

SHALAM

We Ar

THE PHO

CHAPTER 8

Magazines

Today you can buy a magazine
about every imaginable interest.
Did you ever wonder how this
mass medium got started?

A SHORT HISTORY OF THE AMERICAN MAGAZINE

Benjamin Franklin is credited with starting the first American magazine, a monthly with the ponderous title of *The General Magazine and Historical Chronicle for all the British Plantations in America.* His first issue, in February 1741, made media history and gave many others the idea of publishing a magazine. Franklin's magazine and its early competitors were almost solid print and would be unlikely to receive a second glance from today's reader, who is accustomed to attractive magazines that depend heavily on the modern inventions of photography and four-color printing.

Within fifty years of Franklin's venture, there were almost one hundred magazines in the United States, including *The American Magazine* published by Noah Webster (better known today for his dictionary than his magazine). Webster, Franklin, and their colleagues were among the early magazine publishers in the United States. The *publisher* is the person who starts the magazine—the person (or group of people) with the idea and the money needed to make the magazine work. The publisher hires an *editor*, who finds articles for the magazine and has the general responsibility for the content of the magazine. The actual writing in the magazine is not usually done by the publisher or by the editor but by writers, both free-lancers who write for a number of publications and full-time staff writers, employees of the magazine.

In the mid-nineteenth century, magazines were read mainly by the educated elite. During this time magazines such as *Atlantic Monthly* and *Harper's* were started as intellectual journals. But even as early as 1840 there were signs of what we today would call mass-circulation magazines. One of the most popular, *Godey's Lady's Book*, edited by Sarah Hale, instructed women about manners, proper housekeeping, and fashion. Even during the Civil War, *Godey's Lady's Book* distributed 100,000 copies and was probably read by four times that many people. Included in its pages were stories and poetry by writers now found in today's textbooks of American literature—Edgar Allan Poe, Nathaniel Hawthorne, and Henry Wadsworth Longfellow.

Godey's Lady's Book instructed women about manners, proper housekeeping, and fashion.

Many new magazines were started around 1880, after Congress passed a bill granting magazines special mailing privileges. Magazines were given a kind of government subsidy because they were "published for the dissemination of information . . . or devoted to literature, the sciences, arts or some special industry." This mailing privilege still exists, in modified form. Five to ten magazines can be mailed at a special second-class rate for the cost of a single first-class letter.

The completion in 1869 of the first railroad line across the entire United States made the national magazine practical. Also, as education spread, more and more Americans were able to read, and the potential audience for magazines was greatly increased. In the 1880s and 1890s, *Ladies' Home Journal, Good Housekeeping, McCall's*, and *Cosmopolitan* began. The *Saturday Evening Post*, founded in 1821, became the most influential and powerful magazine in the nation after it was bought by Cyrus Curtis, who also published *Ladies' Home Journal*. Curtis made the *Post* a reflection of American life and presented in it a probusiness image, "America for Americans." The *Post* published writers such as P. G. Wodehouse, Sinclair Lewis, F. Scott Fitzgerald, William Faulkner, and Ring Lardner.

The *Saturday Evening Post* had no serious competition as the largest magazine until 1932, when a small black-and-white magazine was issued from a Greenwich Village basement. It was the *Reader's Digest*. The *Digest* promised an article for every day of the month and caught the public's fancy almost immediately. Today the *Digest*, founded by Lila and DeWitt Wallace, has the second largest circulation in the world with over 18 million readers in dozens of different languages.

In 1923 Henry Luce published the first issue of a weekly newsmagazine called *Time*. The magazine helped the news make sense; it provided clear summaries of the succession of confusing events called news. *Time* was a success and gave rise to later successful imitators, such as *Newsweek* and *U. S. News and World Report*. In 1936 Luce started *Life* magazine, which brought vivid pictures of World War II into the homes of Americans in that

HARPER'S NEW MONTHLY MAGAZINE.

No. CXXVII.—DECEMBER, 1860.—Vol. XXII.

[First Paper.]

A PEEP AT WASHOE. BY J. ROSS BROWNE

WHEN I inform the reader that I have scarcely dipped pen in ink for six years, save to unravel the mysteries of a Treasury voucher; that I have lived chiefly among Indians, disbursing agents, and officers of the customs; that I now sit writing in the attic of a German villa more than eight thousand miles from the scene of my adventures, without note or memorandum of any kind to refresh my memory, you will be prepared to make reasonable allowance for such a loose, rambling, and disjointed narrative as an Ex-Inspector-General can be expected to write under such adverse circumstances. If there be inconveniences in being

pretelevision era. *Look*, with a similar slant, began publication the next year, and both thrived on superb, vivid photography.

From the end of World War II until the late 1960s, magazines attempted to be a truly mass medium, appealing to everyone. But then well-known and successful general-circulation magazines, such as *Saturday Evening Post, Life,* and *Look*, shocked their readers by announcing they were going out of business. (Later, all three had revivals. *Life* and *Saturday Evening Post* have survived as monthlies with limited circulations.) In general, by the seventies magazines that attempted to appeal to everyone found it increasingly difficult to compete with television as a general entertainment medium. By the eighties, the great circulation race slackened to a slow walk. Instead of a few gigantic magazines reaching tens of millions, the current trend is toward the specialized magazine for a small but interested audience. Increases in the cost of paper, printing, and postage have made magazines too expensive for advertisers who want to reach most of the nation with their sales message.

MAGAZINES TODAY

At the beginning of 1989, the ten magazines with the largest paid circulation were:
Modern Maturity
Reader's Digest
TV Guide
National Geographic
Better Homes & Gardens
Family Circle
Woman's Day
Good Housekeeping
McCall's
Ladies' Home Journal

So many magazines are published in the United States that no one knows exactly how many exist. Every day at least one new publication is born and another dies. There are currently at least 12,000 different magazines published, ranging from *The Biscuit and Cracker Baker* and *Auto and Flat Glass Journal* to *People* and *Sports Illustrated*.

Most magazines are sold by subscription and/or through newsstands. Neither the subscription rate nor the newsstand price alone is sufficient to enable a magazine to survive and show a fair profit. Magazines make much more money from advertising than they do from what the readers pay for each copy. A few publications, usually intended for very specialized audiences, such as doctors or teachers, are actually given away. These controlled circulation magazines assure potential advertisers that their message will be delivered to a guaranteed number of doctors or history teachers in the country. At the other extreme are specialized magazines and newsletters that contain no advertising and are supported completely by subscription prices that run to more than $100 yearly.

The majority of magazines contain both advertising and editorial content, such as articles, columns, and cartoons. In this way, magazines resemble newspapers, television, and radio. All these media have some kind of content (shows, news, music) mixed with, and economically supported by, advertising.

The editorial content of magazines is created by their own full-time staff, by free-lance writers, or by both. Some publications written by a full-time staff are *Time*, *Newsweek*, and *Mad*.

However, a completely staff-written mass-circulation magazine is the exception. Most magazine articles are written by free-lance writers. Publications receive thousands of unsolicited manuscripts through the mail; their writers range from professional, often-published authors to students who submit school assignments that a teacher considers worthy of publication. The odds are always against the free-lancer who sends out unsolicited manuscripts. However, thousands of free-lance articles are published each year. (*Unsolicited* means that no one at the magazine asked for the article—it simply arrived in the mail. On many occasions a magazine will originate an article idea and solicit an author to write it. *Unagented* means that no literary agent was involved. Professional writers often use a literary agent—a per-

Tips to Writers from Writer's Market

SEVENTEEN, 850 3rd Ave., New York NY 10022. Editor-in-Chief: Midge Turk Richardson. Managing Editor: Mary Anne Baumgold, 80% freelance written. Works with a small number of new/unpublished writers each year. Monthly. Circ. 1.9 million. Buys one-time rights for nonfiction and fiction by adult writers and work by teenagers. Pays 25% kill fee. Pays on acceptance. Publishes ms an average of 6 months after acceptance. Byline given. Computer printout submissions acceptable; prefers letter-quality. Reports in 6 weeks.

Nonfiction: Roberta Anne Myers, articles editor. Articles and features of general interest to young women who are concerned with the development of their own lives and the problems of the world around them; strong emphasis on topicality and helpfulness. Send brief outline and query, including a typical lead paragraph, summing up basic idea of article. Also like to receive articles and features on speculation. Query with tearsheets or copies of published articles. Length: 1,200–2,000 words. Pays $50–150 for articles written by teenagers but more to established adult freelancers. Articles are commissioned after outlines are submitted and approved. Fees for commissioned articles generally range from $650–$1,500. Sometimes pays the expenses of writers on assignment.

Photos: Kay Spear Gibson, art director. Photos usually by assignment only.

Fiction: Adrian LeBlanc, fiction editor. Thoughtful, well-written stories on subject of interest to young women between the ages of 12 and 20. Avoid formula stories—"My sainted Granny," "My crush on Brad,"—heavy moralizing, condescension of any sort. Humorous stories and mysteries are welcomed. Best lengths are 1,000–3,000 words. Pays $500–$1,000.

Poetry: Contact teen features editor. By teenagers only. Pays $15. Submissions are nonreturnable unless accompanied by SASE.

Tips: "Writers have to ask themselves whether or not they feel they can find the right tone for a *Seventeen* article—a tone which is empathetic yet never patronizing; lively yet not superficial. Not all writers feel comfortable with, understand or like teenagers. If you don't like them, *Seventeen* is the wrong market for you. The best way for beginning teenage writers to crack the *Seventeen* lineup is for them to contribute suggestions and short pieces to the

son, usually located in New York—who knows the best markets for articles. Agents sell manuscripts to publishers and receive for their services an agreed-upon percentage [often 10%] of whatever the author is paid.)

Anyone can submit an article or an idea to any magazine and hope for publication. If the article or story is published, the writer will be paid anywhere from $20 to $2,000, depending on the circulation of the magazine and its payment policies.

Most writers who send in unsolicited articles receive a standard form letter called a rejection slip; sometimes an editor will send a letter with the rejection. Rejection by one magazine does not mean that the idea or manuscript is unpublishable. There are many other reasons for an editor's rejecting it. Many articles have been successfully published after having been rejected by dozens of magazines.

The odds are against the free-lancer who sends out unsolicited manuscripts.

New Voices and Views section, a literary format which lends itself to just about every kind of writing: profiles, essays, exposés, reportage, and book reviews."

STOCK CAR RACING MAGAZINE, Box 715, Ipswich MA 01938. Editor: Dick Berggren. 80% freelance written. Eager to work with new/unpublished writers. For stock car racing fans and competitors. Monthly magazine; 120 pages. Circ. 400,000. Pays on publication. Publishes ms an average of 3 months after acceptance. Buys all rights. Byline given. Query for electronic submissions. Computer printout submissions acceptable; prefers letter-quality. Reports in 6 weeks. Free writer's guidelines.

Nonfiction: General interest, historical/nostalgic, how-to, humor, interviews, new product, photo features and technical. "Uses nonfiction on stock car drivers, cars, and races. We are interested in the story behind the story in stock car racing. We want interesting profiles and colorful, nationally interesting features. We are looking for more technical articles, particularly in the area of street stocks and limited sportsman." Query with or without published clips, or submit complete ms. Buys 50-200 mss/year. Length: 100–6,000 words. Pays up to $450.

Photos: State availability of photos. Pays $20 for 8x10 b&w photos; up to $250 for 35mm or larger color transparencies. Captions required.

Fillers: Anecdotes and short humor. Buys 100 each year. Pays $35.

Tips: "We get more queries than stories. We just don't get as much material as we want to buy. We have more room for stories than ever before. We are an excellent market with 12 issues per year. Virtually all our features are submitted without assignment. An author knows much better what's going on in his backyard than we do. We ask that you write to us before beginning a story theme. If nobody is working on the theme you wish to pursue, we'd be glad to assign it to you if it fits our needs and you are the best person for the job. Judging of material is always a combination of a review of the story and its support illustration. Therefore, we ask for photography to accompany the manuscript on first submission."

PUBLISHING AN ARTICLE

How do you get that great story or article published?

If you have an idea for a story or an article for a magazine, how can you go about getting it published?

The first step is to decide which magazine is best for the idea. If you have an idea for an article about horseback riding, for instance, you certainly would not submit it to *Popular Mechanics*, any more than you would submit an idea about your custom car conversion to *Horsemen's Journal.*

The best way to select the proper magazine is to read that magazine frequently and become familiar with the kind of articles it publishes. Another helpful guide to finding the best magazine market for an article idea is a book called *Writer's Market*, revised yearly and available at most libraries. This book lists magazines and their addresses, and tells what kinds of articles the magazine needs and how much it will pay per word or per article.

Once the writer has picked a magazine, the typed manuscript can be sent along with a cover letter explaining that the article is being submitted for possible publication. (If the writer wants the article back, a self-addressed, stamped envelope should be enclosed.) Another approach is to send a "query" letter. A query letter explains the article idea, presents an outline, and perhaps includes a portion of the article. If the magazine responds positively, the writer completes the article and then submits it to the editor. Very often the editor will return the manuscript, suggesting minor or major changes before it is finally accepted for publication. Once accepted, the article will probably be published anywhere from one to eight months later.

After you have spent many hours writing your great magazine article, and weeks or months waiting for a reply, an answer like this might come back clipped to your manuscript:

_____ Magazine

Thank you for letting us read your manuscript. We regret that it does not meet our current needs.

Thank you for your interest in our publication.

The Editors

MEDIALAB

Magazine Publishing Today

1. Prepare a query letter to some magazine with which you are familiar and propose an article suitable for its audience. Select one or two alternatives that would also be suitable.

2. Either as part of this course or in connection with a creative writing course, send query letters and/or manuscripts for feature articles to magazines that specialize in publishing student writing. Develop a screening process to make sure that only the class's best efforts are sent out to magazines. High school students can have magazine articles published; many classes have been successful in this project.

3. Using either *Writer's Market* or another reference source, find the name and address of a magazine that interests you. The magazine should be one you have not read before, perhaps one that is not readily available in your town. Write for a sample copy, explaining that it is for a school project; be sure to send the amount listed as the single copy price. Keep the magazines in a classroom collection for the duration of this course so others can see the variety that is available.

4. Find out if any magazines are published in your area (use the local *Yellow Pages*). If so, find out what kind of magazines they are. If possible, invite someone from a magazine to talk to the class or arrange a tour of the editorial offices.

5. The *Readers' Guide to Periodical Literature* is a handy index to magazine articles published in hundreds of popular magazines. It is a valuable research tool but does not index even 20 percent of all the articles written each year. Many other periodical indexes exist to cover more specialized fields. There is an index for magazines in the arts and humanities, one for film magazines, and dozens of others. Find out which indexes are available at the largest public library in your area and examine them. For each one, describe the kind of magazine included and the kinds of articles indexed.

6. *Debate*: Magazines are more valuable and useful than newspapers or television.

Cover

Advertisement

MAGAZINES AND THE MARKETPLACE

Advertisers often choose magazines rather than other media because of the specific demographics that magazines can provide. "Demographics" is the measurement of the kinds of people who read the publication—their age, income, interests, and the like.

If, for example, you wanted to sell a kit to chrome-plate an automobile engine, the best place to advertise would probably be in a special-interest magazine. You could select from the many magazines read by people interested in cars—for example, *Hot Rod, Motor Trend,* or *Car and Driver.*

If you advertised on television or radio or even in a general magazine such as *Time* or *Reader's Digest,* your money would be spent to reach millions of people who wouldn't want to chrome-plate their engines even if you supplied the kit free. Magazines, by limiting their audiences to specialized interests, create the best possible market segments for advertisers.

Mass-circulation magazines used to engage in circulation wars to obtain as many readers as possible. The more readers a magazine had, the more it could charge for each advertising page. But magazines with millions of readers, such as *Look*, went out of business because, with their general appeal, they couldn't offer advertisers the specific kind of audience they wanted. On the other hand, magazines could not compete with television in the numbers game—the millions of viewers who might see one commercial. These magazines, then, did not stop publication for lack of readers or because of poor quality in the editorial content, but because of too little income from advertising. While mass-circulation magazines aimed at everybody have been going out of business or struggling to survive, specialized publications have prospered.

In order to fill as many pages as practical with advertising, magazines themselves advertise to the business community. Some of these ads give an idea of the aims of magazines that relate to both the editorial content and the advertising.

The purpose of a magazine is to deliver readers to advertisers; but those readers have to be potential buyers. The *Rolling Stone* advertisement in this section is part of the successful "Perception/Reality" promotional campaign, designed to convince potential advertisers that *Rolling Stone*, a magazine once associated with the anti-establishment voice of the sixties (exemplified by "hippies") now is number one with young, affluent people —potential customers who might even qualify for "yuppies."

Magazines survey readers to study their purchasing habits; this research is called demographics. For example, *Reader's Digest* knows that its male readers influence 49 percent of all salad dressing purchases. *Architectural Record* magazine knows its readers account for 90 percent of all money spent on architect-planned buildings.

In recent years, the city-specific magazine has regained popularity. Most of the nation's largest cities have a magazine bearing the city's name. The magazines deliver a unique audience of usually upscale readers for local advertisers.

The number and circulation of magazines are currently at an all-time high. One reason for the new-found success of magazines is that they can deliver an audience not well-reached by television. Magazines can "target" better educated, more affluent readers who prefer reading to watching television.

To further serve their demographic needs, large magazines use sophisticated computer modeling and printing plants to customize both editorial and advertising content. For example, each issue of *Time* is really over fifty different magazines. Some of the editorial and ad content appears in each edition, but other ads and articles are limited to editions targeted to specific geographical areas such as the Midwest or the West Coast edition—or to readers who fit carefully-defined demographic profiles, such as corporate executives.

Perception.

Source: by Fallon McElligott from <u>Rolling Stone</u> magazine.

Reality.

If your idea of a Rolling Stone reader looks like a holdout from the 60's, welcome to the 80's. Rolling Stone ranks number one in reaching concentrations of 18-34 readers with household incomes exceeding $25,000. When you buy Rolling Stone, you buy an audience that sets the trends and shapes the buying patterns for the most affluent consumers in America. That's the kind of reality you can take to the bank.

MEDIALAB

Magazine Marketing

1. Do you see any way in which advertisers might influence the content of magazines?

2. Find out which magazines are the most popular with members of the class. Why are these the most read? What kinds of ads do they contain?

3. What kinds of advertisers might now place ads in *Rolling Stone*, due to the new image of the readers projected by the "Perception/Reality" series?

4. Imagine you are a potential advertiser considering the various geographical and demographically-targeted editions of *Time* magazine. Given the following list of products to market, select editions of *Time* you would target for advertising the following: surfboards, computerized phone systems, hiking boots, medical equipment.

5. Have each person in the class select a different magazine and do a "profile" of it. To "profile" the magazine, find out the following information by using the reference guide *Writer's Market,* or the Standard Rate and Data Service *Consumer Magazine* volume 5, available at most public libraries.

Title.

Subscription and newsstand price.

Frequency of publication.

Does the magazine accept free-lance articles?

If so, what is the pay?

If so, what is the pay?

What kind of articles are published?

Who is the intended audience?

How much does a full page of advertising cost?

How many pages are there in a typical issue?

How many ad pages are there in a typical issue?

(Add up partial pages and include the cover ads in your count.)

What percentage of the total magazine is advertising?

What is the estimated yearly income of the magazine? (To estimate income, multiply the subscription price by the number of subscribers.

Add to this the estimated amount spent in the magazine by advertisers.)

What kinds of products are advertised most?

What is the publishing philosophy that governs the choice of articles?

What does an advertiser pay to reach one person when a single full-page ad is bought?

WRAP-UP

The mass medium of the magazine, like the newspaper, has a long history. Magazines started as intellectual journals, like *Harper's* and *Atlantic Monthly*. In the late 1800s mass circulation magazines, such as *Ladies' Home Journal* and *McCall's*, had their beginnings. You have discovered that, from the twenties into the 50s, the *Saturday Evening Post*, *Life*, and *Look*—with huge circulations—served the function television serves today and provided a visual record for millions of people of what was happening around the world. These magazines became household words. Many of today's magazines are more specialized. In this chapter, you have learned about the process of getting a magazine article published, and how businesses can effectively place ads in magazines targeted to specific audiences.

CHAPTER 9
Radio

What did people do before there was television? Ask someone over fifty—the answer is radio.

A HISTORY OF RADIO

November 2, 1920: Radio as a mass medium is born.

Beginnings

Radio was the first of the electronic mass media. It shaped our expectations of what a mass medium could deliver and paved the way for an incredibly fast acceptance of television by the 1950s.

Before 1920, most radio broadcasts were the property of either the Navy or amateur radio hobbyists. Then, on November 2, 1920, station KDKA in East Pittsburgh, Pennsylvania, broadcast the first nonexperimental public program. From a small transmitter housed in a shack atop a six-story building, KDKA told listeners the results of the national election that day, in which Warren Harding became the twenty-ninth president.

Only a few hundred people had the equipment needed to hear KDKA, but radio as a mass medium had been born. KDKA still exists today, serving Pittsburgh. And its owner then, Westinghouse Electric Company, is still very much in the radio business.

Within a year radio became a national craze. Some called the invention a "wireless telephone," others "radio telephone" or simply "wireless." People bought crude receivers by the tens of thousands. The earliest sets required headphones; only later did top of the line models include loudspeakers that would allow a whole family to hear the broadcast. Reception was poor, static ever present, and programs were few and infrequent. Nevertheless, two years after the first KDKA broadcast, there were 1 1/2 million radios in the United States and more than 500 broadcast stations.

Corporations and wealthy persons quickly obtained federal licenses to broadcast. Some of the earliest license holders included Ford Motor Company and Westinghouse. By the end of 1922, 70 newspapers as well as an equal number of universities owned radio stations.

Radio soundmen of the 1920s provided audio background realism with a pistol, a gong, and lip microphones.

Without mass media, sports would have remained primarily a local interest.

WOR Program Schedule May 29, 1922

10:30 A.M.—"Packing the Week-End Bag," by Vanity Fair

11:30 A.M.—"Smiles," by J.E.K.

12:30 P.M.—A period of song selections from the recordings of Alma Gluck and Homer Rodeheaver

1:30 P.M.—During this period the numbers requested by our radio audience will be played

2:30 P.M.—Richter String Quartet: Beethoven Quartet, op. 18, No. IV, first and second movements, and "Andante Cantabile."

3:30 P.M.—Carl Bannwart, Superintendent of Olivet Sunday School, ex-President of the Presbyterian Union, will speak on "The Man with a Handicap."

4:30 P.M.—Ruth Dale, soprano: "The Awakening," "The Morning-Glory Song," "There Are Fairies at the Bottom of the Garden."

5:30 P.M.—A talk to Boy Scouts

5:40 P.M.—A talk on timely vegetable garden topics, by Charles H. Nissley, Extension Specialist in Vegetable Gardening from the Agricultural and Extension College at New Brunswick, N.J.

6:30 P.M.—Sky pictures for the kiddies, by Mr. Radiobug.

6:45 P.M.—Good-night stories for the children by Uncle George of The Newark Ledger.

Programming

Early programming was primitive by today's standards. There was much recorded music (often classical), many lectures, and some news. Here is the program schedule of station WOR in Newark, New Jersey, as it appeared in the *New York Times* on May 29, 1922:

Early broadcasters had no guidelines as to what kinds of programs to air. Early television stations imitated previous radio successes, but early radio was truly a frontier. Only a month after

Early radio sports-news casters, Graham McNamee (at the microphone) and Phillips Carlin (with field glasses), broadcasting a Notre Dame–Army football game.

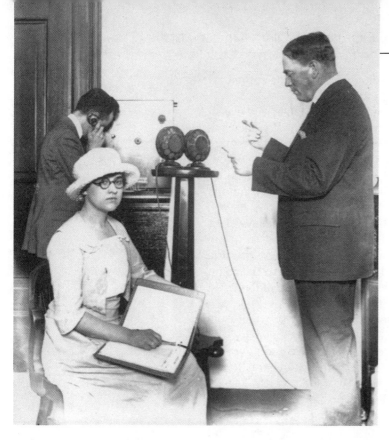

The microphones in an early broadcast studio were a far cry from the miniaturized models used today.

KDKA's broadcast, the Texas A&M University station broadcast the first college football game. A few months later KDKA broadcast the first church service, and the first radio debate on record came from WJH in Washington, D.C., on the argument that "The Daylight Saving is an Advantage." Early radio drama consisted mainly of dramatic readings. We take sound effects for granted in radio and television today, but the techniques had to be invented from scratch. Thunder was created by shaking a thin sheet of metal, and the sound of rain was created by rolling dried peas down a cardboard tube.

Music was the most popular type of programming on early radio, and it remains such today. Many radio pioneers believed radio would bring culture and art to the masses. Opera and classical music were quite common on 1920s radio compared to their very selective place today.

Variety and comedy shows became popular around 1922. Names such as Ed Wynn, Fibber McGee and Molly, Amos 'n' Andy, and the Gold Dust Twins were household words.

The first linking of radio stations into a *chain* (later known as a network) was in January of 1923 to broadcast a concert both in New York and Boston. The music was played in New York and was broadcast by WEAF to New Yorkers. The show was also carried by long-distance telephone lines to Boston's WNAC where it was aired for Bostonians.

Calvin Coolidge used a network of more than 20 radio stations to broadcast his words around the country. These first networks

A typical radio dramatization of the 1920s was "The Little House Family," with Betty Garde (left) and Kenneth Daigneau (right).

were small, however, and could reach few households compared to today's total coverage of the country.

Radio did succeed in bringing music, both popular and classical, to thousands who had no access to live music. It also succeeded in creating a national interest in sports. Without mass media, sports events would remain primarily of local interest. Radio (and later television) helped create national heroes out of sports stars and gave rise to the fan who knew all about nationally famous teams.

Boxing was a popular sport in the 1920s, and the heavyweight championship fight between Jack Dempsey and Georges Carpentier on July 2, 1921, became a radio event. The ringside announcer telephoned his "blow-by-blow" account to the radio station. The radio announcer wrote down the account and relayed the description to an audience of thousands.

Early baseball games were covered by a play-by-play announcer reading a ticker-tape account of the game in a different city. The announcer would try to make the event sound live and appropriate sounds would be added to give the "game" a live quality.

Only four years after the first KDKA broadcast, Dr. Lee De Forest (inventor of the vacuum tube, the predecessor of the transistor) announced that "radio has passed through the fad stage and has become a utility."

> Radio succeeded in bringing music, both popular and classical, to thousands who had no access to live music.

Financing Radio

Radio was exciting and filled with potential. But how were radio stations to survive financially? How could music, sports, and talent be paid for? Entertainers agreed to perform on radio because of the publicity it generated. But as quickly as 1922, the members of the American Society of Composers, Authors and Publishers (ASCAP) demanded to be paid for the right to air their music. Stations were asked to pay annual fees from several hundred to several thousand dollars yearly. This same system of fees paid to ASCAP by radio stations and then distributed by ASCAP to its members remains in effect today.

In 1925, however, radio was not as profitable a medium as it is today. A national debate raged over how to finance our radio system. Some favored the European method, which was to charge a tax on every radio sold. The tax would then be turned over to radio stations by the government. Others thought radio could be supported by subscriptions or memberships. Radio pioneer David Sarnoff of the Radio Corporation of America (RCA) argued that the freedom of radio meant listeners should not have to pay fees. But who would pay the bills?

That question was answered by the discovery that businesses were willing to pay for time to advertise on radio. The first radio commercial was a long announcement by an apartment complex

> The first radio commercial was aired in New York on WEAF in August of 1922.

in New York aired on WEAF in August of 1922. The fee for the commercial was $50. The idea caught on and stations that aired advertising were called "toll stations."

Businesses agreed to sponsor specific shows. Often the corporate name was attached to the show or the performers—the Eveready Hour, the RCA Victor Hour, the Goodrich Silver Chord Orchestra, or the Philco Playhouse.

Herbert Hoover in Washington, D.C., talking over a telephone to a New York audience.

Regulations

The rapid growth of radio caused problems. Frequencies overlapped and some channels were not usable because of interference from competing stations. Some sort of government regulation was needed to keep radio growing in an orderly way. In 1922, Herbert Hoover, then secretary of commerce, called a series of radio conferences to act as arbitrator between conflicting interests hoping to exploit radio. Hoover played a major role in developing a radio system controlled by business yet closely watched and regulated by government.

His efforts led to the Radio Law of 1927, which created the Federal Radio Commission (FRC). In 1934 the FRC was replaced by the Federal Communications Commission (FCC), which still exists today.

The Federal Communications Commission has the power to license radio stations and control many of the technical aspects (transmitter power, wavelength, antenna height) of broadcasting. The FCC has other powers, but in recent years they have been downplayed in favor of industry self-regulation.

Call letters are assigned to radio stations by the FCC. Generally, call letters of stations west of the Mississippi River begin with *K* and those east of the Mississippi, with *W*.

Edward R. Murrow was a pioneer in radio newscasting. From a CBS station in London he broadcast the events of World War II.

The Rise of Networks

The history of radio has been one of a struggle between business interests out to make as much profit as possible, and concerned citizens and the government seeking to ensure that the airwaves are used for the public good. Business interests are firmly in control of broadcasting, but the courts and the FCC occasionally show strength.

For example, the Radio Corporation of America dominated early radio broadcasting and manufacturing. In the late 1920s the RCA network was the largest. Its name—National Broadcasting Company (NBC). Around 1927, RCA president David Sarnoff gave a cold shoulder to George Coats and Arthur Judson, two people who ran a talent agency that supplied performers to NBC. Coats and Judson formed their own network, the Columbia Broadcasting System (CBS).

In 1943, RCA operated two radio networks—the Blue network and the Red network. The struggle between the courts and business was won by the courts in this instance. The Supreme Court ruled NBC had to sell its Blue network. RCA sold the network to Edward Noble, who renamed it the American Broadcasting Company (ABC). Today NBC, CBS, and ABC dominate network radio and television. All three networks have origins in NBC and Radio Corporation of America.

News

The 1920s were dominated by entertainment programming. Only with World War II did news on radio become popular. Radio commentators, such as Edward R. Murrow, Dorothy Thompson, and H. V. Kaltenborn, brought the war home. Network broadcasts enabled Americans to hear the sound of battle and the voices of Hitler, Mussolini, Chamberlain, and Churchill. On the home front, Franklin Roosevelt's fireside chats gave the nation a sense of leadership as it gathered around the radio.

After World War II radio news declined in importance, to be replaced by today's *rip and read* journalism. A rip and read newscast is so named because the announcer rips paper from the wire service teletype machine and reads it over the air. In the 1950s the stars of radio news joined the exodus to the exciting medium of television.

Dick Clark, one of the most popular disc jockeys of all time, choosing a record early in his career in Philadelphia.

Recorded Music

Radio station owners feared that television would put an end to the popularity of radio. Television did change the nature of radio programming. Much early television was simply transplanted radio; it was often the same people and content as radio but with a camera added. So what was radio left to broadcast?

The type of program (called a format) that saved radio had its roots in a 1930s program called "Make Believe Ballroom." The program contained mainly recorded music with talk or information between records. The format was inexpensive to produce and appealed to radio station owners struggling to fill air time without spending much for talent. Variations on the "Make Believe Ballroom" format evolved into today's disc jockey show and radio's almost complete dependence on recorded music.

Slowly, the disc jockey program evolved into music aimed at segments of the listening population rather than at everyone. Some programs catered to Top-40 hits, ethnic music, "easy listening", old standards, rock, or a balance referred to as MOR (middle-of-the-road). Radio became a specialized medium aimed at limited segments of the population.

Television did not put an end to radio, but it did take over the role of *The Mass Medium*. Radio today is healthy and lively as a specialized mass medium.

MEDIALAB

Comparing Radio—Past and Present

1. Talk to people you know who remember the early days of radio. Ask how it changed their daily activities. Ask what programs they enjoyed and if they remember how radio was replaced by television.

2. Use old newspapers, magazines, books, and other library reference aids to find an article on radio written during the 1920s. Read the article and write a brief summary. Explain how or if the author fully understood the potential for radio as a mass medium.

3. Look at the radio schedule from the *New York Times* of May 29, 1922, that appears on page 256. How do the programs differ from today's radio programs? How did radio programming influence early television?

4. Radio dramas are still available today on tape cassettes. Listen to an old radio show and write an essay arguing that old radio shows are more entertaining than many of today's television programs. (Do your best on the essay even if you don't agree with the argument).

5. How would life today be different if radio had not become a mass medium? (Assume that if radio were not a mass medium, there would be no television.)

6. How would radio be different if we had adopted the European system of taxing the purchase of radios? Be aware that this system allows the government to control the flow of income to radio stations.

7. Explain how television helped create the radio disc jockey.

8. Who controls radio programming today—the audience, the government, radio station management, advertisers, or singers and groups with the best-selling records? Support your answer.

9. Examine your local radio stations and explain how they attempt to reach certain segments of the listening audience.

Rate Card

This is an example adapted from a Standard Rate and Data Service publication showing the advertising rates of an AM radio station. Notice the mention of this station's "sister" station on FM.

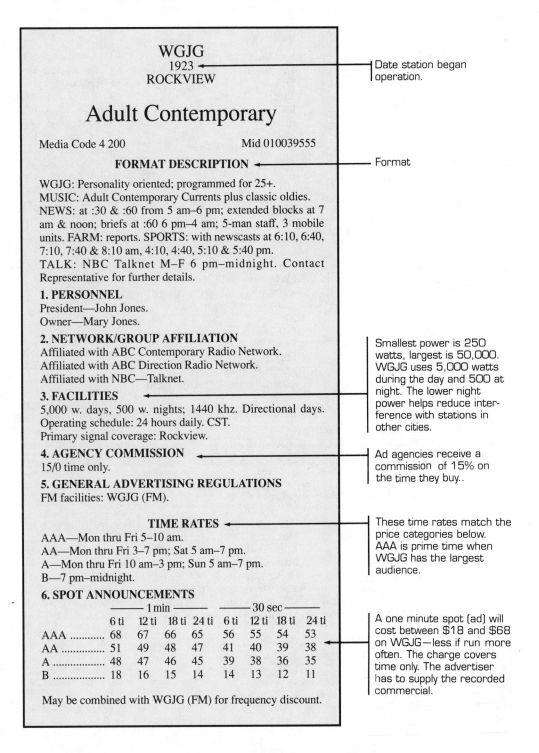

WGJG
1923 ← Date station began operation.
ROCKVIEW

Adult Contemporary

Media Code 4 200   Mid 010039555

FORMAT DESCRIPTION ← Format

WGJG: Personality oriented; programmed for 25+.
MUSIC: Adult Contemporary Currents plus classic oldies.
NEWS: at :30 & :60 from 5 am–6 pm; extended blocks at 7 am & noon; briefs at :60 6 pm–4 am; 5-man staff, 3 mobile units. FARM: reports. SPORTS: with newscasts at 6:10, 6:40, 7:10, 7:40 & 8:10 am, 4:10, 4:40, 5:10 & 5:40 pm.
TALK: NBC Talknet M–F 6 pm–midnight. Contact Representative for further details.

1. PERSONNEL
President—John Jones.
Owner—Mary Jones.

2. NETWORK/GROUP AFFILIATION
Affiliated with ABC Contemporary Radio Network.
Affiliated with ABC Direction Radio Network.
Affiliated with NBC—Talknet.

3. FACILITIES ←
5,000 w. days, 500 w. nights; 1440 khz. Directional days.
Operating schedule: 24 hours daily. CST.
Primary signal coverage: Rockview.

Smallest power is 250 watts, largest is 50,000. WGJG uses 5,000 watts during the day and 500 at night. The lower night power helps reduce interference with stations in other cities.

4. AGENCY COMMISSION ←
15/0 time only.

Ad agencies receive a commission of 15% on the time they buy..

5. GENERAL ADVERTISING REGULATIONS
FM facilities: WGJG (FM).

TIME RATES ←
AAA—Mon thru Fri 5–10 am.
AA—Mon thru Fri 3–7 pm; Sat 5 am–7 pm.
A—Mon thru Fri 10 am–3 pm; Sun 5 am–7 pm.
B—7 pm–midnight.

These time rates match the price categories below. AAA is prime time when WGJG has the largest audience.

6. SPOT ANNOUNCEMENTS

	1 min				30 sec			
	6 ti	12 ti	18 ti	24 ti	6 ti	12 ti	18 ti	24 ti
AAA	68	67	66	65	56	55	54	53
AA	51	49	48	47	41	40	39	38
A	48	47	46	45	39	38	36	35
B	18	16	15	14	14	13	12	11

A one minute spot (ad) will cost between $18 and $68 on WGJG—less if run more often. The charge covers time only. The advertiser has to supply the recorded commercial.

May be combined with WGJG (FM) for frequency discount.

This 1932 listing of radio programs from the *Los Angeles Times* shows the variety of programming and the number of stations broadcasting at that time.

THE DIAL

(From Programs Submitted by Stations)
ALPHABETICALLY ARRANGED
(C)—Denotes chain broadcast.

6 to 8 a.m.

KFI—New York stocks, 6:30; Dr. Selxas's health exercises, 6:45; organ (C,) 7:30; Van and Don (C,) 7:45.

KFWB—Exercises, 7:45.

KHJ—News briefs, 7:15.

KMPC—Setting-Up Exercises, 6:30; Top o' the Morning Club, 7.

KMTR—Eye-Opener, 7.

KNX—Sharples' Gang, 6:45.

KTM—Records. 6.

8 to 10 a.m.

KECA—Exercises, 9.

KFI—Merrie Men and Glenn Sisters (C,) 8; Little Orphan Annie (C,) 8:15; Wings of Song (C,) 8:20; Village Barn Orch. (C,) 9; Beautiful Thoughts (C,) 9:15; Farmers' Union (C,) 9:30.

KFWB—Musical Clock, 8; Hollywood Plaza Ensemble, 9.

KHJ—Shell Happy Time (C,) 8; Hallelujah hour, 8:30; Madison String Ensemble (C,) 9:30.

KMPC—News, 9; John Brown, 9:15.

KMTR—Stock quotations, 8; stock forecast, 8:05; Eye-Openers, 8:15; naval time and Economics, 9; U.C.L.A. hour, 9:45.

10 a.m. to 12 noon

KECA—News, 10; Physical Education, 10:45; Spanish lesson, 11:45.

KFI—Launching S.S. Santa Paula (C,) 10:30; Women's Magazine of the Air (C,) 11:15; French, 11:30; market reports, 11:45.

KMPC—Air Ambassador, 10:30.

KMTR—Mayor Porter, 10:30.

KNX—Eddie Albright, "Be Young and Happy," 10:00; Week-end Preludes (Francia White, songs,) 10:30.

KRKD—Mayor Porter, 10:30; news, 10:45.

12 noon to 2 p.m.

KECA—International release (Germany) (C,) 12; King Kamehaha Birthday Special (C,) 1; Bunny's Family, 1:45.

KFI—Agriculture, 12; Western Agriculture Special (C,) 12:15; news, 1; Stringwood Ensemble (C,) 1:15.

KFWB—Piano, 12; news, 12:15; organ, 12:30; "Child Psychology," 1; songs, 1:15; organ and soloist, 1:30.

KHJ—Ann Leaf, organ (C,) 12; The Times' world-wide news, 12:30; Christian's Orch. (C,) 12:45; Duchin's Orch. (C,) 1; Saturday Evening Frolic (C,) 1:30

2 to 4 p.m.

KECA—Records.

KFI—Tom and Jimmy, 2; the Nomads (C,) 2:30; Footlight Fantasies (C,) 3; Songs of the Sea, 3:30; news, 3:45.

KFWB—Fiction, 3.

KHJ—Arthur Jarrett, songs (C,) 2; Martin's Orch. (C,) 2:15; Aldershot Tattoo (C,) 2:35; Belasco's Orch. (C,) 2:50; Hall's Orch. (C,) 3:15; Do-Ra-Me (C,) 3:30; Street Singer (C,) 3:45.

KNX—Bookworm, 2; records. 2:30; Matinee Mirthquakers (Karla Snell,) 3.

KMPC—Italian Village, 2:30; Banjo Boys, 3.

KMTR—Records.

KRKD—Musicale, 3.

4 to 6 p.m.

KECA—News, 4; Big Brother, 5; Dr. John Snape, 5:30.

KFI—Elsa Behlow Trautner, songs (C,) 4; Al Gale, accordion, 4:15; Civic Concert (C,) 4:30; Harlem Fantasy (C,) 4:45; Lyric string trio, 5; First Nighter (C,) 5:30.

KFWB—Organ, 4; Syncopators, 5:15.

KHJ—Armenian National Musical Society (C,) 4; Four Eton Boys (C,) 4:15; Tea Dance (C,) 4:30; Isham Jones' Orch. (C,) 5; The Times' world-wide news, 5:15; Skippy, 5:30; Black 'n' Blue (C,) 5:45.

KMPC—News, 4:30; Miniature Musicales, 5.

6 to 7 p.m.

KECA—String trio, 6:30.

KFI—Lucky Strike hour (C,) 6.

KFWB—Lorna Ladd interviews Kay Van Riper, 6:15; organ, 6:30; "Growin' Up," 6:45.

KHJ—Music that Satisfies (Ruth Etting) (C,) 6; Columbia Public Affairs (C,) (Manuel Roxas), 6:15; Coral Islanders (C,) 6:45.

KMTR—Twilight Melodist, 6; Paradise Isle, 6:30.

KNX—News, 6; Concert Orchestra, 6:15; "O-o-h! Elmer," 6:30; Merna Kennedy and Lew Cody, 6:45.

KRKD—Records.

7 to 8 p.m.

KECA—Tom and Jimmy, 7; talk by Merle Thorpe (C,) 7:15; string orchestra, 7:30.

KFI—Amos 'n' Andy (C,) 7; Choraleers, 7:45; Bank of America Good Times (Katherine Edson, (C,) 8:15.

KFWB—Tone Etchings, 7; Worthless Talks, 7:30; piano duets, 7:45.

MEDIALAB

Thinking About Radio Programming

1. A station's format describes the type of music it plays or the kind of programming it usually broadcasts. A "Top-40" format station programs those records currently in the top 40 in terms of record sales. Other common formats include MOR (middle-of-the-road), Easy Listening, Rhythm and Blues, Country, All News, News/Talk, Contemporary Hit Radio (CHR) or Rock, Foreign Language, or Classical. Find out what format each station in your area uses.

2. After you have determined the formats of the local stations, try to determine which segment of the audience each station reaches the most. For example, a daytime-only station with "Easy Listening" music and hourly stock market reports probably is most interested in attracting people listening in offices or people at home who want "relaxing music".

3. Make a list of the products advertised during one hour on one station. Various students should choose various stations to monitor. Examine the lists and find the relationship between the products advertised, the station's format, and the intended audience.

4. The rates advertisers pay for radio time depend on the size of the audience and the time of day. Find out what rates your local stations charge for commercial time. These can be checked at many large libraries in a reference book entitled *Spot Radio: Rates and Data*, produced by Standard Rate and Data Service, which lists all the radio stations in the country with detailed information about programming and ad rates. Refer to the sample rate card shown in this section for an interpretation of terms used.

5. Find out which radio station is the most popular among students. Which is the most popular among parents? Do you think that when you become a parent your listening tastes will have changed? Explain the reasoning behind your answer.

6. How does the most popular station in your area decide which songs to play? To find out, you might call the station or write a letter for the entire class. If possible, invite a speaker from the radio station to talk to the class about radio programming.

7. A portion of an old radio directory is reprinted on page 264. It appeared in a 1932 newspaper. Such complete radio program listings are no longer published in newspapers. Notice how the programming or scheduling was similar to that of television today. What changes in our society or in broadcast media might prompt different TV program scheduling in the future?

RADIO TODAY

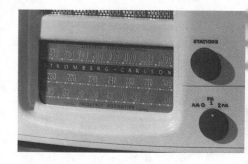

After World War II, radio still resembled today's television in many ways. People listened to specific programs and radio was dominated by the three major networks. But the growth of television and the increased number of radio stations changed the nature of radio.

With so many radio stations available, it was no longer possible for one station to deliver a large enough audience to make a network profitable. There were not enough advertising dollars to go around. In addition, the energies and the development dollars were being spent on the more glamorous medium of television. So radio lost network-supplied programs and became a local medium.

Local stations turned to phonograph records, disc jockeys, and "rip and read" news broadcasts to survive. Some stations tried talk shows, sports broadcasts, even all news. They needed inexpensive programs that would attract local advertisers. The formula worked and was later refined to what is sometimes called "narrowcasting." *Broadcasting* means sending out a signal to attract everyone; *narrowcasting* means carefully selecting music to attract a certain segment of the population to deliver to advertisers. A young audience is gathered by playing rock music, a somewhat older audience with middle-of-the-road programming, and the mature market with easy listening.

In fact, the formula worked so well that the 1960s saw the greatest growth yet in radio's revenues. But no medium is immune to technical changes, not even as old a medium as radio. The early 1960s saw a new kind of radio—FM (frequency modulation). At first FM was of interest only to hobbyists and music nuts interested in something called "hi-fi." There were very few FM sets and even fewer stations; many played only classical music. Existing AM (amplitude modulation) stations took out an FM license and broadcast the same program on both outlets.

Over 1,000 radio stations have their entire day (and night) programming produced on tape by an outside source. All the local stations needs is a tape player, and an announcer to read ads.

In the mid-1960s the Federal Communications Commission decided that AM stations that owned FM outlets should not be allowed to broadcast the same signal on both stations all the time. The FCC wanted to encourage a greater diversity of programming to serve the public. Limits were placed on the amount of time an AM station could simulcast. This ruling created a demand for a new type of programming, different from AM.

The programming void was filled by "underground rock" formats, by so-called "free-form" radio, and often by creative combinations of music, talk, interviews, and off-beat humor. Some stations narrowed their intended audience to certain sections of a large city instead of the whole metropolitan area. Today FM is overwhelming AM stations as much as television overwhelmed radio in the 1950s. This development is due, in part, to different programming; also important to note is that FM has some significant technical advantages.

Most radios can play FM signals in stereo; AM stereo began in the mid 1980s, but most radios still cannot take advantage of the improved sound.

AM stereo began as an effort to recapture some of the audience lost to FM. The stereo does improve AM sound; in technical terms it offers a broader bandwidth—close to that of FM. The sound is not as good as the best FM, but it is close enough to close the quality gap. AM stations now have to offer unique programming to attract listeners who have grown up on FM. FM has a higher frequency response than AM; that is, it allows a greater range of sounds to come through to the loudspeaker. FM is also better suited to large cities since its transmissions are less subject to interference from electric motors, storms, bridges, and office buildings.

In 1990 only 25 percent of radio's total audience listens to the AM band. An AM/FM radio is now almost standard equipment in cars, and many of the portable radios worn as headsets are FM only. So the battle for a share of the audience continues. First radio had to survive the invention of television; now AM radio has to find a way to avoid obsolescence in the face of the better sound of FM stereo.

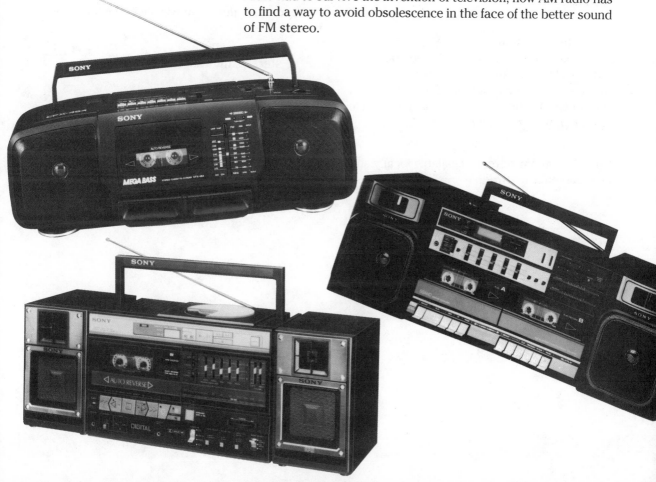

MEDIALAB

Analyzing Modern Radio

1. There are two kinds of commercial radio broadcasting—AM and FM. The two represent ways of transmitting radio waves. Twenty years ago, FM was almost unknown. Only the largest cities had FM stations and few people listened to them. But today FM is the fastest-growing kind of broadcasting. In large cities there are more FM than AM stations.

   Find out what FM stations operate in your area. What is the frequency of each, what are each station's call letters, and what format does each use?

2. Are there any educational FM stations, such as a public radio or school-affiliated station, in your area? (Educational FM stations are usually found on the lower, or left-hand, part of the FM tuning band.) If there is a public radio station in your area, research its history and format.

3. Find out if AM stereo is available locally and what audience it attracts.

4. Research the difference between AM and FM. What are the advantages and disadvantages of each? Take a survey in your class to find out which is more popular.

5. The history of mass media shows that new technology is often seen as a threat to a particular medium. But the new medium (or the technical improvement to an old medium) often does not replace a medium so much as change it. How do you think each of these technologies or trends has affected or will affect the future of radio?

   stereo simulcast (TV and radio)
   videodiscs
   MTV (Music television)
   AM stereo
   satellite transmission

WRAP-UP

Radio became a mass medium in 1920 with the first public broadcast from a station in Pennsylvania. In this chapter you have learned that radio pioneered the program formats—such as music, sports, news, drama, and comedy—that you see on television today. The creation of the FCC and the rise of three dominant networks—NBC, CBS, and ABC—were discussed, and you learned how radio is financed. Looking at radio today, you've studied the histories of and differences between AM and FM stations and learned the difference between *narrowcasting* and *broadcasting*. Finally, you've analyzed your local radio stations and thought about your own listening habits.

CHAPTER 10

Recordings

From Edison's experiments with the phonograph in the late 1800s to today's complex technology, the medium of recordings is constantly changing.

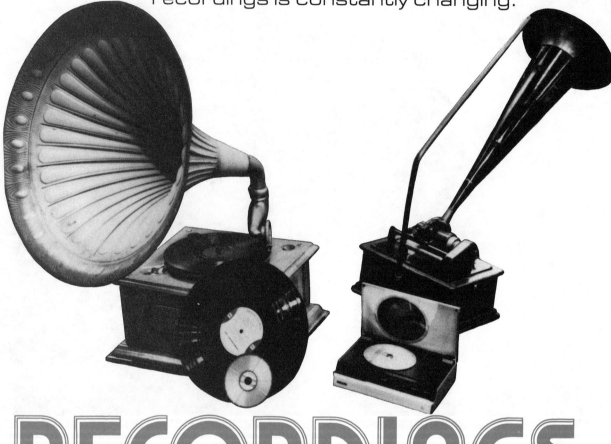

RECORDINGS

From Tin foil to Lasers

In December 1877 Thomas Edison built a machine that recorded and played back sound. The phonograph (from Greek words meaning *sound* and *writer*) was hand cranked and played a cylinder of tin foil. Sound quality was crude, but the machine drew crowds at vaudeville shows. Of course, there were no practical uses for the machines, so Edison stopped making the phonograph.

Ten years later Emile Berliner patented a system using flat discs instead of cylinders. Although not a household name, Berliner laid the foundation for today's record industry. His flat disc could be mass produced from a master, whereas Edison's cylinders were necessarily one-of-a-kind originals. The shellac-coated disc also produced better quality sound compared to the original cylinder. Berliner created a machine to play his new flat discs and called it the gramophone, a name still heard today in Europe. Berliner founded the Victor Talking Machine Company and began selling "Red Seal" recordings, a brand name still used today.

In 1917 Americans bought 25 million discs, spurred by the first recording superstar, opera singer Enrico Caruso. To most Americans, music before 1920 meant classical music. There was no rock music or top-40 radio, so opera singers who provided many listeners with a link to the "old country" became mega-stars. The 78 rpm (revolutions-per-minute) discs broke easily and lasted less than 10 minutes a side, so to record an entire symphony or opera took a series of discs packaged in an album. Although today's CDs are not in albums, the term remains to describe a larger collection of songs from which a single or, hopefully, hit single is culled.

Enrico Caruso

RADIO AS A THREAT TO RECORDINGS

The history of any mass medium is one of conflict between technologies competing for public favor. In the late 1920s, the rise of radio threatened the recording industry. Radio sound was clearer than the record and its music was live. Radio stations broadcast big band music from live pick-ups and the quality was vastly superior to the still thin and raspy sound of records. The recording industry saw radio as a fatal threat. Since radio was used much like television today, record companies feared the public would have less time to play recordings. Remember, car and portable radios were still far in the future. Radio did hurt record sales, but some salvation arrived in 1948, when Columbia records introduced the 33 1/3 rpm long-play record (the LP), developed by Peter Goldmark. The improved record could hold over 20 minutes of music per side, was not as fragile as the 78s, and featured much-improved sound. Goldmark invented the LP because he was a music lover unwilling to put up with listening to a Brahms' concerto while changing and flipping the six records in the album. Goldmark stated "There was no doubt in my mind that the phonograph. . . was murdering Brahms, and I felt somehow impelled to stop this killer in its shellac tracks."

> There was no doubt in my mind that the phonograph . . . was murdering Brahms, and I felt somehow impelled to stop this killer in its shellac tracks.
>
> —PETER GOLDMARK

Stereophonic sound was first marketed in 1958 and quickly made "mono" obsolete.

Around 1950, television emerged as the leading mass entertainment medium. Radio had to change in order to survive. Early television simply "stole" programming from radio. Westerns, soap operas, crime and detective shows, and quiz shows began on radio. To survive, radio switched to music programming. And where did the music come from? Why, records, of course. Radio, a medium that was originally seen as fatal competition to recordings, embraced records as its content. Even today, recordings are the main content of radio.

The recording industry quickly learned that radio was an excellent way to promote its records. A record that was played often on radio sold more copies than other releases. The radio and recording industries became partners instead of enemies.

MAGNETIC RECORDING AND EDITING

Before 1950, recordings were made by producing a master disc directly from the live performance. The method did not permit editing. If a musician hit a wrong note, the only alternative was to start over. In other words, recordings before 1950 had to be what are called real-time performances. A three-minute song was just that—a recording of a song that took three minutes to sing. Magnetic recording was introduced to the record industry first in 1947 from a German invention called the magnetophone. What we call tape recording is a newer medium than the phonograph, and one that revolutionized music and the record industry. Tape recording brought editing to the recording industry.

Tape recorders for consumers were of the reel-to-reel variety and were expensive and inconvenient. But in 1964 the cassette was introduced and it revolutionized the recording industry. Cassettes meant that anyone could easily make tapes. Tape changed the recording industry in two ways: First, it made possi-

ble a new kind of multitrack music, and second, cassettes became to recordings what the photocopy machine was to the printed page.

Before the 1950s popular music on record meant mainly one of four types of music—classical, which was by far the largest-selling category; recordings from Broadway musicals; popular music by crooners, such as Perry Como, Bing Crosby, Kate Smith, Louis Armstrong, and Dinah Shore; and big band jazz by the Glenn Miller band, Tommy Dorsey, Benny Goodman, and many others. A common feature of recording artists before 1950 was the need for real-time talent. To make a record required the ability to play an instrument or sing without error—it required technical ability with voice or an instrument. Tape recording, with its ability to erase mistakes and manipulate sound, made it possible for stars with less than extraordinary musical ability to record hit songs. Editors (called sound mixers) and record producers could take a live performance and alter it drastically to produce a sound that would sell on records. Record producers combined editing with newly electrified instruments to effectively record a new kind of music, labeled rock 'n' roll by Cleveland disc jockey Alan Freed in the early 50s.

Cassettes became to recordings what the photocopy was to the printed page.

The second contribution of tape recording was in its role as an audio copy machine. When music was distributed only on flat discs, copying was not a problem. No machine existed for consumers to make their own duplicate discs. But cassettes made copying as easy as pushing a few buttons. Today, estimates are that over 80 percent of blank tape sold is used to make duplicates of copyrighted music. Record companies estimate losses of as much as two billion dollars a year to copying. One offsetting effect of copyable music is that it makes popular music part of our electronic environment. Music is democratic, available to everyone, instead of being limited to those fortunate enough to buy expensive equipment or hire professional musicians. The Supreme Court ruled in 1984 that home taping does not violate the copyright law, and the recording industry still seeks ways to recover income lost to taping.

compact discs

I don't think we're that many years from the point where 90 percent of what has been an acoustic market will be a digital market.

—RAYMOND KURZWEIL

More than any other medium, recording is the history of new technological developments that seem to save the medium whenever sales lag. The invention of the compact disc by Sony in 1982 again saved lagging sales. A mere six years after its introduction, sales of CDs surpassed those of LPs. A compact disc consists of music converted to a digital code that is then read by a laser beam. A compact disc stores information in the form of 16-bit digital "words." So "1010101011110011" is a bit of information that can be run through a digital-to-analog (D/A) converter to make a sound. A compact disc stores 44,100 of these 16-bit words to make just one second of music for one channel. The optical pickup of a CD player reads data from the disc at the rate of over 4.32 million bits per second!

These discs were far more convenient than the LP, did not require turning over to hear the other side, and were quieter than vinyl records when played on inexpensive equipment. Early CDs were quite expensive because few processing plants existed to create the new medium. Even when supplies loosened, record companies found that consumers viewed the silvery discs as a premium product for which they willingly paid premium prices. Compact discs replaced the LP in a surprisingly short time because of their convenience to consumers and their profitability to record makers, and because Japanese manufacturers sold CD players at reasonably low prices.

Record companies also liked the fact that consumers could not create their own CDs—it was a "read only" medium. But innovations in technology in the 1980s led to the introduction of CDs that could be erased and rerecorded.

MUSIC VIDEOS

Music videos began in European dance clubs. They were produced by record companies to give both new and established groups added exposure, in other words to help sell more records. Some were sent to the United States where they were used as fillers between movies on cable-television outlets. In 1981, Warner Cable sent its Music Television (MTV) by satellite into cable homes. The 24-hour cable service introduced new music (much of it new wave European) to Americans.

Radio stations found their listeners demanding the music already seen and heard on MTV. Record companies quickly discovered that MTV sells records. In fact, a 1983 survey showed MTV as the most influential factor in determining record purchases.

Early videos were low-budget productions but artists such as Billy Joel, Paul McCartney, and Michael Jackson quickly produced high-budget minimovies. Michael Jackson's *Thriller* generated nearly 20 million dollars in revenue, and music videos became a

Michael Jackson

product themselves. Music videos became a testing ground for new film techniques and were on the cutting edge of special effects. Techniques perfected in music videos soon became part of television commercials and later influenced movies, TV shows, and political advertising.

So far, music videos on videocassette or laser videodiscs do not compete with sound-only CDs or tapes. The next technical advance that will "save" the recording industry will be a disc that combines high-quality sound with video. Such discs exist now, but are not yet available at a mass-market price.

Synthesizers & Digital Music

The electrification of musical instruments and the invention of the digital synthesizer is changing both music and the recording industry. The first synthesizer to gain acceptance was named after its inventor, Robert Moog. It was intended to aid in producing classical music but was quickly adopted by rock musicians, composers for commercials and sound tracks, and discos.

Synthesize means to *put together*. A synthesizer puts together elements of sound, such as attack, decay, sustain, and release. The digital synthesizer uses a microprocessor to store the code for these bits.

Digital synthesizers create a wider variety of sounds than almost any acoustic instrument. At first they were used only to copy sounds, for example, to reproduce the sound of a bell or saxophone. But today, synthesized sounds that are electronically unique compete with traditional musical instruments. The entire sound track for one of the 1980s most popular television series, "Miami Vice," was produced by Jan Hammer on a synthesizer.

Acoustical instruments, such as the piano, violin, guitar, and wind instruments, produce rich and complex sounds, but each of these instruments has limitations. Each can play only one sound at a time and is very limited in how that sound can be modified. A violin can produce vibrato, but not much else. A saxophone or trumpet can be muted, but variations on the basic sound are very limited. A piano is the most complex and can be changed by pedals or by mechanically altering the strings or hammers. Each instrument requires considerable physical dexterity to play. A

The entire sound track for "Miami Vice" was produced on a synthesizer.

pianist has to have agile fingers and practice many hours daily to become proficient. Another drawback to acoustic instruments is that so much skill and special technique is needed to master one instrument that musicians must choose to specialize rather than express themselves in a dozen different instruments.

Synthesizers, on the other hand, can change sound in almost unlimited ways. Sound can be layered and played polyphonically. Raymond Kurzweil realized both the strengths of acoustic instruments and the value of the synthesizer when he crossed the synthesizer with a computer to produce a digital synthesizer. His early Kurzweil 250 set out to reproduce the sound of a piano and add digital effects to create and carefully control almost any sound. By using digital technology his machines can reconstruct acoustic sounds and create new sounds. Almost every popular hit today includes a new synthesized sound to catch the public's ear.

To compose the great music of the past required extraordinary skill and coordination. Imagine George Gershwin composing the orchestral version of *Rhapsody in Blue*. He had to write the music as he imagined it in his head. He would write out the notation (drawing notes is a painstaking process), have it printed (no photocopy machines back then), gather some willing musicians (either by having many musician friends or deep pockets) to study and play the piece, hear his work for the first time, and make changes. The changes had to be imagined in his head. He would send the musicians home, rewrite the entire score in order to make changes, get the musicians back to try out the revised version, and so on.

Imagine Mozart on a synthesizer.

If he were writing today with a sampling synthesizer he could hear the work as it was being composed. He could recreate any sound of the orchestra to hear how it would sound alone or in concert with other instruments. He could change notes at the touch of a few keys or mouse buttons. Instead of tedious hand-written notes, he could move ready-drawn notes on a computer screen and have the score printed out. Changes in notes can be made and printed out in a matter of seconds. In short, digital technology removes some of the considerable barriers to music composition. Making music easier to compose enables more people with musical ability to become the composers of tomorrow's music. Synthesizers remove some of the need for physical coordination necessary to play musical instruments while composing. That means a composer or musician with the musical ideas of a Beethoven or a Gershwin, but without their physical dexterity or patience, might produce the greatest music of the twenty-first century.

RECORDINGS AS COMPARED TO OTHER MEDIA

The development of the medium of recordings mirrors the history of film, painting, and photography. At first painters and photographers were content to try to imitate reality. They tried to capture in paint or on film what the eye could see, to make images lifelike. Once that skill was developed, they moved beyond capturing still life and into creating a new reality. Many modern paintings and photographs resemble nothing the eye can see. A comparison of the best paintings and photographs of the first artists in these media with those of modern artists shows very clearly the change that took place. Sound reproduction is also moving into new worlds. The music played on home reproduction systems of the future may be as different from the top tunes of today as heavy metal is from Gregorian chant.

MEDIALAB

Recordings

1. Choral director Ray Coniff has said, "The simple fact is that people today get a lot better sound on records than they do in live concerts." Do you agree or disagree? Why?

2. Concert pianist Glenn Gould has said that "concerts as they are now known will not outlive the 20th century." Do you agree or disagree? Why?

3. Compare and contrast the film editing process in the movie industry and the sound mixing process in the recording industry. You may want to do some research at the library.

4. Who are some of the best known companies producing recordings today?

5. There is a trend in music today toward the more engineered (digital) and electronic sound and away from the simple, acoustic (nonelectronic) sound. Even when you attend a live concert, you usually hear electronically amplified sound. Consider the idea of completely electronic music. For example, will the traditional instruments such as drum and guitar be replaced by more sophisticated electronic devices? Can computers be programmed to play electronic music? How will electronics change music in the next 100 years?

6. Play some recordings that illustrate completely electronic music. Do you think this will ever replace today's music? Why or why not?

7. Find different versions (record, tape, and CD) of the same song and explain how their sound or production is different.

8. Prepare a report on DAT (digital audio tape) and how recorded sound will change in the next ten years.

9. Are the lyrics to today's songs important or are the "sound" and the "beat" more important? Do today's songs attempt to say important things in their lyrics? Historically, the lyrics to popular songs go through cycles of being mainly nonsense for a period of time and then slowly changing to lyrics that are very meaningful. Which phase are we in today? Discuss the recording industry's new policy of labelling recordings containing potentially offensive lyrics.

10. Do you think audio-cassettes will be used for music in ten years?

THE RECORDING INDUSTRY

Radio station programmers play those recordings that are selling best around the country. But recordings rarely become best-sellers until they are played on the radio. The more a song is played on radio stations, the more copies it will sell—and the more it sells, the more radio stations will play it more often. Thus a hit is born.

Billboard magazine is a weekly publication for the music and home entertainment industry. Among its many listings is a top album chart.

Billboard TOP POP ALBUMS™

FOR WEEK ENDING DECEMBER 23, 1989

Compiled from a national sample of retail store, one-stop, and rack sales reports.

★★ NO. 1 ★★

THIS WEEK	LAST WEEK	2 WKS. AGO	WKS. ON CHART	ARTIST — LABEL & NUMBER DISTRIBUTING LABEL (SUG. LIST PRICE)*	TITLE
1	2	1	40	MILLI VANILLI ▲5 ARISTA AL 8592 (9.98) (CD) 6 weeks at No. 1	GIRL YOU KNOW IT'S TRUE
2	1	2	8	BILLY JOEL COLUMBIA OC 44366 (CD)	STORM FRONT
3	3	3	12	JANET JACKSON ▲2 A&M SP 3920 (9.98) (CD)	JANET JACKSON'S RHYTHM NATION 1814
4	6	17	4	PHIL COLLINS ATLANTIC 82050 (9.98) (CD)	...BUT SERIOUSLY
5	4	4	75	PAULA ABDUL ▲4 VIRGIN 90943 (9.98) (CD)	FOREVER YOUR GIRL
6	5	5	8	NEW KIDS ON THE BLOCK ▲6 COLUMBIA FC 40985 (CD)	HANGIN' TOUGH
7	9	8	13	AEROSMITH ▲ GEFFEN 24254 (9.98) (CD)	PUMP
8	7	6	23	THE B-52'S ▲ REPRISE 25854 (9.98) (CD)	COSMIC THING
9	14	14	11	NEW KIDS ON THE BLOCK ▲ COLUMBIA FC 45280 (CD)	MERRY MERRY CHRISTMAS
10	15	12	33	TOM PETTY ▲2 MCA 6253 (9.98) (CD)	FULL MOON FEVER
11	8	7	15	ROLLING STONES ▲ COLUMBIA OC 45333 (CD)	STEEL WHEELS
12	12	13	10	LINDA RONSTADT (FEA. A.NEVILLE) ▲ ELEKTRA 60872 (9.98) (CD)	CRY LIKE A RAINSTORM, HOWL LIKE THE WIND
13	13	10	14	MOTLEY CRUE ELEKTRA 60829 (9.98) (CD)	DR. FEELGOOD
14	10	11	5	WHITESNAKE GEFFEN GHS 24249 (9.98) (CD)	SLIP OF THE TONGUE
15	11	9	14	YOUNG M.C. ▲ DELICIOUS VINYL 91309 ISLAND (9.98) (CD)	STONE COLD RHYMIN'
16	16	22	4	RUSH ATLANTIC 82040 (9.98) (CD)	PRESTO
17	18	16	32	RICHARD MARX ▲3 EMI 90380 (9.98) (CD)	REPEAT OFFENDER
18	21	26	5	ERIC CLAPTON DUCK 26074 REPRISE (9.98) (CD)	JOURNEYMAN
19	20	19	23	CHER ▲ GEFFEN GHS 24239 (9.98) (CD)	HEART OF STONE
20	19	18	25	SOUL II SOUL ▲ VIRGIN 91267 (9.98) (CD)	KEEP ON MOVIN'
21	25	42	4	BOBBY BROWN MCA 6342 (9.98) (CD)	DANCE!...YA KNOW IT!
22	17	15	10	TRACY CHAPMAN ▲ ELEKTRA 60888 (9.98) (CD)	CROSSROADS
23	22	21	46	SKID ROW ▲ ATLANTIC 81936 (9.98) (CD)	SKID ROW
24	23	23	6	JOE SATRIANI RELATIVITY 1015 (9.98) (CD)	FLYING IN A BLUE DREAM
25	24	20	12	TEARS FOR FEARS ▲ FONTANA 838 730 1 POLYGRAM (CD)	THE SEEDS OF LOVE
26	29	28	21	BABYFACE ● SOLAR FZ 45288 E.P.A. (CD)	TENDER LOVER
27	49	102	3	QUINCY JONES QWEST 26020 WARNER BROS. (CD)	BACK ON THE BLOCK
28	30	37	21	NEW KIDS ON THE BLOCK ▲ COLUMBIA FC 40475 (CD)	NEW KIDS ON THE BLOCK
29	27	25	20	ALICE COOPER ● EPIC OE 45137 E.P.A.	TRASH
30	28	29	8	LUTHER VANDROSS EPIC E2 45320 E.P.A. (CD)	THE BEST OF LUTHER: THE BEST OF LOVE
31	26	24	24	BAD ENGLISH ● EPIC OE 45083 E.P.A. (CD)	BAD ENGLISH
				...ON HENLEY ▲ GEFFEN GHS 24217 (9.98) (CD)	THE END OF THE INNOCENCE

THIS WEEK	LAST WEEK	2 WKS. AGO	WKS. ON CHART	ARTIST — LABEL & NUMBER DISTRIBUTING LABEL (SUG. LIST PRICE)*	TITLE
55	70	100	17	MANNHEIM STEAMROLLER AMERICAN GRAMAPHONE AG 1984 (9.98) (CD)	THE INCRED...
56	59	105	3	ROB BASE PROFILE 1285 (9.98) (CD)	LIK...
57	61	59	38	MADONNA ▲2 SIRE 25844 WARNER BROS. (9.98) (CD)	MO...
58	53	54	15	RED HOT CHILI PEPPERS EMI 92152 (9.98) (CD)	A VERY SPECIA...
59	75	131	20	VARIOUS ARTISTS SPECIAL OLYMPICS SP 3911 A&M (9.98) (CD)	FC...
60	51	48	12	TINA TURNER ● CAPITOL 91873 (9.98) (CD)	THE GREAT RADIO...
61	54	56	26	HEAVY D. & THE BOYZ ▲ MCA 42302 (8.98) (CD)	DIRTY ROTTEN FILTH...
62	65	63	40	TESLA ● GEFFEN GHS 24224 (9.98) (CD)	N...
63	58	51	43	WARRANT ▲ COLUMBIA FC 44383 (CD)	HAPPY ANNIVERSARY...
64	64	58	11	RANDY TRAVIS ● WARNER BROS. 25988 (9.98) (CD)	
65	68	69	7	VARIOUS ARTISTS GRP 9596 (9.98) (CD)	
66	56	55	34	GREAT WHITE ▲2 CAPITOL C1-90640 (9.98) (CD)	
67	62	64	7	THE CURE ▲ ELEKTRA 60855 (9.98) (CD)	
68	71	70	64	BON JOVI ▲5 MERCURY 836 345 1 POLYGRAM (CD)	AN...
69	60	52	75	BOBBY BROWN ▲5 MCA 42185 (8.98) (CD)	GREA...
70	80	108	4	RANDY TRAVIS WARNER BROS. 25972 (8.98) (CD)	
71	92	195	3	CHICAGO REPRISE 26080 (9.98) (CD)	THE...
72	66	65	25	PRINCE ▲2 WARNER BROS. 25936 (9.98) (CD)	
73	67	60	5	PAT BENATAR CHRYSALIS 21715 (9.98) (CD)	
74	74	78	6	SOUNDTRACK GRP GR2-002 (10.98) (CD)	
75	102	—	2	SOUNDTRACK WALT DISNEY 64038* (8.98) (CD)	
76	76	81	4	3RD BASS COLUMBIA FC 45415 (CD)	
77	78	89	15	JOE COCKER CAPITOL 92861 (9.98) (CD)	NOTH...
78	69	61	5	TERENCE TRENT D'ARBY COLUMBIA OC 45351 (CD)	
79	96	—	2	CHUNKY A MCA 6354 (9.98) (CD)	STORYTELLER/COMP...
80	82	87	9	SEDUCTION VENDETTA SP 5280 A&M (8.98) (CD)	
81	88	103	3	ROD STEWART WARNER BROS. 4-25987 (39.98) (CD)	
82	84	156	3	DURAN DURAN CAPITOL 93178 (9.98) (CD)	
83	NEW▶		1	TECHNOTRONIC SBK 93422 (9.98) (CD)	
84	87	98	27	PAUL McCARTNEY CAPITOL C1-91653 (9.98) (CD)	
85	86	92	5	ROBERT PALMER ISLAND 91318/ATLANTIC (9.98) (CD)	
86	89	91	4	JODY WATLEY MCA 6343 (9.98) (CD)	
87	72	60	15	ELTON JOHN ● MCA 6321 (9.98) (CD)	G...
88	114	129	4	EDDIE MONEY COLUMBIA OC 45381 (CD)	
89	81	75	6	SIR MIX-A-LOT NASTY MIX 70150 (9.98) (CD)	
90	73	62	9	ICE-T SIRE 26028/WARNER BROS. (9.98) (CD)	
	93	74	29	CLINT BLACK RCA 9668-1-R (8.98) (CD)	
				GINA BELLE COLUMBIA FC 44367 (CD)	

MEDIALAB

Looking at the Top Pop

1. Obtain a current issue of *Billboard* from a large newsstand, or by ordering one copy from *Billboard*, BPI Communications, Inc., One Astor Plaza, 1515 Broadway, NY, 10036, $7.95. Determine if any of the recording artists on the chart on the previous page are still listed. Why do the most popular records change so fast? The big hits of five years ago are hardly heard at all today—why not?

2. Using the preceding Top Pop® list or a more current *Billboard* list, go through your own music collection and check off the recordings you own. Would it be fair to say that, if the class as a whole owns quite a few of those on the list, its taste in music is "typical" and conforms to that of teens across the country?

3. Have each person in class go through his or her own record collection and write down the name of the record company that made each record, tape, or CD (for example—Warner, Motown, Bell, etc.). Note how many recordings are owned by students and how many are from the most often listed companies. The ten largest companies account for over 75 percent of all records sold. Some of the the largest record companies are Warner Communications, CBS, RCA, Capitol, MCA, Motown, Polygram, and London Records.

4. Does the pattern of class ownership of albums resemble the national pattern? If not, what circumstances might explain the difference?

5. If you have a favorite recording next year, it will very probably be one that has been selected and approved by the handful of people who make the final decisions at the five largest record companies. If you have a favorite television program next year, it will probably be one that has been selected and approved by the handful of people who make the final decisions at the three networks. Most of the money you will spend to go to the movies next year will go to a few of the largest film companies. Do you see any problems in this arrangement? Why does this concentration exist in the media industries? Does it exist in other industries?

6. Rock 'n' roll gave birth to the recording industry as *BIG* business. Do you see any current trend in music or entertainment that might serve to capture consumer dollars the way rock 'n' roll did in the 1950s?

7. Take a survey of buying habits in the class. How many people buy albums and how often? How many buy blank cassettes and make recordings? How many buy CDs or video discs? How many spend money on video games or computers that might otherwise have gone for recordings?

ROCK, RICHES, AND THE RECORDING INDUSTRY

Before the 1960s, the dream of many teenagers was to become either a big-time ball player or a movie star. Since then a new dream for many teens began to occur. Every neighborhood has at least one group of a few high school students who play music together and call themselves a group or a band. The dream of many of these groups is to land a recording contract, to become famous, and to tour the world living as only multimillionaire rock stars can.

No doubt some of the neighborhood groups who now play at local dances for $300-500 will become tomorrow's superstars. But their dreams of success in the future should be tempered with knowledge of how the recording industry operates and what it takes to survive. Allan Parachini talks about the myth of the rock star and the reality of the struggling musician versus the recording industry in the following article.

R E A D I N G

Rock & Riches

by **Allan Parachini**

Adapted from the original article

Those kids are all making a bundle, right?

The houselights dim; the clamor of the crowd falls to a low buzz—low enough that the anticipatory coughing can be heard amid the hum of the PA system. In a moment the show will begin. It makes no difference what band is about to play, and it doesn't matter where. What is about to be unleashed, like a genie out of a bottle, is an IMAGE—magical, mysterious, and glamorous—one of many raised up by that energetic cultural force known as Rock, swathed in clouds of sumptuous glory, lauded in hymns of hyperbolic praise, and flattered by the proliferation of those smaller-scale imitations known as Lifestyle. This pantheon of heros and heroines has no parallel in contemporary culture, and we must go back to the early days of the silver screen—of Valentino, Pickford, and Garbo—to find anything like it. What it is is *myth*, a highly selective metaphor about life, of which both performers and their audiences, romanticized and romanticizing, are at once creators and consumers.

But myths are like Chinese boxes, one nestling inside the other on into infinity. The myth immediately inside the myth of the Rock Star is that of Untold Riches, and there is just

enough truth (though not much) to it to make it an effective magnet, drawing young people to New York, Los Angeles, Nashville, or wherever else music is made and recorded to declare themselves in on a piece of the action, a slice of the fabulous take.

They arrive in Los Angeles, for instance, by battered car or bus, check into the YMCA, and hit the street. They walk up to Yucca Street, or Vine near Hollywood Boulevard, look in the Yellow Pages under "Records," and start feeding change into a payphone. Then they wait, lounging on the sidewalk outside a liquor store, having given the payphone as "a number where I can be reached," for the return call that never comes. They have a common desire—a career in the music business—and a host of very uncommon, often highly original, misconceptions about just what that business is. They are, in short, as much prisoners or victims of their myth as any Fortyniner ever was, feeding their hopes on the good news of occasional rich strikes and ignoring the multitudinous evidence of failure all around them.

Rod Stewart, who once slept on a Spanish beach because he couldn't afford a hotel room, who used to play

professional soccer to support his music habit, now earns millions. At the top, the money piles up like winter snow in Donner Pass, and the bulldog tenacity that keeps so many musicians struggling up the lower slopes is fueled by the expectation that they too will eventually, if only they hang on, get to frolic in it. What are their chances?

Record companies sell almost two *billion* units in the United States each year. There are about 200 releases certified "gold" (meaning they sold 500,000 copies for an album, 1,000,000 copies for a single). Such figures translate very readily into Big Money, of course, and the myth has it that the musician is first in line to collect. And myth it is, for there are very few performers indeed in the most favored position.

The performer derives revenue primarily from two sources: live performances and record royalties. He may also earn something from song-publishing royalties (if he writes his own material), since there will then be royalty income from others who perform his songs and from radio stations that play them on the air as well. But before the musician realizes any income whatsoever, he must normally commit a percentage of all his earnings "up front" to a manager, unless he is clever enough to handle his own business affairs—including negotiating complicated contracts with record companies and booking agents; insuring that the provisions of those contracts are fulfilled; securing the most favorable possible terms for such seemingly incidental arrangements as production, promotion, and marketing of records, travel provisions for performance tours, and even the reservation of recording-studio time . . . .

For most musicians, a professional personal manager is an absolute necessity. Managers normally retain between 10 and 15 percent of the musician's entire gross income and can in some cases get as much as 20 or even 50 percent. Accountants (more and more indispensable the higher the sales figures get) are another accoutrement, and they get $300 to $800 a month. Such people are necessary not only to help the performer retain a reasonable part of his initial gross, but also to interpret the complex financial systems that appear to be peculiar to record companies; they

are needed to make certain the musician does not, plainly and simply, get ripped off . . . .

Managers are not a race of white knights, of course. Their ranks are heavily populated by the shady and by the inept, either of whom can leave a client musician, in the manner of one of those bilked innocents in an old prize-fight movie, with no return whatever for his efforts, gold record sales or no. Selection of a good (honest, capable) manager is therefore one of the music business' biggest risks.

But to return to the question of income. Record royalties, unlike the fees paid for live performances, are established contractually between record companies and musicians for periods of between one and five years. Gross royalties are computed on a base of 90 percent of the wholesale . . . price of each record actually sold. Retail discount prices do not bear on royalties. The performer gets between 5 and 18 percent of 90 percent of retail, say (depending on the terms of his contract), and though there are several ways to compute the

amount, they generally work out to about [$.70-$2.00] per album. The record producer gets a 3 or 5 percent royalty, which may in some cases be deducted from the musician's share, and the a-&-r (for "artists and repertoire") man who signed the artist to a record contract in the first place frequently gets 2 or 3 percent, normally from the record company's gross.

Under the royalty system, the *potential* for income from a record that sells well is actually not bad (more than $250,000 for a gold album for example), and if a musician has written his own songs, he receives an additional gross of 1 1/2 cents per song, per record, in song-publishing royalties. Normally, the manager has unobtrusively procured for himself some of the publishing proceeds; if he is honest, he has also done as much for his client. Otherwise, the naive musician may likely find that he has unknowingly signed away some or even all of the potential publishing income as part of a cash "advance" in an innocent-looking contract with a music-publishing firm or even his own record company.

Record companies have established what seems to be a unique sort of company-store relationship with their artists, one that tends to cut handsomely into the income potential of royalties. First, the record companies normally try to charge back to the artist as much of the actual cost of recording and marketing a record as possible. Such costs can amount to about $20,000 (for the most modestly produced album) to as much as $100,000 (for an over-produced spectacular). They include studio time, union pay for extra musicians, and other expenses too numerous and too unimaginable to mention—even the cost of the recording tape is levied against royalties. The record companies also charge their artists for some of the expenses of promoting and publicizing the resulting recording, including, for example, press parties

and the cost (from $750 to $1,500 per month) of retaining a private publicist. A modest tour may also be underwritten by the record company—and charged against the royalty gross; even a short introductory series of engagements in small clubs can run to as much as $50,000.

What results is in many cases an arrangement that would be bitterly familiar to any old-time Appalachian coal miner. Some recording acts owe so much of their soul to the company store that they never overcome their indebtedness; they can only watch helplessly as the royalties of their successful later records are eaten up in mid-career by early advances. Then too, determining the number of copies of a record actually sold is a task of no little difficulty. Records are distributed on consignment, meaning that unsold goods may be returned—for full credit—by individual record stores to small distributors, by small distributors to large, and large distributors to the original

record company. The consignment arrangement is a necessary one, since without it distributors and their clients would probably never gamble on a first release by an artist they had never heard of, or even on a great second release by someone who had bombed with his first. The problem

with this system is that it can take at least several months, and at times as much as several years, to determine accurately the exact number of copies of a recording sold. Record companies manage this situation to their advantage, often withholding a portion of royalties against the possibility of such returns . . . .

Though it is true that there is a comfortable living to be made in music (from $50,000 to $100,000 a year) for a small number of anonymous, unglamorous studio musicians (usually older, always highly skilled), the performing musician whose name appears on recordings and concert billings is usually not nearly so well off. Musicians are, in general, people of fragile egos and are often afflicted with a profound naivete. Those who can learn to adapt to the *business* of music survive—sometimes—and a few, very few, can move beyond that to the Big Money. But, for the most part, what the uninitiated see when they look up from the orchestra or down from the balcony is an illusion. Those are not dollar signs, but just the beam of a Super Trouper spotlight reflecting off a guitar purchased through an advance against royalties.

MEDIALAB

Rock and Reality

1. What mass media help to spread the image of the rock star as glamorous and rich, with a wild lifestyle? Why aren't the thousands of other recording artists written about as much?

2. Based on the article you just read and the graph on this page, approximately what percentage of the money you spend on records, tapes, or CDs actually goes to the performing artist(s)?

3. What do you think is the motivation that drives popular musicians most—the desire to make good music or the desire to make big money?

4. Make a class presentation on the realities of the recording industry. The presentation can be based on library research, or based on some real-life experience.

5. Do people in other media (television, film, writing, art) have managers?

6. After reading the article, draw up a class list of qualities needed to become a rock star.

7. What qualities are different from those needed to be an outstanding business leader, like Donald Trump or Rupert Murdoch?

WHERE YOUR RECORD, TAPE, AND CD DOLLAR GOES
(figures are industry averages)

Recording/royalties—Includes studio costs, fees to the musicians, tape editing, and arranging. Royalties include payment to the copyright owners for lyrics or music and royalties paid the artist when the record is sold. The artist or group typically receives between 5 to 10 percent of 90 percent of the retail price for each album sold. Top name stars can command a royalty of as much as 18 percent. Recording costs are usually charged to the artist and are deducted from later royalties.

Manufacture/package—Includes cost of the material in the final product (tape, CD, or record) and packaging.

Retail cost/profit—Includes the cost of bringing the recording to the store, the overhead of the sales outlet (record store), and the store's profit.

Distributor's profit—Distributors are middlepersons between the record companies and the retail outlets.

Advertising—Includes press releases, newspaper ads, posters, and space advertising.

Record company—Includes both profit and overhead of the record company.

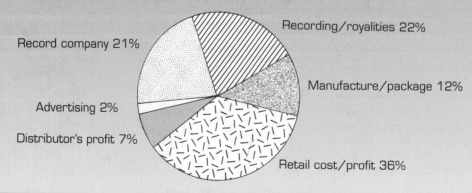

Record company 21%

Recording/royalties 22%

Advertising 2%

Distributor's profit 7%

Manufacture/package 12%

Retail cost/profit 36%

WRAP-UP

Recordings had their beginnings in 1877 with the invention of the phonograph by Thomas Edison. From cylinder to flat disc to 78 rpm, records evolved; by the 1920s they had become a popular medium. At first records were perceived as a threat to radio. However, with the invention of the LP, records soon became the content of radio programming. The early 1950s were an exciting time for the music and recording industry, with two major developments—magnetic or tape recording and rock 'n' roll. The development of audio cassettes and, later, compact discs further revolutionized the recording industry. In this chapter, you have researched facts and figures about the medium of recordings and looked at recent developments such as synthesizers and electronic music. You've surveyed your peers and thought about why buying and listening habits change, plus you've looked at the myth of the rock star and the reality of the recording industry. You can now better understand the ever-changing medium of recordings.

CHAPTER 11
Media Control

Who controls mass media in the United
States? First, take a look at the U. S.
government and the Bill of Rights.

GOVERNMENT AND THE MEDIA

In one sentence of the Bill of Rights, you will find the most significant statement about the U.S. government and the media. The First Amendment to the U.S. Constitution says: "Congress shall make no law. . . . abridging the freedom of speech, or of the press; or the right of the people peaceably to assemble . . . .

The First Amendment does *not* say that anyone can say anything. It says simply that Congress shall make no *law* that prevents (abridges) a person's freedom to speak. One reason for the First Amendment's existence is that a democracy needs an informed electorate who can vote and make decisions. Freedom of speech and freedom of the press exist not only for the speaker or the owner of the press but also for the audience. In other words, part of freedom of speech is the right of the people to have access to a variety of viewpoints and opinions.

Freedom of speech, like any freedom, is not absolute. No modern society has ever existed that did not impose some kind of restrictions on the press, on free speech, and on the right of the public to have information. If a newspaper owner writes and publishes a scathing attack on someone, calling him or her "a crook without morals and a danger to our society," that person could take legal action against the publisher. An attack on another person in print (or pictures or speech) that damages his or her character or reputation and is without truth is called *libel*. A person so attacked can sue the source of the libel for damages.

Freedom of speech and the press exists to promote a free exchange of information and opinions. According to Thomas Jefferson, one of the framers of the Constitution, the public interest could be best served by a society in which there were numerous newspapers free to express themselves without fear of government censorship. The citizens would have to make up their own minds and would be able to do so because they were able to consider the various viewpoints on important public issues. Citizens could also use these newspapers and pamphlets to make known their own views.

But in 1787 Thomas Jefferson and the others at the Constitutional Convention could not foresee the invention of electronic media and mass broadcasting. They could not see into the future and realize that by today major cities would have a free press controlled financially by only a handful of individuals. They could not foresee that printing a newspaper would become a multimillion-dollar industry or that there would be a device such as television that gives citizens very little opportunity to talk back.

Freedom of speech, like any freedom, is not absolute.

NEWSPAPER FREEDOM

Freedom of the press is a long-established tradition for newspapers in the United States and remains today a carefully guarded right. In recent years one of the questions raised concerning newspaper freedom is the right of reporters to conceal their sources of information. In several cases reporters have gone to jail rather than reveal their sources. The reporters contended that if they were forced to reveal sources, they would be less able to report the news in the future. People who might talk to reporters if they could remain unknown would often remain silent if courts could force reporters to tell who they were. Such a law would hamper

In 1969 the Supreme Court made it clear that the Bill of Rights is not for adults only.

the flow of news to the people and would, in effect, be a restriction on the public's right to know. On the other hand, such a privilege might place the reporter above the law and interfere with the judicial process. Some groups advocate a "shield law" that would protect reporters from court orders to reveal their sources, and such laws do exist in some places.

Another issue regarding newspaper freedom concerns school papers. In the sixties students at some colleges and high schools claimed they were being denied the constitutional right to freedom of speech and a free press. School officials argued that the school newspaper was an extension of the school and administrators had the right of control, just as they had control over rules of discipline.

In 1969 the Supreme Court made it clear that the Bill of Rights is not for adults only. The Court clarified the First Amendment rights of students in the ruling in *Tinker v. Des Moines Independent School District.* The case involved three Iowa high school students, aged 13 to 16, who wore black armbands to school to protest the war in Vietnam. They were asked by school authorities to remove the armbands but refused and were suspended from school.

The Supreme Court sided with the students and observed that wearing an armband is symbolic speech and is thereby protected by the First Amendment. More important, the Court held that students are indeed "persons" under the Constitution and have fundamental rights that school authorities must respect. According to the ruling, the freedom of speech and freedom of the press applied to students and student publications. In 1988, however, the *Hazelwood School District v. Kuhlmeier* case came before the Supreme Court. In this landmark decision, the Supreme Court ruled that administrators may exercise "editorial control over the style and content of student speech in school activities, so long as their actions are reasonably related to legitimate pedagogical concerns." This latest decision has, therefore, somewhat restricted the freedom of the press—as far as student speech and school-associated student newspapers are concerned.

Freedom of speech exists not only for the speaker but also for the audience.

broadcasting freedom

Electronic broadcasting is still in its infancy. Many people alive today remember the very first radios, and the early days of television are still part of the memories of many adults. Because of their relative newness, radio and television have no long tradition of First Amendment rights. The subject of broadcasting freedom is still very complicated and controversial.

The complications exist because the airwaves, unlike printing presses, are a limited resource. There are a limited number of television channels in each city (although the technology now exists to expand this number considerably), and even the number of radio frequencies is severely limited. In any city, the people who control the radio and TV stations could assemble easily in an average classroom. Since both television and radio are basically one-way communication devices, great care must be taken to assure the "free exchange of information and opinions" that so concerned Thomas Jefferson. But how can the government act to ensure this free exchange without setting itself up as dictator of what people may hear and see? This problem remains unsolved.

In many countries, the government owns and completely controls all radio and TV stations. In the United States, these outlets are privately owned; anyone with a few hundred thousand dollars can own a small radio station; TV stations cost more, often in the millions. If there were no central control over broadcasting, the result would be chaos. So many broadcasters would fight for the limited amount of airspace (a handful of TV channels, 97 AM frequencies, and about 120 FM channels) that stations would interfere with each other, and few people would get clear reception from any station. In the early days of radio this is precisely what did happen, as many amateurs and basement scientists set up their own radio stations. Finally, confusion grew so great that in 1934 the Federal Communications Commission was established to regulate broadcasting.

According to U.S. law, the airwaves are owned by the people. They are a natural resource like air and water and cannot be bought or sold by individuals or corporations. The FCC grants licenses to qualified groups or individuals to use the airwaves for the purpose of "serving the public good." Licenses are granted for a limited number of years and are renewed if the station can prove it has indeed served the public interest. Radio and TV stations are required to ask the people in their broadcast areas for criticisms and suggestions for improvement of their programming.

According to U.S. law, the air waves are a natural resource like air and water and cannot be bought or sold.

Other FCC Functions

The FCC controls broadcasting by deciding which of the many applicants for a radio frequency or a TV channel will be granted a license. Once the license is granted, the FCC does little to control program content.

The FCC does, however, require each radio and TV station to program time (how much time is not specified) in each of the following categories:

1. Opportunity for local expression (time for people in the local areas to express themselves on the air)

2. Development and use of local talent

3. Programs for children

4. Religious programs

5. Educational programs

6. Public affairs programs

7. Editorials (expressions of opinion) by the license holder

8. Political broadcasts

9. Agriculture programs

10. News

11. Weather and stock market reports

12. Sports

13. Programs for minority groups

14. Entertainment

The First Amendment to the Constitution states, "Congress shall make no law . . . abridging the freedom of speech, or of the press." The Communications Act of 1934 forbids the FCC from censoring broadcasters. In spite of these general laws, broadcasting is controlled, and some of these controls appear to be censorship.

The FCC is not allowed to tell radio or TV stations which programs to carry or avoid. Hundreds of court cases have been handed down that support the "keep the government out" belief. Still, the FCC does control some areas of program content.

An FM station may not duplicate the programming of an AM station for more than 25 percent of its weekly air time if the town has more than 25,000 people. This rule exists to force owners to create a greater variety of programming.

The FCC has no clear laws about the broadcasting of obscenity or profanity, but the U.S. Criminal Code does. The code imposes a fine or imprisonment for material that is clearly "offensive to community standards."

The FCC does forbid subliminal advertising. *Subliminal* means "below the level of consciousness." The most common subliminal technique is to flash one or two frames of film on a screen during a movie. The frame might say something like "Drink Fizzie." It would pass so fast that no one in the audience would be aware of having seen the message. Some psychologists believe that such a message still registers on the brain in spite of its "invisibility." Even though no evidence exists to show that so-called subliminal advertising works, it is banned by the FCC.

The FCC also requires commercials to be broadcast at the same level of sound as the surrounding program. Some TV stations have been known to turn up the volume for commercials, especially those shown late at night. This practice is illegal and TV stations argue it is not done, yet many viewers report that commercials are often louder than the show.s.

The Public Health Cigarette Smoking Act of 1970 forbids radio or television advertising for cigarettes and small cigars; but even before Congress acted, the FCC required stations to carry commercials about the dangers of smoking.

No laws exist to prevent the advertising of alcohol on television, yet broadcasters limit commercials to beer and wine and do not advertise hard liquor, such as whiskey.

Advertisers and broadcast stations themselves control the number of commercials per hour and their content.

> The FCC requires commercials to be broadcast at the same level of sound as the surrounding program.

DEREGULATION

What happened to broadcasting in the 1980s? One major trend was deregulation. Ronald Reagan's presidency brought with it a wave of decreased government control. The concept behind broadcast regulation in America before the Reagan presidency was that broadcasters were public servants entrusted with the airwaves. The airwaves were considered to be owned by the people. The government regulated TV and radio stations to be sure they served the public good. Stations were required to devote time to public service programs and to serve local communities. Station owners were required to own a station for at least three years before selling it; this rule was intended to discourage quick buying and selling simply for fast profit.

After deregulation, rules still exist, but they are far less demanding of station owners. The marketplace was allowed to exert its own controls. Government, during the Reagan years, followed a hands-off policy toward broadcasters. The Fairness Doctrine, instituted in 1959 by the FCC to ensure that radio and television present all sides of an issue and avoid "slanted news", was dismantled in 1987. Congress passed a bill to limit advertising during children's programming to 10.5 minutes an hour on weekends and 12 minutes on weekdays. The bill also required broadcasters to provide educational programming for kids in order to insure license renewal. The bill was vetoed by President Reagan during his last term and did not become law.

GOVERNMENT CONTROL OF ADVERTISING

Advertising in the United States is not as strictly controlled by the government as it is in other countries. In some European countries the "Unfair Competition" law prohibits advertisers from making "water is wet" claims. Some laws also forbid ads that might lead to a wrong conclusion. Even "so what" claims such as "margarine packed by hand" are forbidden under these laws, since packing margarine by hand gives it no extra advantage.

In Sweden the "truth-and-nothing-but-the-truth" Marketing Practices Act gives the government strict control to ensure that ads are scrupulously honest.

In the United States the federal agency charged with some degree of advertising regulation is the Federal Trade Commission (FTC). The FTC has limited power but reserves the right to take court action and order advertisers to cease and desist from what it considers deceptive advertising. The advertiser usually agrees to "sin no more"; if violations continue, the FTC can assess a civil penalty of up to $10,000 per day. In recent years the FTC has become less strict with advertisers, but has levied penalties and has even required a few advertisers to run corrective ads to make up for misleading claims made in their past advertising.

Other than broadcasting and advertising regulations, the federal government exercises little control over mass media. Newspaper, magazine, and book publishers are subject to U. S. laws, but there are few specific regulations or controls on what they can print.

CONTROL BY SOURCES

All mass media are controlled in some way by their sources. Newspapers can print only the news delivered to them or that their reporters uncover. Television programs and films are controlled by their producers and directors; magazine articles are subject to the complete control of editors, writers, and publishers. As media content passes through these hands, it is influenced by the normal human biases and perceptions.

Each medium has within it people who act as censors, although the word *censor* is rarely used. No magazine or book publisher has an official censor as an employee, yet the gatekeepers— all those who must pass judgment on the suitability of articles and photos— act in a way as censors.

Motion picture production is subject to several levels of censorship. The scriptwriter, the director, and the producer of a film control its contents so as not to produce a film that too many people will find revolting or disgusting. Their consideration in censorship is not so much to protect the public morals as it is to maintain a good box office.

In the 1960s the motion picture industry found that parents were afraid to allow their children to go to movies because they had no way of knowing whether the film was suitable for youngsters. A voluntary rating system was established to rate films: G—suggested for general audiences; PG—parental guidance suggested; PG-13—all ages, but parents urged to give special guidance to those children under 13; R—restricted, persons under 17 not admitted unless accompanied by parent or adult guardian; and X—persons under 18 not admitted. Many theaters interpret these ratings very strictly and will demand proof of age for admission to R or X-rated films. The rating system is voluntary and does not in itself carry the force of law.

Some cities and counties have local boards that screen all films about to play in the city or county. They have the power to demand that certain scenes be eliminated or that a film be banned altogether. The power of these censor boards has decreased in recent years, especially in large cities.

Each of the three major television networks has a censor who watches commercials and programs for scenes or words that might offend viewers. Feature films are often edited for television to remove some of the violence, sex, or language in the original version. Local television stations also have the right to refuse network programs, although they rarely do.

The reason for television's self-censorship is that the medium is public, open to anyone who turns on a TV set, including young children. Motion pictures, books, and magazines are usually less restrictive since to gain access one has to pay admission or purchase a copy.

Radio stations often refuse to play songs the station director feels have double meanings, encourage drug use, are unpatriotic, or are in some way in bad taste. During listener call-in shows, many radio stations use a seven-second delay system. With such a system, callers actually speak to a tape recorder that plays their calls over the air several seconds later. This delay is introduced so the program director can bleep out offensive words or cut off possibly libelous remarks.

In a recent development, the recording industry has responded to pressure from parent groups and record retailers by instituting a voluntary, uniform parental warning label program. Labels will be affixed to records, cassettes, and compact discs containing possibly objectionable lyrics. The use of the label is at the discretion of the record companies and individual artists. The Recording Industry Association of America, a trade association whose members produce 90 percent of the records sold in the U.S., hopes this voluntary control measure will eliminate the possibility of government action—that is, legislation requiring such labeling.

Economic Control

Magazines, newspapers, television, radio stations, and book publishers—all, with a few rare exceptions—share one common goal: to make money. This fact controls to some extent the content of these media.

With the exception of book publishing, all these media receive most of their income from advertising. The question thus arises: does advertising in any way influence the content of mass media?

One illustration of economic influence is the true case of the Car-Puter Company's attempt to buy ads in major newspapers and magazines. Car-Puter supplied customers with a computer print-out of dealer costs on any new car, including options. The company also supplied the name of a local automobile dealer

who, through a special arrangement would sell the customer the car for about $150 above dealer cost. The company charged the consumer $5 for this service, which is legitimate and helpful to consumers. However, when Car-Puter attempted to run a small ad, they were refused by most newspapers as well as by some magazines.

The ads were refused without a detailed explanation. The newspapers claimed they had a right to turn down any advertising—and they do. But the reason for the refusal most certainly was related to the fact that automotive ads are an important source of income for newspapers and magazines. Car-Puter Company would not be approved of by other auto advertisers.

As another example, sponsors of television programs are not likely to buy time for programs that attack business. Sponsors carefully monitor network TV shows. A group called "Stop Immorality on Television" asked major TV sponsors about their "moral stance" on the programs they sponsored. Gillette replied that "we try to see that our advertising runs in programs that are suitable for general family viewing." Eastman Kodak commented that they preview all scripts before the airing of a program: "If we find a script is offensive, we will withdraw our commercials from the program." Special interest groups, like the PTA, can and do exert pressure on program sponsors.

Although advertisers have no formal censorship power, they can exert great influence on the kinds of programs that networks will offer the viewers. A TV network would think twice before showing a documentary exposing the faults of the over-the-counter-drug industry, because so much of the network's advertising revenue comes from painkillers and headache remedies.

A question often asked at networks is "Will the show gain sponsors?" The importance of this question can easily limit consideration of another question: "What is in the best interests of the public?"

Newspapers and magazines vary widely in the amount of control they allow advertisers to exert. Some keep news and ads completely separate and will report the problems and failings of local food chains or auto dealers even though these provide the paper with thousands of dollars yearly in advertising revenue. Some newspapers, however, still have a policy of not "biting the hand that feeds them." If the health department closes or issues a warning to a local food store or restaurant, such papers will ignore the story for fear of hurting the advertiser's reputation. A story about a shady car dealer or home builder might go unreported if that company is a large advertiser in the newspaper.

Such control is less frequent now than it used to be, but it still exists, especially among smaller newspapers struggling to stay in business.

The recording industry puts pressure on radio stations to play their songs. Every time a radio station plays a recording, the exposure is as good as or better than an ad. The more radio stations play any given song, the more it sells. Record companies can give away free recordings but are not supposed to give money to stations as an inducement to play the records. There have been many instances in the past of record companies slipping a little extra money ("payola") to disc jockeys to gain air time for a song. The practice is less common now.

Audience Control

The ratings game is a deadly serious business.

The most common kind of control over mass media is the one most often overlooked—control by the audience. If few people watch a TV show, it dies. If only a few hundred people subscribe to a city newspaper, it stops publishing. If a film is a box office flop, similar films will be less likely to receive backing.

A complicating factor in audience control or censorship of the mass media is the fact that no two people in the same mass audience experience a program or news story in exactly the same way. Each member of the audience brings prejudices, biases, and a lifetime of experiences that shape his or her feelings and reactions to the content in the media.

An interesting experiment suggests exactly how important this factor is in control-by-the audience. A special slide viewer was constructed with one hole for each eye; a person looked into it as into a pair of binoculars. In the slide viewer were two pictures, one for each eye. One slide pictured a baseball player and the other a bullfighter. First, a group of American teachers looked into the viewer and were asked what they saw. Next a group of Mexican citizens looked and reported what they saw. The results? More Americans reported seeing the baseball player, while more Mexicans reported seeing the bullfighter. The experiment points out that people see what they have been taught to see.

Every time we look at a picture, an inkblot, a cloudy sky, a painting, a film, or a newspaper, we see those things that are most comfortable to see. We see only what fits our view of the way the world should be and we filter out those things that don't seem to fit. This process of selective seeing is called perceptual filtering.

Each time a newscast shows a police officer struggling with a young person, the viewing audience gives the event a variety of interpretations. Some see the event as yet another example of police brutality, while others see young punks getting what they deserve; some see law and order at work, while others see society falling apart.

No matter how much the government or advertisers attempt to control mass media, there is no way to ensure that the audience will agree with what is presented or even see the same thing as the people next door.

In addition to the process of perceptual filtering, the media consumer controls the content of the media by selecting which program to watch, which magazines to subscribe to, which books or records to buy, which newspapers to read, or which radio stations to listen to. Each decision to use a mass medium can be thought of as a sort of vote approving that medium's content.

The owners of any media outlet keep a constant record of the size and type of audience they attract. The number of units sold is the main measurement for magazines, books, newspapers, records, and films. Television and radio must rely on estimates of audience numbers called ratings.

A number of companies offer ratings services to television and radio. The largest and best known company is Nielsen Media Research Company—so much so that ratings are sometimes called Nielsens. The Nielsen ratings have been accused of reflecting only the habits of those who watch a lot of television. But the networks have found this system the best available and so the Nielsen ratings usually determine a program's future—or lack of it.

The ratings list shown on the next page indicates the popularity of certain shows at the end of 1988. For the "Bill Cosby Show," for example, the rating was 27.9. This means that 27.9 percent of all households with a television watched the "Bill Cosby Show."

Each decision to use a mass medium can be thought of as a sort of vote approving that medium's content.

Top 15 Regularly Scheduled Network Programs

Total U.S. TV Households	AA%
1. Bill Cosby Show	27.9
2. A Different World	23.4
3. Cheers	22.8
4. Roseanne	22.3
4. Golden Girls	22.3
6. 60 Minutes	22.2
7. Who's the Boss?	20.8
8. Growing Pains	20.2
9. Empty Nest	19.8
10. Murder, She Wrote	19.3
11. Dear John	18.3
12. Head of the Class	18.2
13. Hogan Family	17.9
14. L.A. Law	17.8
15. Alf	17.5

Men 18 +	AA%
1. 60 Minutes	16.4
2. NFL Mon. Night Football	15.7
3. CBS NFL Football Gm. 1	15.0
4. Bill Cosby Show	14.3
5. Cheers	12.8
6. NFL Game 2	12.6
7. Murder, She Wrote	11.9
8. CBS NFL Football Gm. 2	11.5
9. A Different World	11.4
9. Golden Girls	11.4
11. L.A. Law	11.2
11. NBC Sun. Night Movie	11.2
13. ABC Sun. Night Movie	11.0
14. Roseanne	10.7
15. NFL Single Game	10.6

Children 2-11	AA%
1. Bill Cosby Show	21.8
2. A Different World	18.2
3. Hogan Family	17.7
4. Alf	17.3
5. Roseanne	15.8
6. Who's the Boss?	15.5
7. Growing Pains	15.2
8. Family Ties	15.0
9. Magical World of Disney	14.5
10. Head of the Class	14.2
11. Garfield & Friends	13.0
12. Muppet Babies II	12.9
13. Pee Wee's Playhouse	12.8
14. Golden Girls	11.5
14. Cheers	11.5

Women 18 +	AA%
1. Bill Cosby Show	21.7
2. Golden Girls	18.8
3. A Different World	17.4
4. Roseanne	17.1
5. Cheers	16.8
6. 60 Minutes	16.6
6. Murder, She Wrote	16.6
6. Empty Nest	16.6
9. Who's the Boss?	15.4
10. Knots Landing	14.5
11. Growing Pains	14.4
12. Dear John	13.7
12. Dallas	13.7
12. Hunter	13.7
15. L.A. Law	13.2

Teens 12-17	AA%
1. Bill Cosby Show	21.3
2. A Different World	19.7
3. Hogan Family	17.2
4. Roseanne	16.9
5. Growing Pains	16.6
6. Head of the Class	16.1
7. Cheers	15.4
8. Alf	14.9
9. Who's the Boss?	14.8
10. Family Ties	13.3
11. Wonder Years	13.0
12. Golden Girls	12.6
13. ABC Sun. Night Movie	12.5
14. NBC Sun. Night Movie	12.2
15. Day By Day	11.2

Nielsen Average Audience
Estimates 2 or more telecasts
(15 mins. or longer)
November 1988

Nielsen Media Research

Surveyors have found people who are part of the random sample living in boxcars, beer trucks, caves, and trees.

Nielsen Ratings

Nielsen Media Research compiles its ratings by installing devices called people meters in 4,000 carefully chosen households. These selected "Nielsen households" are given small gifts for their help and assistance in paying for TV repairs. Households that have been in the sample for 24 months are replaced in order to increase the total number of households and prevent skewed or inaccurate measurements. The randomly-selected group of households must mirror the interests and characteristics of the entire population. Nielsen selects households at random but sends surveyors to locate each sample. Surveyors have found people who are part of the random sample living in railroad boxcars, beer trucks, caves, and trees. Over half the randomly-selected "families" cooperate with the ratings effort.

Nielsen households are equipped with a people meter. It is a small device containing a sophisticated microprocessor that sits atop the television set. Each household member's age, sex, and

Nielsen's people meter is an electronic device used to measure viewing habits of a household. (Photo courtesy of Nielsen Media Research)

other demographic information is programmed into the Nielsen people meter. An accompanying remote-control device records who is viewing. Both have a series of buttons, one for each member of the household and guest viewers. Each household member pushes the assigned button when beginning to watch television.

Advertisers can thus determine if the members of a specific target audience—say, men aged 25 to 54 who watch the first basketball game of the season—continue to watch through the finals.

Nielsen is also developing an audience measurement system that is passive, meaning it requires no viewer button pushing. An infrared scanning system scans the viewing area in a room in seven seconds, detects and records heat generated by people, and processes the information. The passive scanner supplements the people meter to determine when someone enters or leaves the viewing area.

Each day Nielsen computers "call" the people meters at 3:00 A.M. to gather information. By 3:15 that afternoon Nielsen produces the daily ratings report, available to clients online.

MEDIALAB

Researching Media Control

1. Do you think the current film rating system (G, PG, PG-13, R, X) is fair and just? What problems would arise if films were not rated? Is it fair to restrict admission to certain films to those under 18 years of age?

2. Act as a group of network censors meeting to draw up a list of examples of things not to be allowed on commercials and programs. What is on that list?

3. Prepare a brief report on mass media (or one of the media) in some country other than the United States. Compare the operation and control of the media in that country with the situation in the United States.

4. Set up small groups to go to the offices of local radio and television stations and ask to see the "public file" concerning license renewal. Report to the class on some of the file's more interesting contents.

5. The following are brief descriptions of actual court cases concerned with media control. Discuss and debate each case and reach a decision of your own before looking at the court's decision at the end of the Medialab.

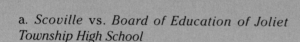

a. *Scoville* vs. *Board of Education of Joliet Township High School*

Two students were expelled for distributing a "literary journal" on school grounds. The magazine contained an editorial critical of the school administration and urged students to disregard school rules. There is no direct evidence that the publication actually caused any disruption in the school process. The students wrote the magazine and sold 60 copies at a price of 15 cents each.

The lower court ruled that the language took the "form of immediate incitement to disregard legitimate administrative regulations necessary to the orderly maintenance of a public high school system." In other words, the magazine was a "clear and present danger" to the orderly operation of the school and so was not entitled to First Amendment protection. The students could reasonably be punished for their conduct.

The case was then taken to a court of appeals. Discuss the case and reach your own decision; then compare your opinion with the actual ruling or decision reached by the court of appeals.

b. *ACT* vs. *TIO*

The Television Information Office (TIO) is an organization that acts as a public relations arm for the television industry. It prepares TV spots, printed reports, and other services designed to enhance the image of television. One of its TV spots (made by TIO and offered free to TV stations to use as public service announcements) pointed out the benefits of TV programming for children. Many stations around the country used the spot.

Action for Children's Television (ACT), a group concerned with improving children's programming and often critical of the television industry, requested that the FCC, under the fairness doctrine (still in effect at that time), order stations that carried the TIO ads also to carry a counter-ad pointing out that children's television is "unimaginative, inartistic, commercial-ridden, and harmful to children." Because the FCC created the doctrine, it—rather than a court made the ruling on this case. How would you decide?

6. Why do you think liquor advertising is limited on television? Remember that a glass of beer or wine contains about the same amount of alcohol as a mixed drink. Could you propose a better approach to the control of advertising for alcoholic beverages?

7. Cigarette advertising is not permitted on television but can appear in newspapers and magazines. Would you favor cigarette advertising as (a) allowed anywhere to protect freedom of speech, or (b) forbidden everywhere since it is a drug and a social menace?

8. Here are typical comments from a network censor about an old NBC series, a Western called "High Chaparral": "Victims of homicide are to be shown with their eyes closed and not positioned grotesquely." "In the montage of the warring Indians being hunted down and shot, take care that this is not overdone so that it becomes a brutal thing; nor should we see Buck [one of the characters] grinning fiercely just before the killing. This would give him the aspect of a sadist." "As the kid is shot and he starts to fall, please avoid sensationalizing the fall as he goes tumbling down the rocks. It will be unacceptable to see the kid bouncing from rock to rock in his fall." "As Maria cradles the dying Ramon in her arms, avoid showing the knife protruding from Ramon's chest."

Do you think these observations are valid or do the observations tend to make the violence that does appear more unreal and therefore more harmful than if it were presented in a realistic way? Support your answer.

9. The chart on page 306 lists the top fifteen regularly scheduled network programs and the audience share for each by various groups. Judging only from the chart, why is the "Bill Cosby Show" top-rated? Remember, base your answer *only* on information from the chart, not from what you know about the show. How many of these shows (ranked as of November 1988) are still popular?

The number in the column labeled AA% (meaning percentage of *average audience*) is a rating; it indicates what percentage of all television sets in use are tuned to that show. Why does the number one show (Cosby Show) in the category of total U.S. TV households have a higher rating number than the number one show in the four other categories?

Decisions (activity 5): In *Scoville* vs. *Joliet Board* of Education, the Court of Appeals found that the expulsion of the students was unjustified and constituted an invasion of their First and Fourteenth Amendment rights.

In *ACT* vs. *TIO*, the FCC denied the argument of Action for Children's Television and emphasized that the fairness doctrine required an overall balance on issues and that ACT had not proved the spots created an imbalance. (Note the FCC's fairness doctrine was dismantled later, as part of deregulation.)

WRAP-UP

How are the media controlled in the United States? As you have learned, mass media have always thrived in the United States because of the freedom of speech and freedom of the press—First Amendment rights. In this chapter you have learned these freedoms are not absolute. The government exerts some control over the media. Media also regulate themselves through censors or gatekeepers. In addition, economic factors control the content and programming of media, along with advertisers and special interest groups. In this chapter you have learned that you can exert control over broadcast media through your viewing habits and perceptional filtering. You've taken a look at Nielsen television ratings and the people meter. Being aware of how mass media are influenced and controlled by government, self-regulation, advertisers, and people, in general, will help you understand how mass media have developed to their present forms.

CHAPTER 12

Media and Our Image of the World

How have mass media formed or influenced your perceptions?

STEREOTYPE

Each person has a mental picture of what the world out there is like. For centuries, this picture was shaped by personal experience and education. These two factors are still present in shaping mental pictures, but there is a third force that assumes an ever-increasing importance. Today, mass media play a major role in teaching people what the world is like.

By pushing aside the limitations of experience and schooling, mass media have created a nation of people who have opinions on just about every subject and mental pictures of places never visited, people never encountered, and events experienced only as tiny images on a television screen. News and entertainment media distribute so much information about the world that many educators claim schools are no longer the main source of learning for most people. Mass media have taken over the role of forming our mental image of the world.

Our mental map or picture of the world is in some areas quite detailed and well developed. But sometimes our picture of the world out there is only a rough sketch with few details. Human psychology seems to demand that the sketch be filled in with details. Once the outline is formed, we use what we are taught by our parents, schools, and mass media to fill in the details. Often what we are taught, though, is stereotype.

Stereotypes provide the illusion that we know our way around in what otherwise would be unknown territory.

A stereotype is an oversimplified idea of something, based on limited experience. For example, for four years, between the ages of 6 and 10, Henry lived in a neighborhood where there was one French family on the block. This particular family was unable to keep a neat house or yard, and people in the neighborhood talked about those "sloppy Frenchies." From this limited experience, Henry generalized that people from France were generally sloppier and dirtier than Americans. Henry never went to France, never met many other French people, and did little reading. When he married and had children, he still made remarks about "sloppy Frenchies." Henry's children also grew up believing that people from France were dirty and sloppy.

The application to an entire group of the qualities of a limited sample of that group is a stereotype. In themselves, stereotypes

Jean Stapleton and Carroll O'Connor played the media-created stereotyped characters of Edith and Archie Bunker in the classic television series "All in the Family."

are a convenient mental device. They help us deal with the vast amount of reality that can never be known in detail. The problem is that most stereotypes contain only a kernel of truth and so are dangerous if taken to be the whole truth.

Stereotypes give people a feeling of security, a feeling that something complex is understood. They provide the illusion that we know our way around in what otherwise would be unknown territory. When the stereotypes we hold (and everyone believes *some* stereotypes) are attacked or challenged, we view this as a personal attack and often actively defend our stereotypes.

Clearly, stereotypes are not limited to the prejudiced or bigoted, to racial categories, or to the unschooled. Many stereotypes are strengthened by the mass media, although at other times those same media replace a commonly held stereotype with a fuller picture. Because of the power of mass media, some stereotypes are rather commonly accepted as the full truth.

Television, for example, often shows cardboard characters—people whose personalities are not developed in the plot.

Television, for example, often shows cardboard characters —people whose personalities are not developed in the plot. These cardboard characters—such as the jolly fat man, the dumb secretary, or the hard-boiled cop—are easily recognized by viewers and can be used for laughs or instant plot development. The constant repetition of such characters tends to condition viewers to expect fat people to be jolly or secretaries, dumb or cops, hard-boiled. People who belong to often-stereotyped groups find it difficult to overcome media-created expectations.

On television, murder, assault, and armed robbery are the most common crimes. In reality, quiet burglaries, clever larcenies, unspectacular auto thefts, and drunkenness are the most common. Video detectives solve 90 percent of their cases. In reality, the figure is considerably lower. On television only 7 percent of violence occurs between relatives. In reality this accounts for 25 to 30 percent of interpersonal violence.

Groups that are often stereotyped include the following:

Scandinavians	"Jocks"	Handicapped people
Poles	People on welfare	Wealthy persons
Women	Jews	Librarians
Texans	Teenagers	Radicals/Conservatives/
Italians	People over 65	Liberals
French	Housewives	Professors
Blacks	Intellectuals	Scientists
Mexicans	Construction workers	Overweight people
Artists	Professional athletes	
"Punk-rockers"	Straight-A students	

Sometimes mass media do replace stereotypes with a fuller picture of a group of people. Stereotypes are easy and familiar, however, and the media will continue to use them as long as audiences accept them.

MEDIALAB

Mass Media and Stereotypes

1. Are stereotypes always bad? Are they always partially wrong? Of what use are stereotypes?

2. Why do stereotypes exist?

3. Find examples of some of the stereotyped qualities of as many of the groups on the list as you (as a class) can. Add to the list other stereotyped groups. A good way to fill in the details about a stereotyped group is to brainstorm each group, starting with the statement, "Most (*name of stereotyped group*) are presented as . . . ."

4. Find examples of stereotypes in any mass medium and bring them to class.

5. As a research project select one group you believe has been stereotyped. Describe the stereotype and bring evidence of its falseness. For example, you might believe that the stereotype of people on welfare being lazy loafers is unfair. As proof you could bring reliable statistics showing that only a small percentage of those on welfare are able-bodied men—most of those on welfare being disabled, elderly, or women with dependent children.

6. Find someone in the class who can tell of a stereotype that he or she has recently learned is not true.

7. Find examples of cardboard characters on television. Explain why you think they are not realistic.

8. How do cartoons use stereotypes for humorous effect?

9. Assume you are the National Minister of Stereotypes in a country where all mass media are government controlled. You have access to whatever media you desire. Devise a media campaign to create a stereotype of a certain group you want to elevate to positions of power. For your campaign to be most effective, the citizens of your country should remain unaware of it, yet become completely convinced of the truth of the stereotype you are creating.

10. Find some group of which you are a member that is the target of occasional stereotyped comments. Refute those stereotypes.

11. Pick some group that is frequently stereotyped on television (women, teenagers, fathers, criminals). Conduct a study by watching as much prime-time television as you can for a week or longer and note each time a member of the group appears in any way on a show or commercial. Take notes on how the person is presented. Compile your notes and present your own report titled "How Television Stereotypes (*name of group*)."

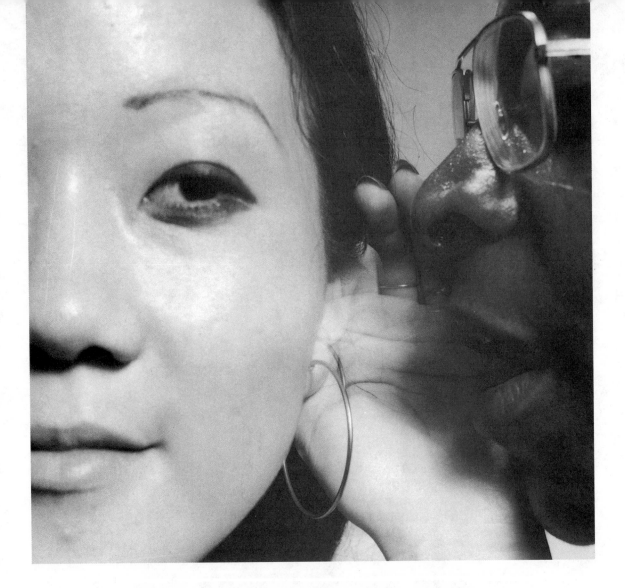

RUMOR AND DISTORTION

Rumors are stories that grow as they go. Rumors fall somewhere between the extremes of gossip and news. Rumors and stereotypes are distant cousins. Both contain some truth combined with a large and often dangerous amount of nontruth. Both can lead people to irrational action, both are often accepted as truth, and both can be created, intensified, or lessened by mass media.

Rumors often start out as truth. A psychologist once planted a rumor in the cafeteria of an Air Force base by asking, "Is it true they are building a tunnel big enough to move B-52's to town?" A half day later the planted question came back to him as a statement: "They are building a tunnel to move B-52's to town." Notice the differences: The original question came back as a statement, without the "Is it true?" at the beginning. Added to the statement was the fact that a tunnel was being built to move B-52's, whereas the original question merely referred to a tunnel big enough to move B-52's. The distortions introduced are typical of those that convert fact to rumor.

1 2 3 *main ways of distorting the truth*

True stories are distorted in three main ways in becoming rumors—sharpening, leveling, and assimilation. *Sharpening* refers to the tendency for items in the original story to become more dramatic. A weapon becomes a loaded gun. A large octopus becomes a sea monster.

Leveling refers to the fact that as the story is repeated, details drop out rapidly at first and then level off to a simple, easily repeatable version.

Assimilation refers to the tendency for stories to be repeated in terms familiar to the person telling the story. A rumor that starts about an event in a European cafe might end up being told in the United States as happening in a fast-food restaurant.

Rumors usually serve some kind of emotional need. One researcher has coded rumors into three basic varieties: (a) pipe dreams, expressing wishful thinking; (b) bogie rumors, arising from fears and worries; and (c) wedge-driving, dividing groups and destroying loyalties.

Pipe-dream rumors seem the least frequent. A common example of a bogie rumor is the sighting of a flying saucer—a report often verified by numerous people. The wedge-driving rumor is particularly popular in politics. During the 1972 presidential campaign, a New Hampshire newspaper attacked a presidential candidate, former Senator Edmund Muskie, for supposedly making an insulting remark about the French-Canadians in the state, calling them "Canucks." The only evidence the paper had was a letter from someone who said he had heard the remark. Though this letter was later discovered to be a fake planted by the opposition, the incident harmed Muskie's standing with French-Canadian voters in the primary election.

Writer Norman Mailer has coined the term *factoid* to describe rumors that have no existence except that they appear in print or in another medium. In spite of their lack of truth, people repeat them as if they were facts. *Pseudo-facts* might be another appropriate term.

A pseudo-fact can cause harm. In 1883, the Brooklyn Bridge had been open only six days when tragedy struck. Even though thousands of people had walked safely across the bridge, rumor had spread that it was unsafe and would collapse. Someone screamed while walking across the bridge, and panic followed as the cry "The bridge is falling" spread. Forty people were injured and twelve were trampled to death as a result of panic caused by that rumor.

Mass media have the ability to cause a rumor to sweep the nation. In 1938 a famous radio broadcast of the drama *War of the Worlds* set off a nationwide rumor that invaders from outer space had landed in New Jersey, causing a small panic.

Since mass media can spread facts quickly, they usually tend to control rather than inflame rumors. For instance, during urban rioting, television and radio have both provided rumor control centers, reassuring viewers and listeners that disturbances were only in certain areas, that fires were under control, that the trouble was not spreading, and so on.

One exception to this tendency serves to illustrate the power of the media and people's belief in television. On the "Tonight" show, Johnny Carson said on national television, "You know what else is disappearing from the supermarket shelves? Toilet paper. There's an acute shortage of toilet paper in the United States."

By noon the next day supermarkets all over the country were faced with a stampede of people buying from 5 to 25 extra rolls. The kind of toilet paper that was in short supply was not the kind sold in stores, but government-issue toilet paper bought only in large lots by bids. Carson had made the point clear that his comment was not a news report but only a humorous speculation. Yet because of leveling, sharpening, and assimilation, within four days there was a real shortage of the better-quality supermarket paper because people were hoarding.

Officials of the Scott Paper Company assured the public to "stay calm. There just isn't any shortage." By the middle of January supermarket shelves were full again, thus assuring shoppers there was no shortage. One TV star watched by millions can start a national spree of toilet-paper buying. One wonders in what other ways the remarks of widely watched TV personalities can influence what people do and think.

MEDIALAB

Routing Out Rumors

1. As a class experiment, conduct a study in the process of rumor creation. One person looks at a picture and describes it to another. The second person, who does *not* see the picture, repeats the description to a third person. The third person repeats the description to a fourth and so on, until a sixth person has received the verbal picture description. The first and last picture descriptions should be tape-recorded for study. Compare the first description with the final to see what differences there are. Are any of the differences explainable as leveling, sharpening, or assimilation? The best kind of picture to use is one from a newspaper or magazine that shows several people doing something.

2. What are some interesting rumors you've read about or heard recently? Note: Gossip is more personal (about someone in the school, for example) than rumor.

3. Find out if your local government has a rumor control center. If so, find out what it does and perhaps invite someone from the center to talk to the class.

4. If there were no mass media, do you think there would be more rumors or fewer? Why? How do mass media serve in time of crisis or disaster to cause or prevent panic and rumors?

INFLUENCE ON LANGUAGE AND THOUGHT

Mass media have had an obvious effect on many facets of every-day life. Here are three ways in which mass media influence language and thought.

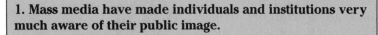

1. Mass media have made individuals and institutions very much aware of their public image.

Do you wish to be more successful? More loved and accepted? Do you want to appear to be a winner? Being a winner is easy, mass media tells us. You don't have to change yourself, just change your image. Put on a different public mask; change the image that others see. The advice is given for individuals moving up the corporate ladder, for lowly politicians who wish to become president, or for aging institutions that need new life.

Mass media present images, not reality. Human beings do not appear on television screens. What we see are only twelve-inch-tall images drained of blood and flesh and converted into electronic signals. Newspaper reporters quote carefully considered words, not deep feelings or honest emotions. Stars of popular music and movies project carefully constructed masks for the masses—the people behind the masks are far less important. The image counts.

Mass media present images, not reality.

Politicians and other public figures who survive on the basis of their images often make statements carefully designed to offend no one. Politicians have always been known for their ability to appear to be all things to all people, but only since mass media have threatened to make every statement public knowledge have they truly mastered the art of public evasion.

Before press conferences, television news coverage, and mass-circulation newsweeklies, what a candidate for office might say to a crowd one day could easily be changed the next, and only the closest observers would notice. Today, however, mass media act as a reminder of what the politician said yesterday or even last year. Such a public memory can be embarrassing. Instead of keeping candidates honest, media memory seems to keep them vague. Many politicians believe the safest way to speak is to phrase statements so they can be interpreted in a variety of ways—all favorable to the listener. Too much of such intentional vagueness, however, can cause the public to see the image of a spineless or wishy-washy candidate.

Politicians and spokespersons for corporations are not alone in their concern for how the public will interpret their words. Professional organizations in many fields encourage their members to choose words carefully so as to create a favorable public image. Janitors have become maintenance engineers, garbage collectors are sanitation workers, and undertakers are funeral directors.

A professional organization concerned with the public image of dentists gave them the following list of words to help them speak their way to a better image:

Do Say	Don't Say
Reception room	Waiting room
Treatment room	Operatory
Consultation room	Private
Case discussion	Case presentation
Necessary X-rays	Full-mouth series
Diagnostic models	Study models
Complete dentistry	Rehabilitation
Treatment or dentistry	Work
Considerable (or small amount of) decay	Cavities, areas, or surfaces
Restoration	Filling
Sedative dressing or medicinal restoration	Temporary filling
Removal	Extraction
Follow-up visit or preventive program	Recall
Prepare the tooth	Grind the tooth
Partial denture	Partials
Primary or foundation teeth	Baby teeth
My assistant	My girl
Fee	Bill
How did you plan	Would you like
Take care of	Pay for
Payment arrangements	Financial arrangements
Agreement	Contract or note
Investment	Cost
Did you want to take care of this by cash or check?	That will be ten dollars.
Three twenty-seven	Three hundred twenty-seven
I recommend	I suggest
The doctor recommends	Doctor would like
Bookkeeper's allowance	Discount
Professional courtesy	Professional discount
Thorough examination	Check up
Mrs. Scott, Doctor is ready to see you now.	Would you like to come in?
Uncomplicated	Simple
Dr. Adams is with a patient right now. This is Ann, Doctor's secretary. How may I help you?	Who's calling please? Doctor is busy. May I help you?
Do you prefer mornings or afternoons?	When would you like to come in?
Doctor's schedule is filled for today. However, she can see you . . .	She's all booked up. She can't see you until . . .

Even teachers (or is it educators?) have tried to use words to influence the way they are viewed by parents. Consider the following helpful hints given to the teachers of a school in New York for talking to parents and writing comments on report cards:

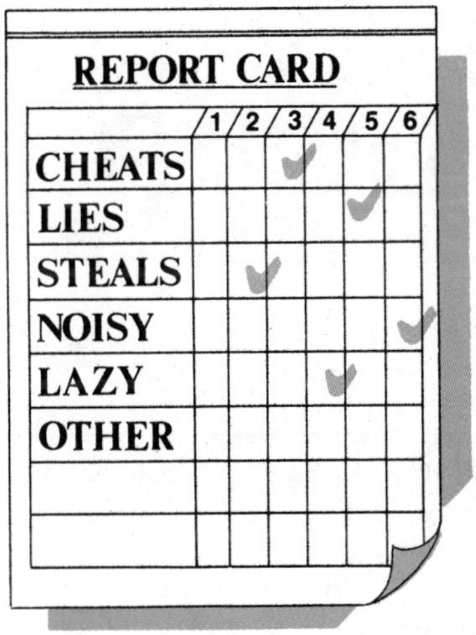

FOR PARENT INTERVIEWS AND REPORT CARDS

Harsh Expression (Avoid)	Euphemism
1. Does all right if pushed.	Accomplishes tasks when interest is stimulated.
2. Too free with fists	Resorts to physical means of winning his point or attracting attention.
3. Lies (Dishonest)	Shows difficulty in distinguishing between imaginary and factual material.
4. Cheats	Needs help in learning to adhere to rules and standards of fair play.
5. Steals	Needs help in learning to respect the property rights of others.
6. Noisy	Needs to develop quieter habits of communication.
7. Lazy	Needs ample supervision in order to work well.
8. Is a bully	Has qualities of leadership but needs help in learning to use them democratically.
9. Associates with gangs	Seems to feel secure only in group situations; needs to develop a sense of independence.
10. Disliked by other children	Needs help in learning to form lasting friendships.

REPORT CARD

	1	2	3	4	5	6
CHEATS		✓				
LIES				✓		
STEALS	✓					
NOISY					✓	
LAZY			✓			
OTHER						

2. Advertising has used some of our most important and meaningful words so many thousands of times that the words may have lost some meaning.

Consider words like:

love   alive

freedom   excitement

Advertising influences words much like inflation influences the dollar.

Sometimes these words are used by advertisers to hint that the product will somehow create freedom, love, or aliveness. The ads often imply that if you use this brand, you will experience freedom; if you apply that brand, you will feel more alive. Such hints or indirect appeals can be attractive to people who fear they are not loved or who frequently feel bored or trapped. Love, freedom, and a sense of aliveness are all very difficult and fragile states of being. They are goals that require struggle and often great effort and even pain.

If we repeatedly hear phrases such as "Fizzle soda tastes like love," or "Love is giving a gift of a fine watch," or "Virginia is for lovers," or "Au Revoir perfume is love in a bottle," doesn't the word *love* mean less when used to express a genuine feeling?

If *freedom* is riding a motorcycle on a dirt hill on a Saturday afternoon, or driving a certain kind of car, or having a no-wax floor, or wearing a certain brand of jeans, then isn't the personal struggle for true freedom somehow made less important?

If being *alive* is drinking a cola, having a second car, or being able to eat caviar while riding on a yacht, then doesn't the word *alive* mean less?

Advertising influences words much like inflation influences the dollar. The constant application of words like *love*, *freedom*, and *aliveness* to everyday products make these words worth less. Today's dollar buys less than the dollar of ten years ago; similarly, today's *love* means less than the *love* of ten years ago.

3. Mass media present models of language for our imitation.

Students in English classes examine grammar, usage, and examples of correct English. However, a few dozen homework assignments, an occasional test, or even a six-week crash course in grammar are tiny efforts in comparison to the thousands of media messages we see and hear every day. Each media message can be considered an example of acceptable grammar and language use. Media users simply spend far more money to present examples of language than any school system.

Many, perhaps most, of the language messages sent through mass media use language correctly and creatively. Ad writers, speechwriters, and newswriters are educated people who know more about the correct use of language than most people.

Many of the slogans, buzzwords or catch phrases, and jingles find their way into the everyday speech of millions. The expressions and speech mannerisms of popular television entertainers or commercials are repeated perhaps millions of times a day by those who formed the original audience. Often our idea of a clever phrase is a copy of one we heard on television the night before.

On some occasions, media "teach" incorrect grammar. Some advertisers seem to feel that the audience they want to reach finds incorrect grammar the normal way of communicating. So to "speak their language," the advertiser will intentionally use incorrect grammar. One cola manufacturer advertised "What's good enough for other folks *ain't* good enough for me." They knew *ain't* is not proper in print but probably felt that potential cola drinkers would find the word the most appropriate. Perhaps they thought "What's good enough for other folks isn't good enough for me" would sound awkward. The cola advertiser may have said, "What's good enough for the masses is good enough for our ads."

The nonword *gonna* sometimes appears in print ads and the word *got* is often used incorrectly. The hair conditioner slogan "You're gonna swear you got more hair" illustrates both. The phrase in proper construction is "You're going to swear you have more hair."

Got is a perfectly acceptable word. It is part of the present perfect "have got." A beer claims, "If you've got the time, we've got the beer." A fast-food chain claims, "We've got the best darned burger in the whole wide world." These are examples of the correct use of *got*. But a car manufacturer who uses the simple phrase "you got it" isn't making a clear statement or one that is grammatically correct. The ad headline "what you want, it's got" would be more correctly written as "it has what you want."

Grammatical errors are relatively easy to find in advertising and in the speech of people on talk shows. Do such mass examples of poor language use have any influence on the way we speak or write? Do the thousands of examples of correct language and grammar do more to improve our language? Perhaps media have little if any effect on our language. What do you think?

MEDIALAB

Recognizing Media Language

1. Find examples in newspapers and magazines of politicians using language to create a favorable public image.

2. Do mass media help keep politicians honest in any way? Support your answer.

3. Give examples of actions people take, words they use, products they buy, and places they go that are chosen to help further their favorable image.

4. Find an example of a public statement given to the mass media by some government agency that uses language to create a favorable image.

5. Analyze a press conference (on tape or film) or a speech by a candidate for public office. Examine that person's use of language.

6. Examine the "say/don't say" list for dentists. Discuss why a particular phrase appears in the "don't say" column. Would you feel differently about treatment from a dentist who used all the "don't say" phrases than you would from one who used all the correct words and phrases?

7. Have mass media in any way presented the dentist unfairly, thus making dentists very concerned about their public image? Explain your answer.

8. If you were a teacher, would you say "Your child cheats" or "Your child needs to learn the rules and standards of fair play"? Why?

9. Do you agree that advertising cheapens certain words? Provide examples that support your answer.

10. Read *1984* by George Orwell and discuss the concept of *doublethink* and relate it to the concept of *doublespeak*, the misuse or distortion of language.

11. In what way does advertising act as a kind of dictionary of everyday life?

12. Find examples of current ads that use incorrect grammar. Are the ads using words that way on purpose, or are they simply mistakes?

13. Is the overall effect of media to improve our use of language or to make correctness less likely? Support your answer.

14. Are the three ways in which media influence our language and thought statements of fact or opinion? Prove your answer.

WRAP-UP

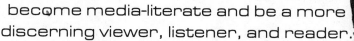

In this chapter on media and our image of the world, you've learned about stereotypes, along with why and how people form them. You've looked at television shows and how characters are often portrayed in stereotypical ways. Rumor and distortion of fact, in relation to mass media communication, have been explored along with the special language that has been created by the media. Looking at advertising and politics, you've learned how words can be trivialized and overused—and distorted. Being sensitive to media language, along with recognizing stereotypes and rumors, will help you become media-literate and be a more discerning viewer, listener, and reader.

CHAPTER 13

New Trends and Futurecasting

Predicting the future or futurecasting is dangerous; it's so easy to be wrong. The following readings serve as warnings for our current predictions about the world of the future.

PREDICTIONS FROM THE PAST

READING

YOUR NEWSPAPER BY RADIO!

This article appeared in *Modern Mechanix* magazine in 1938. Over fifty years later we still receive newspapers in much the same way.

A private newspaper with any spot in your home as the press room, the world's best editors and reporters on your staff, and the radio as your copy boy—this is not the dream of Jules Verne—but an actual accomplishment, available today to anyone in the United States owning an ordinary radio receiver.

No thundering press will deafen you when your paper is printed, but instead, equipment contained in a small, attractive box will silently print your "latest edition" while you sleep, completing it in time for reading at breakfast.

Facsimile transmitters and printers have been announced by two manufacturers, Finch Telecommunications Laboratories, Inc., of New York City, and RCA Victor, of Camden, N. J.

Predicted to be in widespread use within the year, many large broadcast stations have started tests with the system, and actual broadcasts on a definite schedule will be an accomplished fact as soon as these tests are completed. Of great significance is the fact that the Federal Communications Commission has granted the broadcasters permission to operate the facsimile equipment on the regular broadcast frequencies. Translated into actual use, this means that when the householder is through listening to his favorite station, he merely turns a switch which will, at the correct time, again turn on the radio for reception of the same station, but this time instead of sounds emitting from the loudspeaker, an up-to-the-minute newspaper will unfold.

At present one of the largest eastern broadcast stations, WOR, is supplying this type of transmission, though not yet on a regular schedule. It is being done both on the regular broadcast channels as well as on the ultra-short waves.

Plans are under way for regular service of facsimile transmissions early this spring.

Among other stations that have received F.C.C. permission to make facsimile broadcasts are WGN, Chicago; KSD, St. Louis; WHO, Des Moines; WGH, Norfolk, Va.; WHK, Cleveland; KSTP, St. Paul; KMJ, Fresno; and KFPK, Sacramento.

The facsimile recorder will be sold at a price no higher than the average good broadcast receiver. When production is increased the price is expected to be reduced to that of the average medium priced midget receiver. With the exception of the recorder, no special equipment is required except the broadcast receiver itself.

This new medium of entertainment and education is not to be confused with television, differing most widely from it in that its operation produces a tangible newspaper on which appears the printed word, photographs, drawings, sketches, and even advertisements. As the newspaper is produced, it can be removed from the machine and preserved if desired, differing from the conventional type only in size.

Briefly, the operation of the transmitter and recorder is as follows: The copy to be transmitted —whether it is pictures, news flashes, line drawings, or comic strips—involves no special printing or preparation because the material itself can be inserted directly into the transmitter. An electric bulb, throwing a spot of light, moves back and forth across the copy to be transmitted. This action is similar to that of the human eye as it sweeps from left to right across a line of type. In its movement across the copy, the spot of light is reflected back into a light-sensitive photo-electric cell. When the scanning light strikes the white portions of the copy, it returns a full reflection to the light-sensitive cell. When it strikes a black area, no light is reflected, while for the shaded areas, a corresponding reflection is obtained.

Because of the action of intermittent light at the cell, these reflections are changed into electrical energy or impulses. At the receiver or recorder, these impulses operate a stylus sweeping in synchronism with the scanning light at the transmitter.

THE MOVIES 100 YEARS FROM NOW

Back in 1924 David Wark Griffith, an American film director often considered the "father of American cinema," looked into his crystal ball marked 2024, and this is what he saw.

In the year 2024 the most important single thing which the cinema will have helped in a large way to accomplish will be that of eliminating from the faces of the civilized world all armed conflict. Pictures will be the most powerful factor in bringing about this condition. With the use of the universal language of moving pictures the true meaning of the brotherhood of man will have been established throughout the earth. For example, the Englishman will have learned that the soul of the Japanese is, essentially, the same as his own. The Frenchman will realize that the American's ideals are his ideals. All men are created equal.

. . . You will walk into your favorite film theatre and see your actors appearing in twice the size you see them now, because the screens will be twice as large, and the film itself twice as large also. With these enlargements, "close-ups" will be almost eliminated, since it will be relatively easy to picture facial expression along with the full figure of the performer. It will always be necessary to picture the face in pictures. It is the face which reflects the soul of a man.

Our "close-ups," or "inserts," as I call them, are sometimes cumbersome and disconcerting. I invented them, but I have tried not to overuse them, as many have done. It is a mechanical trick, and is of little credit to anyone.

We shall say there are now five elaborate first-run picture theatres on one New York street, Broadway. In 2024 there will be at least forty. Cities of 1,000 will average at least six. Cities of 20,000 and thereabout will have over a hundred. By virtue of its great advantage in scope, the motion picture will be fitted to tell certain stories as no other medium can. But I must add that the glory of the spoken or written word in the intimate and poetic drama can never be excelled by any form of expression.

In the year 2024 our directors of the better order will be men graduated from schools, academies, and colleges carrying in their curriculum courses in motion-picture direction. Our actors and actresses will be artists graduated from schools and colleges either devoted exclusively to the teaching and study of motion-picture acting or carrying highly specialized courses in acting before the camera. This is inevitable.

It really seems to me a bit humorous now to realize how

narrow a place in our everyday life the film is playing, despite the great rise in attendance in the last few years. One hundred years hence, I believe, the airplane passenger lines will operate motion-picture shows on regular schedule between New York and Chicago and between New York and London. Trains, which will be traveling twice or three times as fast as they do now, will have film theatres on board. Almost every home of good taste will have its private projection room where miniatures, perhaps, of the greater films will be shown to the family, and, of course, families will make their albums in motion pictures instead of in tintypes and "stills." Steamships will boast of first runs, which will be brought to them in mid-ocean by the airplanes, and I may add that almost all subjects in our schools will be taught largely with the use of picture play and the educational animated picture.

By the time these things come to pass, there will be no such thing as a flicker in your film. Your characters and objects in pictures will come upon the screen (which by then may not even be white, and certainly may not be square, or look anything like what it does now), and they will appear to the onlookers precisely as these persons and objects appear in real life. That much-discussed "depth" in pictures, which no one as yet has been able to employ successfully, will long since have been discovered and adopted. The moving canvas will not appear flat, but if a character moves before a fireplace you will recognize the distances as between the character and the fireplace. Likewise, in landscapes, you will feel the proper sense of distance. Your mountain peaks will not appear to rise one on

D. W. Griffith

top of the other, but will appear exactly as if you stood and looked at them. Of course these are merely details that will require long and intense study and experiment, but they will come. In other words, from the standpoint of naturalness, motion pictures one hundred years from now will be so nearly like the living person or the existing object pictured that you will be unable, sitting in your orchestra seat, to determine whether they are pictures of the real thing.

By a perfection of the studio lighting system, film will be smooth before the eye as if it were a stationary lighted picture. By that time the studios will have changed

greatly, and instead of actors being forced to work before great blinding lights, which now at times register 117 degrees of heat, we shall have "cold" lights. We are experi-menting in these already. Our studios will be great spreading institutions, as large as many of the cities surrounding New York. I think that one hundred years from now there will be no concentrated motion-picture production such as our Hollywood of today. Films will be made in various cities, most of which will be located near to New York.

Now let us prepare for a small-sized shock. One hundred years from today it will cost perhaps twice as much as it costs today to see the really first-class cinema. It is perfectly proper that it should. Time, effort, energy, and preparation put into pictures at that time will have advanced greatly. I am just honest enough to say that I do not at the moment understand how more time, effort, energy, and preparation could have been put into my own pictures; but, then, for the average large picture play this will hold true. The average supposedly high-class film play in 2024 will be on view at not less than $5 a seat.

In looking into the crystal I have seen many things which I have not touched upon here. Perhaps they would be too tedious to bring out and discuss. But of one thing I may place myself on record plainly and without qualification. The motion picture is a child that has been given life in our generation. As it grows older it will develop marvelously. We poor souls can scarcely visualize or dream of its possibilities. We ought to be kind with it in its youth, so that in its maturity it may look back upon its childhood without regrets.

MEDIALAB

Thinking About Predictions

1. The 1938 magazine article "Your Newspaper by Radio!" is typical of thousands of glowing articles and press releases predicting wonderful benefits just around the corner from a new invention. The article predicts the newspaper-by-radio system will be "in wide-spread use within the year." Almost 50 years later, the system still is not in operation. Why doesn't this wonderful new invention exist in millions of homes today?

2. The popular press often reports on new technology more with the eye of a cheerleader than of a critical evaluator. Find examples of current articles that predict marvelous benefits from a new invention. Evaluate the device with a critical eye.

Evaluate the new invention from an economic viewpoint by asking these questions: Would production of the invention cost so many millions of dollars that only the largest corporations could afford to experiment with it? Can the invention make a profit for its producers? Who would be most

threatened by the invention? Would there be a great demand for the invention or would it be little more than a toy for the rich?

3. What current mass media supply much the same services promised by newspaper-by-radio?

4. Review the description of how the newspaper-by-radio invention works. What modern device does it resemble?

5. After reading D. W. Griffith's essay on the movies, discuss the various predictions that have come true and the predictions that have not.

6. Try futurecasting: Look ahead 100 years and then write your own brief essay on the future of movies.

HOW VIDEOTAPE HAS CHANGED THE FACE OF FILM

Most revolutionary changes in mass media are not totally new inventions that sweep the world. Instead, they are changes in already existing media. The recording of visual images began with the use of film and remains that way today, although many improvements have been made over the first crude films. The medium of film had no challengers to its supremacy until the invention of videotape. Videotape raises the possibility that film may go the way of horse-drawn buggies, the stagecoach, and high-button shoes. Going to a video rental store has become a daily habit for some people. This trend, coupled with the general decline in movie theater attendance in recent years, has inspired the medium of film to new technological heights and made movie theater owners very conscious of customer service.

Currently both film and videotape are used extensively on television, but feature-length movies are still made with film rather than videotape. More and more television commercials and television series use videotape rather than film, especially when the effect of something happening *right now* is desired or there is a limited budget. In order to understand the advantages and differences of videotape and film, a comparison is necessary.

Videotape can show what is. Film can show only what was.

COMPARISON OF FILM AND VIDEOTAPE

Videotape	Film
No images can be seen on videotape; used and unused tape appear identical. Tape is opaque.	Images can be seen when film is held to the light, since film is transparent.
Unused videotape is not damaged by light, but can be ruined by magnetism.	Unprocessed film is easily damaged by light, but not affected by magnetic waves.
Tape can be viewed immediately after shooting.	Film needs to be chemically treated (developed) before viewing.
Tape can be erased and reused.	Film can be used once and is not erasable.
Video loses quality with enlargement. Large video images lack detail when compared to film projected on a movie screen.	Because film is transparent, it can easily be enlarged by a projector for viewing in large groups.
A videotape can easily be copied onto another tape.	Film can be copied onto another film only through an elaborate chemical process in a film laboratory.
Videotape can be edited and manipulated electronically without physically cutting the tape.	Film must be physically edited by cutting and splicing.
Videotaping has been made easy for the amateur with the invention of the camcorder.	Shooting movie film requires technical knowledge of lighting, angle, camera operation, and so on.
The quality of the videotape image is limited by the quality of the monitor. Even the most advanced monitors lag far behind the resolution (clarity) of a projected film.	A movie film camera produces refined images with a high degree of resolution.

MEDIALAB

Film vs. Video

1. Judging from the information you just read, what are the advantages of film over videotape? What are the advantages of videotape over film?

2. While watching television, you may be able to tell the difference between material that is filmed and material that is on videotape. How would you describe that difference? However, you will not be able to tell videotape from a live broadcast.

3. Are most commercials on videotape or film? Most weekly programs? Do you have any idea why this is true? What about daytime television dramas?

4. Make an educated speculation of the future of film and videotape. Before trying such futurecasting, you may wish to survey your class and find out why a person may choose going to a movie theater over renting a videotape, or vice versa. In addition, you may want to research local movie theaters and determine if any recent changes or improvements have been made to attract more customers.

5. What effect has the affordable pricing of videotape and videotaping equipment had on the medium of film?

6. Try an experiment in class: Using a movie camera and a camcorder, film and tape the same scene or bit of action. Watch the videotape and the film as a class and discuss the differences.

THE NEW MEDIA

Holography

Holographic film looks like a piece of clear plastic about the size of this page. But if that piece of plastic is held up so that a laser beam can pass through it after first going through a special lens, the plastic reveals an amazing sight.

Appearing on the plastic is an utterly realistic three-dimensional picture—say, for example, of a child's alphabet block. Looking down into the picture, you can see the top "A" of the block. As you move your head around, you can see the other sides of the block, even the back and bottom. Holography may well be the most important addition to photography and film since color. The word holography translates roughly from the Greek, meaning "the whole picture."

To add to the aura of magic, that piece of plastic could be removed from the ruby-red laser light and cut into one-inch squares. When each tiny square is put into the light, the entire picture remains intact.

Holographs can be made so real that a viewer can walk around an image and be convinced it is real. If a holograph is made of a scene that includes a magnifying glass, viewers will see a magnifying glass that actually works. As viewers move their heads, whatever appears behind the magnifying glass will be enlarged.

You now see holographs in many places—on keychains, on baseball cards, on credit cards, and so on. If holography can be made practical for film and television, movies in the future might be projected all around the audience instead of on a two-dimensional screen.

Fax

Facsimile machines aren't new, but improved and less-expensive models hit the marketplace in 1987 and revolutionized the way the world does business. Facsimile is the new Pony Express, the fastest way to send documents over a distance. Fax (short for facsimile) machines transmit documents over phone wires from one fax machine to another. A few newspapers offer experimental fax versions of the morning edition. Some grocery stores and carry-out restaurants use a fax to take orders, many radio stations

Many radio stations now take song requests by fax. One Los Angeles station gets up to 500 faxed requests a day from listeners.

accept faxed play requests, and NASA faxes instructions to orbiting space shuttles. Today, nearly 100 million messages travel daily over phone wires and the phrase "fax it" is part of our vocabulary.

Fax is a personal rather than mass medium. But advanced machines can be programmed to send the same message to hundreds of machines (often during nighttime hours when phone rates are lower) thus creating a fax network. In 1989, fax networks played an important role in the student demonstrations in China and in the revolutions in Eastern Europe. The fax is also used to spread the word of new scientific discoveries. Future improvements in speed and quality could make fax a threat to traditional mail delivery systems.

HDTV

Television in the 1990s could see the most dramatic change since 1954, the year color was introduced. High-definition television (HDTV) promises a picture as clear as that on a movie screen with stereo sound matching that of the finest CDs. HDTV is already operative in Japan, where the system was demonstrated with daily hour-long broadcasts to publicly placed HDTV screens.

HDTV's technology is digital—it has more in common with a computer than a traditional TV set. The implications of HDTV go far beyond merely bigger screens and clearer pictures. According to the American Electronics Association, HDTV means "an eventual merger of communications, computers, and entertainment into interrelated high-resolution digital technologies and markets. The resulting electronics-based industry may well underlie the world's economy and shape its political organization in the 21st century."

The prime obstacle to HDTV is that it is not compatible with our existing broadcast system. The FCC has ruled that HDTV must be compatible with existing sets, just as the first color transmissions had to be compatible with older black-and-white receivers. HDTV requires more than an improved TV set—it needs a whole new broadcast system. The current American broadcast system (called NTSC) scans a picture tube 525 times with a resolution of about 300 dots per line. Current European sets use a more advanced system and scan 625 lines per image. HDTV, in comparison, will feature over 1,000 lines per image and 1,000 dots per line.

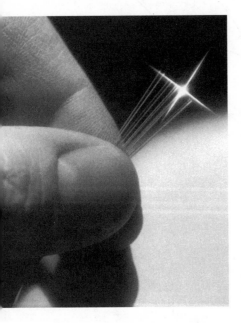

Fiber Optics

Fiber optics, simply put, is a better cable. A fiber optic cable uses silklike strands of glass to carry pulses of laser light. One pair of glass filaments, thinner than a human hair, can carry 24,000 telephone calls simultaneously at the speed of light, compared to 20 by regular copper cables. In 1980 there were no fiber optic cables; today, over a million miles of cable is in place. Fiber optic cables have a greater bandwidth than copper cables, so they can carry video information along with voice data.

Telephone companies could deliver TV shows or movies directly to homes through fiber optic cables. Currently, telephone companies are forbidden by law from offering such services. Telephone companies with fiber optic networks could offer at a lower cost the same services now supplied by cable operators.

With a nationwide fiber optics system, the kind of communication seen on network TV programs such as "Nightline" could become a reality for businesses. Three or four people anywhere in the world could see *and* hear each other in a videoconference.

Direct Broadcast Satellites

If you owned your own home satellite dish back in August of 1989 you could have tuned to GE Satcom F2R, Transponder 13, at 71 degrees west longitude, 3960 megahertz, vertical polarity—and seen the future. The future consisted of digital pictures transmitted from Voyager 2 during its flight past the planet Neptune and of live news conferences by Voyager scientists. The transmission by-passed TV networks and beamed the programs via satellite directly into the home of anyone with a correctly tuned backyard satellite dish.

Direct broadcast satellites (DBS) avoid the traditional media gatekeepers such as networks and television stations. A transmitter in Europe with a satellite uplink could beam programs into the United States. Governments could broadcast propaganda programs, and terrorists and nationalists could state their case in the court of worldwide public opinion.

The technology for DBS exists now. Satellites that send stronger signals mean that homeowners can use smaller satellite dishes. Some DBS broadcasting already exists in Europe where there is economic incentive to overcome national borders. Older satellite dishes the size of a house are being replaced with smaller dishes hardly more visible than the standard rooftop TV antenna. A more technically correct name for a home satellite dish is TVRO, which stands for TV Receive Only earth station.

In 1990 four media conglomerates—NBC, Cablevision, Hughes Broadcasting, and Rupert Murdoch's News Corporation —announced a one billion dollar venture to bring direct broadcast satellite service to the U.S. by the mid 1990s. The satellite, called Sky Cable, will deliver up to 108 broadcast channels to homes equipped with a "satellite dish" no bigger than a table napkin.

The satellite feed will carry high-definition television and digital sound, according to the plan. Television networks currently use DBS to relay transmissions, but not to broadcast directly to consumers.

Simulation of a family watching a television program transmitted by the above Sky Cable satellite (artist's rendition) and delivered to the home by a small receiving dish mounted on a windowsill. The satellite is due to be launched and the system in full operation by the mid-1990s.

Digital Everything

The media buzzword of the late 1980s continues into the 1990s— *digital*. Digital technology is replacing older analog technologies in all mass and personal media. Virtually any message (voice, images, music) can be stored, transmitted, and manipulated in digital form. You should understand the difference between digital and analog.

Digital means that information is reduced to binary form, to digits of zeroes and ones, to a flow of switches that are either on or off. Digital is not a medium; it is a way to store and process data. Once converted, the data are stored in a computer's memory or saved on a magnetic medium such as a floppy disk. This conversion to digital form takes place in a microprocessor. Digital recorders, cameras, and other devices require a built-in microprocessor.

Analog means information is mirrored or echoed rather than stored. Photography, video, film, photoreproduction, tape recording, radio, television, and most existing media are built on analog technology. A photocopy machine (such as a Xerox™ brand you might find at a local library) illustrates analog technology. Through a complicated system of lights, mirrors, heat, and chemicals, the copier produces an image (an "analogy") on paper.

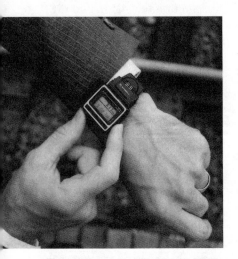

The wrist watch pager, introduced by Motorola in 1990, is an example of a new communications medium created through digital technology. The phone number to be called appears on the LCD (liquid crystal display) screen.

In analog technology, each copy loses some information. A photocopy is not as clear as the original; this loss of information is a measure of the weakness of the process. Some copies are much better than others; at its best, analog technology can be very good.

If you make a copy of the copy, even more information is lost—the copy is much less clear than the original. If you continue to make copies of copies, each following generation will be "worse" than the previous until you have a very faint image. If you make a copy of a tape recording some quality is lost in the dubbing. A videotape dub is not as clear as the original tape; a dub of a dub often has poor color and quality. This loss of quality in succeeding generations is one disadvantage of analog technology.

Another problem is that very little can be done to change the original data. A photocopier can enlarge or reduce but little else. A tape recorder can faithfully record the data of a sound but cannot manipulate that sound. Digital technology overcomes both these problems.

Compare the analog process to that of a digital copier. Such a copier does not yet exist for ordinary consumers, but it will in just a few years. The digital copy machine scans the original and produces a series of binary instructions stored in memory or on a disk. You could make a copy on paper, but you could also store your copy on a magnetic medium much like a credit card. The storage card could hold hundreds or thousands of pages ready to convert to paper when and how you want. The copy, if you could see it, would look like computer code. To make a visible copy you would feed the computer code to a digital-to-analog converter. If you make a copy of the computer code, no quality is lost. Copies of copies will have exactly the same degree of information (quality) as the original.

You've already made digital copies of information if you have worked with a computer. Let's say a friend writes a computer game and makes you a copy on a floppy disk. When you use the game on your computer there is no difference between your friend's original and your copy—that's a digital copy. The copy was made by transferring and translating digital code, not by making a mirror image of the actual game as it appears on-screen. If you copy your disk and pass it on to someone else, that second-generation copy is identical to the original. Even a thousand generations later, the copies will be identical as long as no errors are introduced in the data.

Not only is your copy identical to the original, you can make changes by changing the computer code. You can reprogram the game to suit your interests or talents.

Digital phone lines are coming. Each phone will convert your voice to a digital stream of ones and zeroes. This means audio quality will be as good as compact discs, even for overseas phone calls.

But if your friend makes a copy of the printed instruction sheet with a photocopy machine, the copy is inferior to the original—that's analog. If you, in turn, copy your photocopy, the quality becomes even worse; in other words, it loses information.

Digital advances are already in the marketplace:

- Personal computers are now commonplace in homes and offices.
- Compact discs use digital technology to reproduce sound.
- Digital audio tape recorders (DAT) store music as binary code.
- Digital synthesizers create and manipulate data to make music.
- HDTV will require digital processing. Some advanced sets now use digital techniques to create picture-within-a-picture effects.
- Digital processors make camcorders capable of various special effects and nearly automatic operation.
- Still cameras are now available that take digital pictures stored on a disc and played back on standard TV sets.

Videotext

The videotext system already exists in Europe and promises to make your TV set the center of household two-way communication. Viewers in homes equipped with videotext can access a computer that displays screens of information through the television. The viewer can make menu selections that open the way to electronic shopping, banking, mail, news delivery, and other services. Notice that this invention is a refinement of the device described in the article you read earlier in this chapter entitled "Your Newspaper by Radio," originally published in 1938.

Computing

In the 1980s computing changed *everything.* The ability of computers to turn information into a stream of binary code influenced all mass media and most areas of life. Unless you camp in the wilderness, computers influence what you do every hour. In 1983 only about 7 percent of white-collar workers used a personal computer (PC); in 1991 that figure rose to over 60 percent. The more computers become a part of daily life, the more important they become. Here are some examples of new uses for computers:

At least one fire department uses a personal computer and mapping software to learn about emergency calls before fire fighters arrive on the scene. Dispatchers download emergency information with a modem to a laptop computer in a van on the fire scene.

Traveling salespeople are increasingly carrying a portable PC as part of their standard equipment. With the PC (with built-in modem) they can query the home office about product availability and enter orders right from the customer's office.

The Library of Congress plans that its American Memories project will make its collection of rare documents available on an optical disk. Digitizing original documents, historic prints, and rare photographs will mean researchers will not have to travel to Washington to use them.

Combining the computer with a telephone hook-up via a modem enables the creation of electronic bulletin boards. Electronic bulletin boards facilitate communication among Vietnam veterans, users of specific software programs, nurses and medical personnel, environmental scientists, researchers studying very specialized areas of science, and thousands of other affinity groupings.

About one-half million employees relocate to other cities each year, and house hunting in a new city is difficult. To ease the task some realtors digitize pictures of houses for sale and prepare a computer file of offerings for potential clients. The computer file can be sent through phone lines to help the employee with the arduous task of house hunting.

The Sony "Palmtop" computer, a compact computer that can recognize hand-written characters; introduced to the U.S. market in 1990.

Traveling salespeople are increasingly carrying a portable PC as part of their standard equipment. With the PC (with built-in modem) they can query the home office about product availability and enter orders right from the customer's office.

Medical illustrators in Chicago use personal computers to "age" pictures of missing children. Pictures of what the children might look like as they grow older have helped recover 17 missing children. The aging is done by formulas and can do in 20 minutes what takes an artist 20 hours.

Law enforcement officers in many states carry in-car computers hooked directly to the state motor vehicle department and to national crime files.

Advanced commercial aircraft carry thousands of micropro-cessors. Some planes are so computer controlled they can land themselves, untouched by human hands.

Many colleges require students to use computers. An increas-ing number of grade schools and high schools require or, at least, offer computer courses. In 1983, Clarkson University was the first to require students to use a PC.

NTN Entertainment Network uses a personal computer to create "interactive sporting events." While watching a football game, viewers can guess what play the quarterback will call, enter the guess into a tabletop terminal, and score points if they're right. Sports bars that participate use a PC and a 2-foot TVRO to pick up the events.

Every Mrs. Fields' cookie store has a PC in the back to track sales, judge inventory, and plan schedules for employees and baking. Store managers can ask questions as specific as how many chocolate chip cookies to bake on a Thursday afternoon in the summer. The computer allows store managers to communicate with corporate headquarters.

Personal computers have revolutionized politics and election campaigns. Every serious candidate for a national political office has to have a computer expert on staff. Computers generate personalized mail and contributor solicitations, and track voting patterns. The three major TV networks use computers to predict the outcome of presidential elections even before all the polls are closed.

Artists use PCs extensively. The ability of a computer to manipulate an image makes it an ideal tool for art. The computer is not merely a convenience in art and graphics —it is now a tool as basic as the paintbrush, airbrush, or canvas.

Designers and architects use CAD (Computer-Assisted Design) programs to speed up the previously tedious task of drawing technical illustrations, cutaway views, blueprints, and floor plans. The computer makes editing these often complex drawings easy.

Currently, computer-generated art is judged either a novelty or a useful special effect in graphic design. But a new medium of expression takes time to be accepted as art. Photography existed for about 150 years before an art museum exhibited photographs. The medium of photography was first seen as mechanical reproduction, not creative expression. Computer art today is seen primarily as a convenience that saves time and money. But the future of computer art might see museums showcasing the finest examples of human creativity created on the digital canvas of the future—a computer screen.

Electronic mail via computers and modems (often called sim ply E-mail) is replacing first-class mail as the businessperson's first choice for communicating. E-mail is much faster and less expensive than a letter sent through the postal service. Phone calls are still the mainstay of business communication, but E-mail is better for short messages and information exchanges. Anyone who has tried to reach a businessperson while he or she is in the office and not on another line knows that a system like E-mail that prevents playing telephone tag is essential.

E-mail is like an electronic message board. The communication is sent using a computer and modem and is "posted" on the recipient's computer. The E-mail can be received even if the addressee is not in when the message is sent. An E-mail "letter" can be sent to many people at once. There are currently about 2 million electronic mailboxes and over 30 million messages are sent every month.

PCs have changed the workplace in many ways. There is a whole new set of jobs designed to integrate people and PCs. Now there are personal computer managers, systems trainers, and LAN (Local Area Network) administrators.

Electronic surveillance equipment provides security in today's world. (Burle Security Products)

PCs have opened the walls of corporate offices. This year well over 5 million people will be "telecommuters" who work from home at least part of the time. A telecommuter, using a computer and usually a modem (a device that transmits data over telephone lines), stays in touch with the corporation while not requiring desk space or the usual office support structures. It is now possible for an executive to live in California and work in New York.

Computers are often used to monitor worker effectiveness. Computers attached to scanners in grocery store check-out lanes can measure exactly the productivity of each worker. Computers often monitor telephone agents who rent cars, make airline reservations, or offer customer assistance. A computer counts how much time workers spend on breaks, measures keystrokes per hour, reads files, and generally acts as an electronic supervisor always looking over the employee's shoulder.

Film animation (the making of cartoons for television or movies) has always been a tedious job requiring thousands of paintings on clear cells just to make a few minutes of film. The computer's untiring ability to repeat itself is well suited for animation. In 1988, the Academy Award for best animated short film was given to *Tin Toy*, a five-minute short that was computer-generated. Sketches for the film were

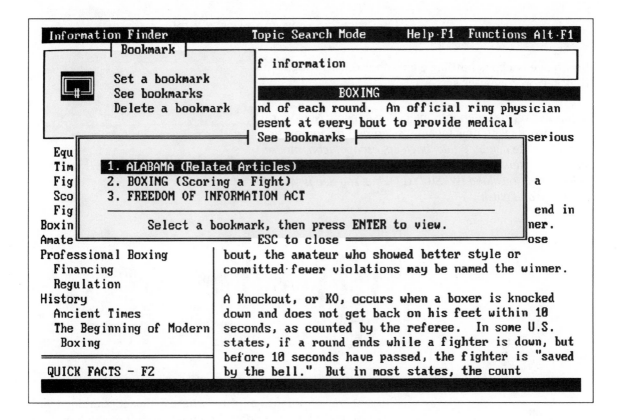

Information Finder   Topic Search Mode   Help·F1 Functions Alt·F1

┌─ Bookmark ─┐
│   │   f information
│ Set a bookmark   �nd of each round. An official ring physician
│ See bookmarks   esent at every bout to provide medical
│ Delete a bookmark   ├─ See Bookmarks ─┤   serious
│   │
Equ
Tim   1. ALABAMA (Related Articles)
Fig   2. BOXING (Scoring a Fight)   a
Sco   3. FREEDOM OF INFORMATION ACT
Fig   end in
Boxin   Select a bookmark, then press ENTER to view.   ner.
Amate   ═══════════ ESC to close ═══════════   ose

Professional Boxing   bout, the amateur who showed better style or
  Financing   committed·fewer violations may be named the winner.
  Regulation
History   A Knockout, or KO, occurs when a boxer is knocked
  Ancient Times   down and does not get back on his feet within 10
  The Beginning of Modern seconds, as counted by the referee. In some U.S.
    Boxing   states, if a round ends while a fighter is down, but
                           before 10 seconds have passed, the fighter is "saved
QUICK FACTS - F2   by the bell." But in most states, the count

A CD encyclopedia display screen. Information Finder™ by World Book helps you quickly find what you are looking for and keep track of related materials.

From INFORMATION FINDER by World Book, Inc. By permission of the publisher.

scanned into a personal computer, then altered on screen and tested. The actual animation was too demanding for a PC, so the film was animated on a mainframe com-puter.

Encyclopedias have always been useful but bulky and expensive. Now encyclopedias exist on compact discs that convert a shelfful of books to a five-inch disc. The CD player (very much like the CD player used for music) is hooked to the computer and can find every occurrence of any word in the entire encyclopedia in a few seconds. The disc can be updated yearly so an encyclopedia can be a subscription item instead of a one-time investment.

Public libraries are in the process of abandoning row upon row of catalog-card drawers in favor of computerized catalogs. Users can search library holdings by typing in a book title, subject, or author. In some systems, the computer will search several area libraries for the book and indicate if the book is on the shelf or out.

Nearly one billion dollars a year is spent on computer games, such as Nintendo®. Plans are afoot for video games on a higher level—games in which you enter a store and play on teams. One plan, called BattleTech, outfits players with two color screens and a computer. The game will be a battle simulation like those in *Star Trek*, with the players in telephone-booth-like cockpits battling each other only through what they see on computer screens.

Computer terms creep into everyday speech. New words (or old words with new meanings) coined by computer users include *default value, back-up, escape, icon, mouse, window, system failure, bug and debug, online, downtime, upload and download, WYSIWYG (What You See Is What You Get), and glitch.*

Futurecasting

Current trends point to a future where a TV set combined with a computer will be the central communication console in each household. Once digital HDTV becomes standard, such blending of the two devices will be inevitable. Looking at telecommunications, Ian Ross, president of Bell Laboratories, predicts that by 1995 data transmission—machines talking to people and machines talking to machines—could account for as much traffic on AT&T's phone lines as voice conversations.

In attempting to predict what the communication media of the future will be like, there are few certainties. Perhaps the only sure thing is that tomorrow's media will be as different from today's as today's are from those of the nineteenth century. You will one day tell stories to your grandchildren of the old days of broadcast television, of the days when you first operated a computer, and of the time when pictures were projected in only two dimensions. The grandparent of the year 2020 might well recall the quaint custom of going to something called movie theaters, the old-time stereo FM radio, the vinyl disc phonograph records, and the days when even large cities had no more than one-half dozen television channels.

Predicting or speculating about the future is more than a mere exercise of imagination. To the unprepared, the future arrives as a shock; to the prepared, the future arrives as a logical extension of the present. To speculate about how the communications media will develop is to take some part in that development. To have considered what is desirable in human communication is to be able to make a value judgment about what the future of mass media should be.

MEDIALAB

Looking at New Trends and the Future

1. Keep a bulletin board or clipping collection on any of the following.

> New uses for fax machines (such as advertising, also known as junk mail)
>
> The process of high-definition television in the U. S.
>
> New applications for fiber optics technology
>
> Satellite broadcasts direct to homes
>
> Digital technology (such as digital radio via satellite, digital video transmission, digital sound, digital photography)
>
> Videotext or any system that uses television as a two-way medium
>
> New uses for home computers
>
> The computer as a library research tool
>
> Electronic mail (correspondence via computer)
>
> The link between CD players and the computer

2. If your school has a fascimile machine, try to arrange a fax exchange (a variation on being a penpal) with a school far away, preferably in another country. You might conduct a survey and compare your responses with those of the other students.

3. Has HDTV in the United States come any closer to reality in the past year? Use research tools such as *Reader's Guide to Periodical Literature* to help answer this question.

4. Find someone in the class who has seen television in Europe or Japan. How does the picture clarity compare with that of American TV?

5. Fiber optics can make the "video telephone" a reality. Do video conferences take place in your part of the country?

6. Find a student who lives in a household with a satellite dish. Have that student report on life with a TVRO.

7. Explain the difference between digital and analog in your own words. Use the clock and an automobile gas gauge as your primary examples. Explain how you react differently to digital as opposed to analog devices.

8. Find the latest example of digital technology changing a consumer product or communication medium.

9. How does digital technology change the concept of a "copy"? If a video image can be digitally altered (without leaving a trace that it was changed), can videotape ever be used to prove an event really took place?

10. A television set could become the heart of an interactive communication system for every household. Does "two way cable TV" exist in your area?

11. Find out how your local library uses a computer to assist research. Can you search the library card catalog with a home computer? Does your library conduct computerized database searches for patrons? Does your library have an encyclopedia or other reference book on a CD-ROM player for patron use?

12. Talk to a "telecommuter"—someone who spends part of his or her workday at home with a computer instead of at an office. Prepare a brief written or verbal report about telecommuting.

13. Ask a working parent, "How have computers changed your work in the past five years?" Prepare a brief written report on the answer—or, as an alternative activity, write a brief essay predicting what the future office or workplace will be like.

WRAP-UP

In this last chapter of *Understanding Mass Media*, you've looked at predictions from the past and realized the risk of futurecasting developments in communication media. You've discovered how technology can change an existing medium, or create a new one. You've studied and researched new media trends and developments in computer technology, television, and telecommunications—you've even tried your hand at futurecasting. Now that you've achieved media-literacy and contemplated the future—you will be better prepared for the many changes awaiting you in the mass media world of the twenty-first century.

Glossary

AM: Type of radio transmission in which the sound wave modulates the height (or amplitude) of the carrier wave. AM is the original form of radio broadcasting; FM is a more recent system.

Animation: The film art of making drawings move. An animated film is often called a cartoon. All film cartoons are animated, but not all animations are cartoons.

ASCAP (American Society of Composers, Authors, and Publishers): Collects fees from recording companies, radio and TV stations, and others who use the music of their members for profit. The fees are distributed to the copyright owners. BMI (Broadcast Music, Inc.) performs a similar service.

Aspect ratio: The ratio of a screen's width to its height. Today's TV screens have a 4 to 3 ratio. Tomorrow's high-definition TV screens will have a 5 to 3 ratio.

Associated Press (AP): A news service (often called wire service) that supplies news and features to thousands of newspapers, and TV and radio stations. Associated Press is a cooperative owned by its members.

Behavioral research: The study of consumer needs and buying patterns. The focus in this kind of research is on what people do. Advertisers conduct such research in order to make ads more effective.

Broadcast: A word borrowed from agriculture originally meaning to cast seeds broadly. Today it means using airwaves to beam radio or television signals.

Cable television: A means of delivering television signals to homes via wire cables, usually buried underground—in contrast to broadcast TV, which delivers programs by airwaves. Cable television requires the set to be physically hooked into the system; broadcast television is available to anyone with a TV set.

CD: A compact disc from which sound is retrieved by a low-power laser beam; made of iridescent plastic.

Celebrity: A person known for being well-known. A "big name," a widely recognized name or face, a media personality.

Claims: The specific part of an ad in which the product claims to be superior or desirable.

Closed captions: Words superimposed on TV programs for hearing-impaired viewers. The captions require a special decoder.

Composition: In visual communication, how the parts of a picture are arranged.

Copyright: Legal protection granted to the creator of literary works, graphics, music and lyrics, recordings, and other audiovisual works. The law allows the creator or copyright owner to distribute and profit from the copyrighted work.

DBS (Direct broadcast satellite): A satellite that broadcasts signals directly to any TVRO (satellite dish on earth) in its path.

Demographics: The study of an audience to determine its characteristics, for example, its age, wealth, or education etc.

Deregulation: The elimination (or lessening) of government regulation in business. One of the key trends of broadcasting in the 1980s was deregulation.

Digital: Information reduced to a binary form of ones and zeroes, or on/off. Once information is converted to a digital form, it can be manipulated, stored, and transmitted by computers and cables.

Downlink: To receive a transmission from a satellite; also, the dish used for the reception.

Drive time: Time of heaviest commuting traffic, usually 7 to 9 A.M. and 4:30 to 6:30 P.M. Drive time is to radio what prime time is to television in term of audience peak.

E-mail: Abbreviation for electronic mail. Computers, telephone lines, and/or communication satellites transmit messages between computers instead of using the postal system to deliver paper-based messages.

Editorial: Opinions expressed by the medium's management. These opinions are clearly labeled as opinions and are often found on the editorial page.

Equal time: An FCC requirement that stations that sell time to one political candidate must sell or give equal time to all qualified candidates for the same office. The provision applies only to candidates for political office. News programs are not required to give equal time to each candidate.

Fax (facsimile): Machines that can convert printed documents into signals carried by ordinary telephone lines. In the United States during 1989, over 50 billion pages were "faxed."

Federal Trade Commission (FTC): Government agency that regulates federal trade, including radio and television broadcasting.

Federal Communications Commission (FCC): Government agency charged with regulating broadcasting in the United States.

Feedback: Mass media communication is mainly a one-way street, a way for the owners of media outlets to communicate to the masses. When there is a response from the public—or *feedback*— mass media communication becomes a two-way street.

Fiber optics: Thin strands of glass that can carry electronic data through pulses of laser light.

First Amendment: Constitutional amendment guaranteeing freedom of speech, press, and religion. It states simply: "Congress shall make no law respecting an establishment of religion, or prohibiting the free exercise thereof; or abridging the freedom of speech, or of the press; or the right of the people peaceable to assemble, and to petition the government for the redress of grievances."

Flipping: Going from channel to channel using remote control. See *grazer*.

FM: Frequency modulation; a type of broadcast signal that contrasts to AM, or amplitude modulation. FM sound is considered superior to AM, but the signal does not travel as far.

Gatekeeper: An individual or group who controls the flow of information or entertainment. The gatekeeper can block, add to, or change information. An example of a gatekeeper is a managing editor of a newspaper.

Grazer: A TV viewer (or radio listener) who often flips through channels, watching several shows at once. Grazing almost requires a remote control.

HDTV: High-definition TV provides a fine-quality, wider picture. Digital technology means more can be done to manipulate the resulting image.

L.O.P. theory: A somewhat tongue-in-cheek theory stating we gravitate toward whichever program we find least offensive at that time—*the least offensive program.*

Mass medium: A means of communicating with a mass of people. Television is a mass medium; the telephone is a personal medium.

Medium: A channel or system of communication or expression. Plural form is *media.* To a communication specialist, television is a medium; to an artist, chalk is a medium; to a sculptor, clay is a medium.

Microprocessor: A tiny silicon chip that can do much of the work of a computer.

Modem: A device placed between a computer and a telephone line. Modems can transmit and receive computer files.

Motivational research: The study of what motivates consumers to buy or not buy certain products and brands. The focus in this kind of research is on the "why" of behavior.

News hole: The amount of space in a newspaper (measured in column inches) available for nonadvertising material.

Pay TV: A system in which the viewer pays either a monthly fee or a special charge for a specific program. HBO (Home Box Office) is an optional pay-TV service for cable subscribers.

PC: Abbreviation for personal computer. Personal computers have improved so fast that they can now perform better than huge, multimillion-dollar computers of years past.

People meter: An electronic diary used by ratings services to measure audience size for TV programs. The people meter also gathers data about exactly who is watching which program at any given time.

Perceptual filtering: A term describing the human tendency to filter out of what we see those elements that do not fit our view of how the world works. We tend to see what we want rather than what is.

Persistence of vision: An image on the eye "persists" for a fraction of a second. This "eye slowness" enables us to see an illusion of movement when we see over 24 images in a second.

Press release: Prewritten "news story" released by a person or organization seeking media coverage; often written by public relations professionals.

Prime time: The times during which television has its largest audience: 8 to 11 P.M. Eastern or Pacific Time, and 7 to 10 P.M. Central or Mountain Time, Monday through Saturday. Prime time starts an hour earlier on Sunday.

Pseudo event: An event staged for the purpose of gaining time or space in mass media. Examples include press conferences, ribbon cuttings, press releases, surveys, demonstrations, awards and contests, and other staged events.

Rating: The percentage of all TV households tuned to a program at once. A rating of 22 means 22 percent of all TV households.

Scene: In film, one or more shots unified by time and place.

Sequence: In film, a group of scenes joined by a common purpose or setting, for example, the chase sequence.

Shot: The basic building block of a film or video. A shot is what happens in front of the camera from the time it starts until it stops. A shot can be a fraction of a second or over an hour. Shots are further defined by the distance of the camera from the subject—long shot, medium shot, close-up.

Soap opera: Dramatic programs originally begun on network radio and transplanted to daytime television—called "soaps" because they were originally sponsored and produced by soap companies. The purpose of soaps was to gather a female audience who would be potential buyers of detergent. Soap companies (Procter and Gamble, for example) still advertise on the soaps but no longer control their content.

Stereotype: An oversimplified description based on limited experience. TV shows often use stereotyped characters who are instantly recognized by viewers, instead of characters developed by plot.

Superstation: A local TV station whose signal is delivered by satellite to cable systems across the country. Examples include WTBS in Atlanta, WOR in New York, and WGN in Chicago.

Syndicates: Agencies that supply features and columns to newspapers. Columnists such as Art Buchwald, Bob Greene, and Ann Landers are "syndicated." The columns and features are sold to newspapers based on circulation. Thousands of features are available, ranging from cartoons to astrology readings.

Synthesizer: In music, an electronic device that breaks sounds into simpler components and reassembles them into new sounds.

Time shifting: The practice of using a VCR (videocassette recorder) to watch a show actually broadcast at some other time or date.

TVRO (TV receive only): A satellite dish that can receive TV signals. Home satellite dishes are TVRO.

UHF: Ultra High Frequency—channels 14 and higher on TV sets. UHF signals do not travel as far as VHF.

UPI: United Press International, a wire service.

Uplink: To transmit to a satellite for relay; also, the dish used to transmit.

VHF: Very High Frequency—channels 2–13 on TV sets.

VHS: Abbreviation for the rarely-used phrase Video Home System. VHS uses half-inch videotape in a cassette format.

Viewer fatigue: Information overload as applied to television commercials. Evidence suggests viewers are seeing more commercials but remembering fewer.

Wire service: News-gathering agency that sends stories to subscribing newspapers, radio stations, and TV stations. Stories were originally transmitted via teletype machines but today are being sent by computer hook-ups. Wire services include Associated Press, United Press International, England's Reuters, France's Agence France-Presse, and the Soviet Union's government-owned TASS.

Zapping: Using the remote control to change a channel when a commercial appears.

Zipping: Fast-forwarding through commercials when watching a program on videotape.

Index

Acknowledgments

Readings

"The Allure of Daytime Television Drama," reprinted with permission of *Popular Psychology*, 1972.

"The Message of the Police Tale," reprinted from *Writing for Television* by Stuart M. Kaminsky, with Mark Walker, Copyright © 1988 by Stuart M. Kaminsky, with Mark Walker. Used by permission of Dell Books, a division of Bantam, Doubleday, Dell Publishing Group, Inc.

"TV Violence *Is* Harmful," by Jesse L. Steinfeld, reprinted with permission from the April 1973 *Reader's Digest*. Copyright 1973 by the Reader's Digest Association, Inc.

"In Defense of Television," and "Some Questions to Ask Yourself About Your Own TV Watching" by Peggy Charren and Martin W. Sandler, from *Changing Channels* © 1983, Addison-Wesley. Reprinted by permission of Peggy Charren, President, Action for Children's Television, Cambridge, Massachusetts.

"Of Directors, Magic, and Waterfalls of Salad Dressing," from *The Best Thing on TV—Commercials* by Jonathan Price. Copyright © 1978. Reprinted with permission of Viking Penguin, Inc. New York.

"In Movies, Hearing Is Believing," (originally entitled "Stick It in Your Ear"), by Frank Spotnitz, published in the October, 1989 issue of AMERICAN FILM. Reprinted with permission.

"What Comics Can Teach You About Movies," by Steve Gerber, reprinted from SUPER-8 FILMAKER, vol. 2, No. 5, 145 East 45th Street, New York, New York 10017.

"The Techniques of the Gag Cartoonist," from *The Fourth Estate: An Informal Appraisal of the News and Opinion Media* copyright © 1971 by John L. Hulteng and Roy Paul Nelson. By permission of Harper & Row Publishers, Inc.

"How to Manage TV News," by Joe Saltzman, full professor of the Journalism department of USC.

"The Accident: A Cross Media Study," an excerpt from THE NEWS BUSINESS by John Chancellor and Walter R. Mears, Copyright © 1983 by John Chancellor and Walter R. Mears. Reprinted by permission of Harper & Row, Publishers, Inc.

Excerpt from *More Language That Needs Watching* by Theodore M. Bernstein. Copyright © by Theodore M. Bernstein. Reprinted by permission of the author and Atheneum Publishers, Inc.

Excerpt from 1989 *Writer's Market*. Copyright © 1989 by Writer's Digest Books.

"Rock & Riches," by Allan Parachini. Copyright © 1974 Ziff-Davis Publishing Company. Used with permission of *Stereo Review Magazine*.

Photographs/Illustrations

Associated Press/Wide World Photos: 120, 260, 261, 267, 321

The Bettman Archive: 12, 13, 14, 20, 34, 121, 196, 240, 255, 256, 257, 259, 266, 273, 279, 312, 313, 335, 337

BPI Communications, Inc./BILLBOARD: 284

Brown Brothers: 259

Photo courtesy of BLOCKBUSTER Video: 226

Photo courtesy of Burle Industries: 350

Film clip courtesy of Calabash Animation: 124

The *Chicago Tribune*: photos © copyrighted. All rights reserved. Used with permission: 198, 218

Click/Brian Seed © 1985: 72–73

Illustration courtesy of ETC Recordings, Bensenville, Illinois: 276

Fallon McElligott from *Rolling Stone*, 1986. By Straight Arrow Publishers. © 1980 Reprinted by permission: 72, 249–250.

Daniel J. Hochstatter: (Illustrations) 10, 16, 24–25, 39, 49, 58, 60, 88, 99, 107, 114, 197, 208, 281, 300

Marilyn Gartman Agency: 1, 12, 13, 227

Photo courtesy of Hughes Corporation Inc.: 343

Reproductions courtesy of Library of Congress: 76, 121

Los Angeles *Times* 1932 © excerpt, reprinted by permission: 264

Vernon McKissack: (Illustrations) 22, 29, 95, 96, 105, 115

"My View" advertisement for Toyo-View camera courtesy of Mamiya America Corporation, Walter Wick Photography, New York, NY, and Poppe Tyson Advertising © 1990: 73, 246

DAREDEVIL cover courtesy of Marvel Entertainment Group: 160

PHOTO DISTRICT NEWS cover courtesy of *Photo District News*; cover photo courtesy of Dennis Manarchy, Advertising Agency, Goodby Berlin and